MIRACLES
and WONDER

MIRACLES
and WONDER

THE
HISTORICAL MYSTERY
OF JESUS

ELAINE PAGELS

DOUBLEDAY

New York

To Alan, with gratitude and love

Contents

Contents

Author's Note

While writing this book, which requires Biblical quotation, I have often included translations from the New Oxford Annotated Edition (Oxford University Press, 2001). This set of translations, chosen and approved by a fine team of scholars, is the one I recommend to our students at Princeton. Exceptions occur, however, when quoting Greek texts from the New Testament, where I often use my own translations instead.

MIRACLES
and WONDER

Introduction

W AS JESUS AN actual person, or a fictional one? What do
we, or can we, know about him, historically speaking?
And how do we know what we think we know; what sources are
available? How has our sense of who he was—or is—changed
over time, and through different cultures?

Questions like these impelled me to head for graduate school,
long after I'd given up on several versions of Christianity, starting
with the Methodist church I knew as a child. Although I loved the
music, including the powerful hymns of Isaac Watts, the passion
for social justice that inspired Methodism's founder, John Wesley,
had been quietly dropped, replaced with an encouragement to
"be nice"—an adaptation of the gospel that apparently sounded
more appropriate for the suburban California town where we
lived.

I was fascinated, though, and somewhat scared, when entering
the nearby Catholic church with my best friend from school: St.
Aloysius Church was far more mysterious, with candles flickering

under a wooden image of Jesus in agony, hanging on a crucifix high above the altar. Then I would wait, seated on a dark wooden bench, while she disappeared into a black box to whisper to someone invisible, who would dole out the penalty for her sins. I was always relieved when we could escape back into the sunlight.

So I gave up on religion, and turned instead to dance, poetry, and music. Nothing I'd seen in those churches could match the power of the Hopi dances celebrated late at night on Christmas Eve at Taos Pueblo in New Mexico, or the performance of *Revelations* danced by Alvin Ailey's company in New York, or the poems of John Donne and Dylan Thomas, or the music of Bach or Aretha Franklin. At the time, I had no idea that stories of Jesus had ignited nearly every one of these artists.

But when I was in high school, a friend invited me to go to San Francisco to some kind of public meeting. To my surprise, we were on our way to a "Crusade for Christ," where Billy Graham, then a handsome, charismatic preacher, addressed over eighteen thousand people packed into the sports stadium at Candlestick Park, while thousands more stood listening in the parking lot. First he warned that what he had to say would sound foolish to intellectual and educated people—and it did. He challenged people who, like my father, a scientist, revered science as the world's highest wisdom. Then he raised his voice to speak of America, but not, as my immigrant grandparents did, as the gold standard for morality and justice. Instead, invoking the prophet Isaiah ("Ah, sinful nation!"), he denounced American leaders for driving our most brilliant young men (he didn't mention women) to build bigger weapons, even after American bombs killed hundreds of thousands of people in Hiroshima and Nagasaki. Shaking his fist, he challenged Christians who use the Bible to justify slavery and segregation.

Then, as an enormous choir quietly began to sing "Just As I Am," the preacher dropped his voice to hushed tones, speaking of our need for God's love, promising everything, even eternal life: all we had to do was go forward and "accept Jesus into your heart." Billy Graham offered nothing less than a new life: I could be "born again," break out of my family and join the family of a heavenly father, who, unlike the earthly one, knew everything about me, even my secret thoughts, but loved me anyway.

That moment, Graham promised, could change everything—burst the confines of the world in which I'd been living and break into a new and expansive universe. Having just turned fifteen, I found this invitation irresistible. Overcome with tears, I walked down to the front with thousands of others, as thousands more sang and roared approval, praising God for all the souls being saved that day. Now all of us who were "born again" shared in a cosmic drama of salvation. That day opened up vast spaces in my imagination that I'd previously entered only through the music and stories of others. It changed my life, as the preacher promised it would—although not entirely as he intended, or, at least, not for as long.

Hearing of this, my parents were upset, and my father was angry, having struggled as a young man to free himself from his family's ferocious Presbyterianism, a hotbed of bitter arguments about salvation and damnation. When he discovered Darwinian science, he quickly discarded religion, which he had assured me is now obsolete, a relic of humanity's superstitious and archaic past. Although he worried, insisting that I'd been duped, I eagerly joined an evangelical church. There I could meet my "brothers and sisters in Christ," and we would hug each other, pray, and praise the Lord, eating fragments of cracker and drinking grape juice from tiny plastic cups as we shared communion, as members of Christ's body on earth.

A year and a half later, though, everything changed. Suddenly devastated when one of my closest high school friends died in a car crash, I went to the church in shock. Members of our close-knit group, at first sympathetic, asked, "Was he born again?" When I said, "No, he was Jewish," they said, "Then he's in hell." Feeling as if I'd been punched in the stomach, I nearly asked, *Wasn't Jesus Jewish?* Unable to speak, and shocked that their sense of God's love had nothing to do with anyone outside the circle of "Bible-believing Christians," I walked out alone, devastated, and never went back.

After that, I again left Christianity behind. Several years later, since I loved to explore literature, drama, and art, I thought, why not apply to the graduate programs in art history at New York University, or in poetry at Columbia, in "Social Thought" at the University of Chicago, or in philosophy at Brandeis? Finding every one of these appealing, I decided to apply to them all, and did.

At the same time, I began to wonder: what is it about the stories of Jesus that once had evoked such powerful responses in me? Although I heard people say that religion was childish, or, as Freud insisted, a delusion, I was curious. What was it that resonated so deeply in my own experience? Was it because of Jesus, and who he was? Was it only Christianity, or could another religious tradition—Buddhism, for example—arouse such powerful responses, and open us to realities beyond our understanding? Hearing of a doctoral program in the Study of Religion at Harvard that offered graduate students the option of exploring Hinduism, Judaism, Buddhism, Christianity, or Islam, I applied there, too.

A year and a half later, I flew across the country to Cambridge, Massachusetts, excited and intimidated but eager to start what would become my life's work—investigating the history of religion. After locating a garret apartment in a house near Harvard Yard, I set out to meet the formidable Krister Stendahl, Professor of New Testament, priest of the Swedish Lutheran Church, recently appointed as Archbishop of Sweden. After a few preliminaries, he suddenly swerved his desk chair to ask a pointed question. Having warned me that women were almost never accepted as doctoral students at Harvard, and that those who came failed to graduate, he asked, "Why did you come here?" Startled, I said that I hoped to find the essence of Christianity. He paused, and, with a severe look, asked, "What makes you think it has an essence?" At that moment, I knew I was in the right place. Although I couldn't answer his question, I realized that I had come here precisely for this: to be asked a question like that; challenged to think in ways I'd never imagined.

I'd chosen Harvard because it was a secular university, where I wouldn't be bombarded with church dogma. Yet I still imagined that if we went back to first-century sources, we would be able to find out what Jesus actually said and did, and how Chris-

5

tianity began. But the first thing I learned in graduate school is that exploring these themes would be far more difficult than we expected. As students, we could not find a simple path to what Stendahl ironically called "play Bible land" simply by digging through history. But I also saw that hope of "finding the real Christianity" has driven countless people, including both the faculty and students on our own team, to investigate how this movement started. And for most of us, our historical investigations also involve a spiritual quest.

First I learned that none of the narratives now called "gospels" were written during Jesus's lifetime. Instead, they were written anonymously, some forty to sixty years after his death. What I thought were their authors' names had been added about a hundred years after they were written, when admirers of these particular "gospels" added names familiar from Jesus's inner circle, to lend them credence. Around 160 C.E., the two called the Gospel of Matthew and the Gospel of John were attributed to Jesus's disciples. The other two in the New Testament were given names of second-generation followers. Mark was traditionally known as a follower of Peter, and Luke was reputed to be a follower of the apostle Paul. And although each of these gospels includes historical and biographical material, their writers set out primarily to spread their faith in Jesus, and to publicize his message—the "good news" (the meaning of the Greek term "gospel")—not to document history.

I discovered, too, that *none* of the surviving first-century sources that mentions Jesus is neutral. For while his devoted followers wrote gospels, prominent members of the Roman elite were writing scathing attacks. The Roman senator Tacitus, for example, and the Roman court historian Suetonius, both intent on composing biographies of famous people, despised Jesus's followers as ignorant and superstitious rabble—people foolish enough, in a Roman critic's contemptuous phrase, to "worship a crucified Jew."

Besides these long-familiar sources, I was enormously fortunate to have access to the famous cache of over fifty ancient texts discovered in 1945, including those we called "gnostic gospels," such as the Gospel of Thomas, the Gospel of Philip, and the Gospel of Truth. Amazingly, these claimed to offer "the secret words of the Living Jesus"—including many sayings familiar from the New Testament, and others that startled and intrigued us. These ancient texts, sealed in a six-foot-high jar, had been hidden in a cave in Egypt. Who put them there, we asked, and why? In an earlier book, *The Gnostic Gospels*, I wrote about our preliminary findings.

These hidden texts remind us of the tumultuous path Jesus's teachings have taken to reach us. Around 312 C.E., as is well known, the Roman emperor Constantine astounded his constituents by taking Christ as his divine patron, and declaring Christianity a legal religion after years of persecution of Jesus's followers. Right after that, a former soldier in the Roman army named Pachomius also declared himself a Christian, and sought to establish a community on earth that might become an "outpost of heaven," inviting several thousand Christian men to build what became one of the earliest monasteries in Egypt, in the town of Nag Hammadi. Many sacred writings were circulating widely among Christians at that time—Paul's letters and the four gospels now in the New Testament, along with gospels attributed to Thomas, Philip, Mary Magdalene, and other disciples—and monks in Pachomius's monastery collected and treasured many of them, and read them aloud during evening devotions.

But about ten years after Roman rulers decreed that "Christians may again exist," Constantine was frustrated to find many of them divided into rival groups, arguing about Jesus: was he a man, or was he God? To resolve such disputes, Constantine invited more than three hundred bishops to codify "orthodox" Christian belief into a standard statement that would become the "Nicene Creed" of those who called their group "catholic" (in Greek, "universal"). This was the founding of the Catholic Church.

Decades after that, when the Catholic bishop of Alexandria discovered that monks in Pachomius's monastery were reading secret gospels along with those read publicly in church, he determined to control what monks were allowed to read. Denouncing as "heresy" the gospels that claim to offer Jesus's secret teaching, the bishop ordered the monks at Nag Hammadi to stop reading them. And although nearly all copies were burned or thrown into the Nile, someone—apparently, monks from the monastery—disobeyed the bishop's order and spirited more than fifty texts out of the library and carefully hid them in a nearby burial cave, where, we were told, they were discovered nearly two thousand years later. The texts we have are few and often damaged, but they are opening up new worlds of insight.

So now, given the opportunity to draw upon a far wider range of sources than those available to many historians in the past, I am excited to return to the questions with which we began: Was Jesus actually a historical person? If so, what kind of person? The answers are not obvious, since our earliest sources are brief, and often contradictory. There are more questions than answers—many gaps in what can be known. But the evidence confirms that he was, indeed, an actual person; everyone among his contemporaries who mentions him agrees on that, whether they speak of him with reverence or contempt.

I began this book with other questions, too. What was the social and political context of Jesus's life in Judea? How is it that Jesus, who lived thousands of years ago, has not gone the way of other beings, gods or humans, like Zeus or Julius Caesar, who populate our culture's remote past? How do so many people relate to him as a living presence, even as someone they know intimately? What attracts people to Jesus today? I decided to ask that last question of anthropologists who work in many different parts of the world, especially where Christian conversion is rapidly expanding—in Africa and Latin America, and also in parts of Asia and the United States. When people tell why they convert, we can see how ingeniously—and how variously—they weave stories of Jesus into the fabric of their cultures, as people have done throughout two millennia.

And since in my own life I've been fascinated with these stories and the art they have inspired, I also ask how contemporary artists engage and transform them. What intrigues someone powerfully enough to write a poem bringing some detail—or some person in the story—to new life? What catches the imagination of artists in every generation and nearly every culture who picture Jesus healing a blind man, or raising the dead? What engages the filmmakers who identify with Jesus so intensely that they picture him as powerful and mysterious, or as suffering doubt and unspeakable agony? Here, then, we conclude by comparing how several contemporary artists engage these stories to respond to current—and perennial—issues like political oppression, race, and gender. Now, as throughout the millennia, these ancient stories have been animated by continual revision.

Much as I would enjoy investigating how these questions have played out through all two thousand years, I know that's impossible. But I cannot resist asking not only "Who *was* Jesus?" but also "Who *is* he?" What intrigues me is the astonishing *persistence* of Jesus, both rediscovered and reinvented. How did the rabbi known as Jesus of Nazareth come to be pictured as the Son of God enthroned in heaven next to the Lord of hosts? Exploring the huge terrain in which Christianity was constructed is a two-way quest—in *Miracles and Wonder,* we will go back to recover, as far as possible, what actually happened, and look forward to see how the gospel writers developed their sources in a way that was powerful and even more compelling than straightforward historical writing.

Only now, after reflecting on the themes, texts, and enigmas of Christian tradition for decades, have I felt ready to engage the stories of Jesus directly. Excited by what I found, I invite you to share in the adventure.

1

The Virgin Birth: What Happened?

Jesus's Family and the Circumstances of His Birth

PERHAPS THE MOST unusual feature of the gospel stories is the virgin birth: What might it mean? How do the gospel writers say that it happened, and why? When I first started to ask these questions, I found many surprises. I'd always assumed that there was only one birth story, having seen different versions merged into one on Christmas Eve in our small Methodist church in California, when we acted out the children's pageant, dressed as angels crowned with sparkling halos, or shepherds or kings with paper crowns, arriving to greet the baby Jesus, a doll cradled by the girl who'd scored the role of Mary. But when I went back to investigate the birth story, I was amazed to see that, although the New Testament gospels of Matthew and Luke agree that Jesus was a royal prince, born in Bethlehem, and that heavenly signs announced his birth, at nearly every other point each tells a very different story.

I was also surprised to see that the earliest written narrative of Jesus's life in the Bible, the Gospel of Mark, tells us nothing about the circumstances of his birth, and nearly nothing about his family background. The same is true of the last of the four New Testament gospels, the Gospel of John, but the other two, the Gospel of Luke and the Gospel of Matthew, tell us a great deal, each offering many details.

Both Luke and Matthew start by telling of Jesus's family and lineage, and relating the circumstances of his birth and youth. Each offers a genealogy that traces Jesus's paternal descent from his father, Joseph, to Israel's royal dynasty, back to King David, circa 1000 B.C.E. As we've noted, both locate Jesus's birth in Bethlehem, the city native to Israel's kings. Both also claim that Jesus's parents received divine visions about their future child and his destiny—heavenly signs, astrological portents that signified the arrival of a divinely appointed "Son of God." Most amazing of all, both Matthew and Luke insist that Jesus's birth involved a miracle unprecedented in the history of the world—a "virgin birth."

To understand what each writer has in mind, we need to read these stories separately. Matthew begins by announcing that Jesus is God's chosen Messiah, setting forth a genealogy that shows his descent from Israel's greatest kings, David and Solomon. Then he tells how *magi,* astrologers from foreign lands, alerted by the appearance of a new star signaling the birth of a future king, travel to Jerusalem bearing royal gifts to honor the newborn prince. But news of the birth of a potential rival terrifies the reigning king, Herod the Great. After convening his entire court, he summons the foreign ambassadors, ordering them to find the child and return to tell Herod how to locate him.

Although a familiar story in Luke's gospel pictures Jesus's parents traveling to Bethlehem, seeking an inn, and finding none, Matthew, surprisingly, says that his parents had a house in Bethlehem, ancestral city of the Davidic dynasty. Then, he says, the heavenly sign, the Christmas star, led the *magi* to their home (Matthew 2:10). Overwhelmed with joy, they enter the house and, seeing the child with Mary, his mother, kneel down to pay homage, opening their treasure chests to offer gold, frankincense, and myrrh. But after they secretly depart from Jerusalem, eluding Herod, the enraged king orders his soldiers to slaughter all male Jewish babies under the age of two—a fate Jesus escapes only because his father, Joseph, immediately takes his family into hiding in Egypt. Only later, after hearing of Herod's death, does Joseph dare return with his wife and child. But, fearing that Herod's son and successor also might threaten the child's life, Joseph moves the holy family from their home in Bethlehem to a rural town in Galilee, where they live incognito until Jesus grows up. As Matthew tells it, this explains why, instead of being recognized as a prince, he is known simply as Jesus of Nazareth (2:22–23).

Luke, too, says a lot about Jesus's family and birth; but, as we've noted, he tells quite a different story. Instead of a royal birth heralded by a divine sign recognized by kings and rulers throughout the world, Luke mentions no star, and no public alarm. Instead, he pictures a pregnant young woman from a rural family, who went into labor while traveling away from home. Having nowhere else to stay in Bethlehem, she and her husband took shelter in a barn, and Jesus's mother had to give birth in a manger; only local herdsmen took note of what happened. But since Luke, like Matthew, insists that Jesus's father was related to Israel's royal dynasty, he says that Mary and Joseph had traveled to Bethlehem, claiming that members of that family were required to pay Roman taxes there.

As Luke tells it, Mary, astonished when the angel Gabriel appears to her to say that she is about to become pregnant, exclaims, "How can this be, since I am a virgin?" Reading Luke's account as an adult raised questions that hadn't occurred to me before. Many Christians love and revere Mary, not only as "Mother of God" but also as someone whose loving-kindness and purity Christian women might seek to emulate. But now, rereading Luke's story, I had to consider other possibilities. What if we suspend, for a moment, the happy fiction Luke presents, and consider how a young woman receiving such a message might actually respond? Isn't it likely that a girl with no sexual experience might be startled and dismayed to hear that she is about to become pregnant, given the potential embarrassment and shame she might suffer? Luke is a writer who, unlike Matthew, focuses on Mary, and wants us to imagine her surprised and delighted. Yet the dialogue he puts in her mouth suggests that she is overwhelmed and simply acquiesces, declaring, "I am the Lord's slave; so be it" (Luke 1:38). Luke's choice of words, the Greek *doulē,* "slave," is often translated into softer terms, like "servant" or the English word "handmaiden." But those hearing this story in Luke's time would likely know that an enslaved woman was required to obey a master's will, even when that meant bearing his child, as it often did. Luke intends to show, however, that the Lord himself could turn a burden into a blessing, even for Mary.

For over two thousand years, Christians throughout the world have merged the two stories into one, to create a composite version that ignores their discrepancies. For, although both birth stories agree on three points—Jesus's lineage, the location in Bethlehem, a miraculous birth—there the similarities end and difficulties begin. And although historians have sought for millennia to verify details of these stories, they have found none—none for Matthew's claim of an unusual astronomical sign; none for any historical record that hints at a massive slaughter of Jewish babies; and none to validate Luke's claim that Jesus's family would have had to pay Roman taxes in Bethlehem. So, when the Roman Catholic scholar Raymond Brown considers the "star" Matthew mentions, he notes that, though ancient Babylonian astrologers "might have associated a particular star with the King of the Jews," there are no records of such an event, or even of such a prediction. Brown does suggest that many of Matthew's contemporaries might have accepted his account, since Roman biographers often associated the sighting of special astronomical signs with the births of great rulers. For example, a silver coin honoring Julius Caesar (c. 40 B.C.E.) portrays him with a special star that signals his divine destiny.

In the seventeenth century, European scientists began to sift through evidence of unusual celestial events, seeking scientific evidence for the "star." The astronomer Johannes Kepler suggested that it must have been a supernova, although there is no record of one from that time. Others have suggested that the star may have been a comet, perhaps Halley's Comet, which appeared in 12 B.C.E. Later, however, when Kepler sighted a conjunction of

Jupiter and Saturn, he noted that the same conjunction, predicted to occur every 805 years, may have happened in 7 B.C.E., when it appeared in the constellation Pisces, and so may have been the Christmas star—a view that some endorse to this day.

Yet, since such speculation is far from conclusive, literary scholars suggest instead that, rather than speaking of astronomical "facts," Matthew assimilated into his narrative the poetic language of such prophets as Isaiah. Writing six hundred years before Jesus's birth, Isaiah envisioned that when the "day of the Lord" dawned, Gentiles would travel to the holy land of Israel, bearing "the wealth of the nations," along with camels and flocks of sheep, bringing offerings of "gold and frankincense" to honor the dawning of the "great light" of God's glory (Isaiah 60:1–7). If that is what prompts Matthew to write the "Christmas star" into his birth narrative, his likely intention is not to deceive his audience into believing something that didn't happen. Instead, convinced that Jesus was, indeed, God's promised Messiah, Matthew may have assumed that events coinciding with his birth would have fulfilled ancient prophecies. And since Matthew intended not only to write a narrative of Jesus's life but above all to show the meaning of his birth and his life, he may well have adopted Isaiah's metaphor, picturing Jesus's birth as the light of a new dawn.

What about Matthew's claim that King Herod ordered his soldiers to slaughter Jewish babies? As noted, historians of the early Roman Empire have searched in vain for any hint of such a government-ordered massacre. Yet Herod was famous for his cruelty, which may have made such a story sound plausible. When he suspected two of his sons, Alexander and Aristobulus, of plotting against him, Herod ordered his executioners to kill them both; he had previously executed their mother, Mariamne, his favorite wife, under similar charges. After that, a popular saying mocked his professed refusal to eat nonkosher food: "Better to be Herod's pig than his son!" Nevertheless, nearly all historians agree that the unprecedented mass killing that Matthew claims to report could not have occurred without any trace remaining in Jewish or Roman historical records.

Instead, here again, as in the case of the "Christmas star," many scholars agree that Matthew models his story of Jesus's birth on literary precedent—on famous passages in the Hebrew Bible, to suggest, for example, that, just as the infant Moses escaped the Egyptian pharaoh's mass slaughter of Jewish babies, so the infant Jesus barely escaped a similar massacre under King Herod (Matthew 2:8–18). As for the third event, which Luke reports— that Mary and Joseph had to travel to Bethlehem to register for taxes—historians of Rome note that, although Roman rulers did inflict severe taxes on Jews around the time of Jesus's birth, they imposed no such travel requirement. So, here again, literary scholars join the discussion, suggesting that Luke includes this detail in order to move Jesus's parents from their home in Naza- reth to Bethlehem in time for his birth, to fulfill the Hebrew Bible prophecies of a Messiah's birthplace.

Matthew's and Luke's birth narratives, then, likely contain more literary adaptation of Hebrew Bible stories than history. This similarity between their gospels shows that, although the New Testament writers often mention historical events, they were not writing primarily to report history, or even biography—not, at

any rate, in ways that conform to Greek and Roman literary conventions. Instead, they were writing, some forty to seventy years
after Jesus's death, primarily to publicize his message. Simply put,
Jesus's devoted believers wrote these narratives to persuade others to "believe in the gospel"—the Greek term *euangelion* translates as "good news"—and join their new movement.

The gospels, then, have that motivation in common. But when
we think of these writings as less than factual, written, in effect, as
propaganda for the movement (intending that term as descrip-
tive, not pejorative), we begin to question startling discrepancies
between them. The earliest written sources that mention Jesus—
the letters of Paul, and the New Testament gospels—all mention
his mother. But apart from the two birth stories we've noted in
Matthew and Luke, only John's gospel briefly mentions Joseph as
Jesus's father. Neither Paul nor Mark ever mentions Joseph's name,
and neither mentions any human father. Noting this absence, Professor Raymond Brown has speculated that Joseph is not a historical figure. He suggests instead that Matthew may have patterned
what he writes of Joseph's receiving messages from angels in his
dreams on the Hebrew Bible story of Joseph "the dreamer," told
in Genesis 37. But if Joseph was not Jesus's father, who was? As we
shall see, many respected scholars regard the birth stories primarily as legends woven from Biblical stories in order to deflect that
embarrassing question.

The mystery begins with Jesus's genealogy. We've noted that
Matthew begins his account with one genealogy, and Luke adds
another—which raises questions we need to investigate. Both
claim to trace Jesus's lineage back to King David, but when we com-

pare them, we cannot help noting that these two accounts clash from the start. Immediately after mentioning Joseph as Jesus's father, each names a different man as Jesus's paternal grandfather; and after that, the two genealogies continue to diverge at nearly every turn (Matthew 1:1–18; Luke 3:23–38). Finally, whereas Matthew claims to trace Jesus's lineage back to Abraham, Luke goes further, claiming to trace it back to Adam, ancestor of the human race, whom he calls "son of God"—a term he also applies to Jesus.

A confusing genealogy is one thing; the bigger question is, why do both writers insist on Jesus's "virgin birth"? Matthew admits that Joseph himself found this claim so outrageous that when he discovered that his future bride was pregnant, and not with his child, he immediately decided to break the marriage contract (Matthew 1:18–19). At this point in Luke's story, however, he mentions nothing of marital discord. On the contrary, Luke wants to interpret what happened as miraculous, an enormous blessing. As he tells it, a young girl who "has never known a man" suddenly, astonishingly, discovers that God has graced her with a unique role in human history. Bursting with joy, she begins to sing a song of praise to God.

How are we to account for these wildly divergent stories, each making such an improbable claim? Apparently, what prompted Matthew and Luke to write these birth narratives were rumors ridiculing Jesus as a bastard—a charge of illegitimacy that Mark's account, written some ten years earlier than the others, seems to confirm. Both Matthew and Luke clearly knew Mark's account very well, since each of them, writing independently, chose to revise it. So, although Mark says nothing about Jesus's birth when he begins his gospel, later, when he does mention Jesus's family, he does so only incidentally, and in ways that embarrassed Jesus's followers. For, after recounting how Jesus's public activities had aroused huge crowds to gather around him, and gained him a popular reputation as a prophet and healer, Mark says that his relatives were alarmed. Mark reports that "his family went out to seize [or "restrain"] him, saying, '*He has gone out of his mind!*'" (Mark 3:21). This episode troubled later Christian translators so much that many chose to translate the phrase that ordinarily means "his family" (*hoi peri autou*) to imply that it wasn't his own family who thought he was insane but only some people "around him." Yet Mark admits that other people also suspected Jesus of insanity—or, as his contemporaries would interpret his actions, that he was demon-possessed. As Mark tells it, "The scribes who came down from Jerusalem said, '*He is possessed by Beelzebub; he uses the ruler of demons to cast out demons!*'" (3:22).

Not long after that, Mark says, Jesus returned to his home town, Nazareth. But when, on the Sabbath, he stood up to speak in the local synagogue, as he had done in other villages, his former neighbors greeted him with skepticism and scorn: "Where did this man get all this? . . . What miracles has he been doing? Isn't this the carpenter, *the son of Mary,* the brother of James, Joses, Judas, and Simon; and aren't his sisters here with us too?" (6:1–3).

Mark says that many who knew Jesus best were offended by him, so contemptuous that "he could not do any miracles there . . . and he was amazed at their refusal to believe in him" (6:3–6). Soon afterward, Jesus left Nazareth, declaring, "Prophets are honored everywhere, except in their hometown, and among their own relatives and family" (6:4–6). Hearing the tale of this visit, Mark's Jewish contemporaries likely would realize that hardly anyone in a patrilineal culture would call a Jewish boy "Mary's son" if he had a recognized father, even one deceased. Instead, Mark admits, Jesus's own neighbors saw him only as a local workman, and his mother as a woman who had many children—five sons, as well as several daughters not regarded as important enough to name— and no father in sight (6:3).

Recognizing these details in Mark's account as extremely troublesome, two of his readers—those we call Matthew and Luke— set out to revise what Mark wrote, apparently intending to replace it with their own versions. Both cut out information they regarded as potentially damaging to their claims about Jesus. Consequently, both Matthew and Luke leave out the story of Jesus's family trying to restrain him, and their concern about his sanity. Even worse, though, was Mark's report of the neighbors calling Jesus "son of Mary." Every one of the later gospel writers leaves out that offensive slur, changing the wording to include a recognizable father. Matthew, for example, changes this sentence to imply that "the carpenter" was not Jesus himself but Jesus's *father*. As he revises Mark's story, then, the neighbors identify Jesus as the son of his supposed father, as well as his mother: "Isn't this *the carpenter's son*? And is not his mother called Mary?" (Matthew 13:55). Luke, too, writing independently of Matthew, changes the neighbors' question to read, "Isn't this *the son of Joseph*?" (Luke 4:22). Finally, John, writing his own version ten to twenty years later than any of the others, claims that they'd said, "Isn't this Jesus, *the son of Joseph, whose father and mother we know*?" (John 6:42).

Noting the embarrassment that these "corrections" are meant to cover up, the historian Morton Smith suggests, "These facts make it probable that Jesus was not the son of Joseph. Had he been so, 'the son of Mary' would never have appeared in a Christian text." Smith goes on to say, "If Jesus' birth was, in fact, irregular"—that is, illegitimate—"he would have been a ridiculed child in the small country town in which he grew up, and we could easily imagine the reasons for his leaving Nazareth." Many scholars note in Mark's narrative a disconnect between Jesus and his family. The Biblical scholar David Flusser observes, "There is a psychological element in the life of Jesus that we may not ignore; his rejection of the family in which he was born; and he expected, even urged, his followers to do that too." For, as we have seen, Mark already let slip that when Jesus was out in public, his own relatives and family had gone out to restrain him and take him home, worried that he might be insane (Mark 3:20–21). Shortly after that, Mark says that Jesus's mother and brothers went to a house where Jesus was speaking to a large crowd. Standing outside, they "sent to him, and called him." But when Jesus was told that "your mother and brothers are outside, asking for you," he refused to go to them, or even to invite them in. Instead, he turned to his audience, asking rhetorically, "Who are my mother and brothers?" Then, looking out at the crowd before him, he declared, "My mothers and brothers are here! Whoever does the will of God is my brother and sister and mother" (3:31–35).

Although later Christian tradition tends to sentimentalize Jesus's relationship with his mother, she does not appear in the rest of Mark's narrative. Luke reports that Jesus urged his disciples, too, to leave their homes, wives, parents, and children, as he had done, "for the sake of the kingdom of God" (Luke 18:28–29). As Luke tells it, Jesus famously declared, "*Anyone who comes to me, and does not hate his father and mother, wife and children, yes, even his own life, cannot be my disciple*" (14:26)—a statement that Matthew modifies ("*Whoever loves father or mother more than me is not worthy of me*" [Matthew 10:37–39]). Even John, who tries to picture a warmer relationship between Jesus and his mother, reports that, early on, he sharply rebuked her, calling her "woman" (John 2:4), and noted that even Jesus's own brothers did not believe in him (7:5). Worse, John reports that Jewish critics snidely implied, to Jesus's face, that they knew he was said to be illegitimate (8:41).

Charges like that are what Matthew and Luke seek to deflect by writing their birth narratives. For Jesus's followers were intensely aware of what hostile outsiders were saying. Rabbinic sources from those early centuries often repeat the derisive comments then circulating: that Jesus was illegitimate, his mother promiscuous. Some go so far as to say that she conceived him with a lover who was not even Jewish—a Roman soldier named Panthera (a name spelled in different ways in various sources). According to one rabbinic report, the distinguished Rabbi Eliezer, teaching around the time Mark was writing, was accused of becoming a follower of Jesus after he reportedly had heard the teachings of a Galilean, spoken "in the name of Jesus, the son of Panteri"—a charge that Eliezer famously denied. This may be the earliest report of many in which Jewish teachers derisively spoke of Jesus as the son of a man named Panthera. Other rabbinic reports say that some Jewish teachers referred to Jesus instead as "Ben Stada," arguing with others, who asked, "Was he then the son of Stada?"—a derisive term, sometimes interpreted as *s'tat da*, "this one was turned away" from her husband, implying that she was promiscuous. Other rabbinic reports suggest that Rabbi Hisda, much later, suggested that "the lover was Pandira," prompting some to spread a rumor that his mother was Miriam (Mary), a hairdresser, effectively accusing her of infidelity.

Hostile reports in early Jewish sources also suggest that Jesus had learned magic in Egypt, having tattoos on his body, as magicians were known to do, indicating that he had undergone magic initiations, and knew spells. A report from the generation after Eliezer shows that some rumors persisted, especially those saying that Jesus practiced magic and that he deviated from Jewish tradition. And Mark acknowledges that even during Jesus's lifetime his disciples invoked his "power name," used to heal or exorcise demons, after Jesus told them to do so. He says that they objected, though, when they heard others outside their group trying to use it as well (Mark 9:38–41). Rabbinic reports from the generation after his death indicate that other people, too, tried to enact healings in the name of "Jesus ben Pantera."

Around two hundred years after Jesus's death, his devoted follower Origen, a brilliant Egyptian teacher, worked hard to challenge these allegations, widely publicized in a popular anti-Christian polemic called *On the True Doctrine*. Its author, Celsus, was a Greek philosopher and follower of Plato who warned that the Christian movement was a dangerous secret cult. Speaking as a patriotic citizen of Rome and devout worshipper of the gods,

Celsus caricatured Christians as ignorant rabble who believed in crazy stories. He also accused them of conspiring to destroy the empire itself by denigrating its culture and demeaning its gods— serious charges indeed. Writing about a hundred years after Jesus's death, Celsus admits that he had strung together what he had heard from Jewish critics of the movement:

> Let us imagine what a Jew . . . might put to Jesus: "*Is it not true . . . that you fabricated the story of your birth from a virgin to quiet rumors about the true and unsavory circumstances of your origins?* Is it not the case that far from being born in royal David's city of Bethlehem, you were born in a poor country town, and of a woman who earned her living by spinning? Is it not the case that when her deceit was discovered, to wit, that she was pregnant by a Roman soldier named Panthera, she was driven away by her husband—the carpenter—and convicted of adultery?"

Stories like that have resonated through Jewish sources from the first century to the present day, while Christians have continued to reject such allegations as unfair attacks fueled by hostility.

At this point, someone might object: Isn't Jesus's virgin birth an essential element of Christian faith? Doesn't the Apostles' Creed, foundational for the Catholic Church, and those later endorsed by Protestant and Orthodox Christians, declare that Jesus was "conceived by the Holy Spirit, born of the virgin Mary"? Church leaders in later times certainly used these phrases to interpret what Matthew and Luke wrote in their birth narratives. But when we look at the gospel writers themselves, we can see, for example, that Matthew, writing circa 80–90 C.E., was not, of course, a "Christian." This is a term he never uses, and likely never heard. Luke, assumed to be the only Gentile among the four evangelists, suggests that outsiders coined the term "Christian" about two generations after Jesus's death to refer to Gentile converts like himself. Matthew, like Paul, is, of course, a follower of Jesus, immersed in the traditions and the Jewish Scriptures, and both Matthew and Luke were writing at least a century before the movement we call "Christianity," much less any Christian creed, was invented.

When I began to investigate the work of various Christian scholars, each sifting through the evidence about the birth stories, I found that they came to opposite conclusions. We've seen that Professor Raymond Brown, who, in 1977, published a massive and learned study of the birth narratives, concluded that the evidence supports the church's theological claim of virgin birth. About ten years later, the Catholic historian Jane Schaberg, the first woman scholar to carefully review the same evidence, along with countless scholarly sources, came to the opposite conclusion. Schaberg suggests that even Matthew's birth story inadvertently acknowledges that Jesus was conceived out of wedlock. When I first heard of her book, I ignored it, as did many other scholars, having mistakenly assumed from the title (*The Illegitimacy of Jesus*) that she had simply written a hostile polemic.

Even now, I hesitate to mention such allegations, lest some readers jump to the conclusion that I endorse them. But we cannot discuss the birth narratives without asking why the stories are written as they are, and how Jesus's birth may have happened. In a book called *The Virgin Birth,* the scholar and Presbyterian minister Tom Boslooper adopts what may be the simplest explanation: that Mary and Joseph, engaged to be married, had begun a sexual relationship before they actually lived together. Thus, he suggests, the child was theirs, conceived early. Reaction to Boslooper's book was swift and harsh: members of the Presbyterian church in which he was ordained charged Boslooper with heresy, and forbade him to preach. Boslooper's study, like Schaberg's, is carefully considered and cautiously expressed. He points out that in some areas of Judea, an engaged couple could have been alone at least once after the engagement agreement, when they could have begun a sexual relationship. Yet, had that happened, as other scholars point out, there would have been no scandal, no blame—and no need to invent elaborate "birth stories."

Furthermore—and surprisingly—both Matthew and Luke explicitly reject that explanation. Each insists that Joseph was not Jesus's father, even if, as Matthew suggests, he later agreed to adopt the child as his own. As many historians have noted, Jewish sources report that Jews in Galilee set far stricter standards for sexual purity than did their groups elsewhere: a Jewish girl arriving to live with her future husband would have to be a virgin. As Brown notes, "Many think that the difference arose because Jewish communities were aware of the danger that Roman troops occupying Judea might rape or seduce a betrothed virgin." Anyone subjected to foreign occupation forces, whether in the first century or the twenty-first, knows that foreign soldiers often target and rape young girls, especially those from poor families in rural areas. Yet Brown dismisses the possibility that Mary faced

27

this threat, noting that Jesus's birth occurred at the beginning of the first century: he writes that permanent Roman garrisons did not occupy Judea until after the failed Jewish revolution, some seventy years later.

But Brown and those who share his view have ignored the facts on the ground in first-century Galilee—facts that no one living in Nazareth at the time could possibly miss. Decades before and after the turn of the first century, various groups of devout and militant Jews were plotting revolution against Rome, a situation that the Jewish historian Josephus documents in detail. Josephus himself, an educated man from an influential priestly family, had served as a general in the revolt that began circa 66 C.E., some thirty years after Jesus's death. Captured and held as a prisoner of war, Josephus, after his release, wrote an account that is sometimes read as taking the Roman side, in which he denounces his fellow revolutionaries as *lestai,* "bandits" or "robbers," a derogatory term he often used for warriors inciting sedition, intent on what he later characterized as a futile and foolhardy rebellion.

Nevertheless, Josephus also wrote a famous history of that war, reporting that around the time of Jesus's birth, usually dated to circa 6–4 B.C.E., King Herod, ruling Judea as Rome's subject king, sought help from Quintilius Varus, the newly appointed governor of Syria, to crush a palace coup and prevent potential threats to Roman power. Josephus writes that soon after this, in 4 B.C.E., when Herod became ill and died, certain "seditious people" incited the crowds pouring into Jerusalem for Passover to violently protest Roman rule. Herod's son Archelaus, who had claimed his father's throne, immediately sent his whole army to put down the riots. In the fighting that followed, Josephus reports, Roman soldiers killed three thousand Jewish fighters before the rest fled into the neighboring mountains.

But when Archelaus failed to pacify his territory, and "ten thousand other disorders" broke out all over Judea, he fled from the province at night and sailed to Rome. Governor Varus, alarmed, sent word to Emperor Augustus in Rome that gangs of militant Jews were now inciting insurrection in Judea, seeking to free their people from Roman domination and exorbitant taxes. Josephus takes special note of Judas the Galilean, whom he describes as a fierce and dangerous revolutionary, hungry for power. Having established his headquarters in the Galilean city of Sepphoris, an important Roman stronghold, Judas incited a crowd of Jewish fighters to attack the government palace. After his men broke into the imperial armory and seized the weapons they found there, arming themselves, another group attacked a nearby Roman fort, and looted the imperial treasury. As Josephus tells it, "The whole district became a scene of fire and blood."

Although Varus commanded four Roman legions, along with auxiliary troops who perhaps numbered some twenty thousand more men, he was worried about protecting them from the threat of more uprisings. So he divided the legions, and marched two of them from Syria toward Galilee. Concerned that he still needed more fighting men to subdue the Judean countryside, Varus secured fifteen hundred more auxiliary soldiers from Beirut, which may have included an expert cohort of Syrian archers, along with other troops from the king of Arabia, and sent these combined reinforcements into Galilee. These soldiers attacked

Judas's men and, after fierce fighting, regained control of Seppho-ris. Then, to punish the city for having allowed Judas to base his headquarters there, Roman soldiers captured and enslaved the entire population, and burned the city to the ground.

Anyone living within a two hour's walk of Sepphoris—for example, in Nazareth, about three miles away—would have seen the fires torching the city, and would have smelled the smoke for days. Later, people from nearby towns would have seen the scorched ruins of the once-great city, and heard horrific stories from survivors. Leaving several thousand soldiers stationed there to stamp out further resistance, Varus marched the others toward Jerusalem, ordering them to burn down the city of Emmaus on the way, to avenge the deaths of hundreds of his men. Subject people knew how Roman armies operated; in words that Taci-tus claims to quote from a defeated British general: "They make a desert and call it peace."

When Varus and his armies reached Jerusalem, many citizens there surrendered to them, having heard how they had devas-tated the countryside. Varus then sent thousands of soldiers back into rural areas to hunt down leading insurrectionists like Judas, who were hiding out in the hills of Galilee. Josephus reports that Varus's soldiers captured and crucified two thousand men—a number that some contemporary historians suggest is exagger-ated, but, in any case, a hideous spectacle. Roman commanders often chose to set up crucifixions in public places, especially on well-traveled roads, intending to punish the Jewish people and to terrify them into submission. Who, passing by, could ever forget seeing a forest of naked men hanging from crosses, their dying cries of agony sometimes lasting for days, their corpses often left as carrion for vultures and wild dogs?

Despite Roman military codes of discipline, Josephus reports that Varus was unable to control the thousands of Roman soldiers and auxiliary troops encamped from Jerusalem to the hills of rural Galilee. Having destroyed Jewish resistance, and then left to patrol and ravage the country, they disobeyed orders, Josephus says, and "had often been disorderly," stealing from the local population, coercing Jewish men into forced labor, and prowling for unprotected women to gratify their sexual needs. As the archeological historian Marianne Sawicki notes:

> Many young people in and around Sepphoris were sexually assaulted when the city was besieged and burned in 4 B.C.E. It is plausible that the mother of Jesus was one of the victims of this violence . . . The archeological evidence of the siege of Sepphoris confirms at least one event during which Roman soldiers combed through Mary's neighborhood, and, following their standard procedure, raped whomever they could catch.

Was Mary, as a young girl from a humble rural family, "one of the victims of this violence"?

We have no way of knowing. But scholars like Brown, who choose to dismiss that possibility, do not mention what Jews bitterly remembered for centuries, and many do even today, as the "war of Varus"—events that occurred around the time of Jesus's conception and birth. What this indicates, at least, is that the charge that Jewish critics so often repeated—that Jesus's bio-logical father was a Roman soldier—is not entirely implausible. The military historian Benjamin Isaac cites Jewish sources that speak of rape by soldiers as a common occurrence in first-century Judea, a fact that may well account for Galilean Jews' intense anxi-ety to protect their daughters' virginity.

And even though some scholars note that the name Pandira/Pantera, with variants like Panthera or Panteri, is of Greek ori-gin, it does occur in Latin inscriptions of the early Roman Empire that mention men with Greek names. Other scholars cite hints of a soldier with that name who may have served with the Roman army in Palestine at the turn of the first century C.E. His grave-stone, found in Germany, which was inscribed with the name Tiberius Julius Abdes Panthera, notes that he served in Palestine in the early first century during some part of Emperor Tiberius's reign, apparently until 9 C.E. The inscription describes him as a Syrian archer from the city of Sidon, in Phoenicia (present-day Lebanon), who had joined the Cohort Sagittariorum ("cohort of archers"). Scholars of the Roman military suggest that his name, Pantera, may indicate that he wore a panther's skin fur to display his cohort's predatory emblem, since his gravestone notes that he served as its standard-bearer. His Latin names, Tiberius Julius, would have been awarded to him later, in recognition of his hav-ing served for forty years in the Roman imperial army, after he was honorably discharged.

Historian Adolf Deissmann suggested that Pantera's unit may have been among those that Varus sent into Judea in 6 B.C.E. to stop the insurrection. We've noted how, after the combined

Roman forces routed the Jewish fighters, they set the city on fire and burned it to charred ashes, before capturing and selling the city's population as slaves. After that, stationed in Judea, the unit was ordered to patrol the territory, and to pounce on any hint of further revolt. Roman soldiers were commonly known to exploit, mistreat, and kill subjugated people, and we've noted Josephus's comment that after Varus's army had finished the exhausting and messy work of crucifying thousands of insurrectionists, they acted in ways that shocked even their commander.

Could this tombstone of a soldier who would have been in his early twenties at the time of Jesus's conception (6–4 B.C.E.) be the only genuine relic of the Holy Family? The historian James Tabor discusses the question of whether this man was, indeed, Jesus's biological father. Yet even Morton Smith, who raises this question, acknowledges that this is unlikely, since the polemical sources that repeat such allegations cannot demonstrate any direct connection with Jesus's mother.

Let's be clear, then: my purpose in mentioning these speculations is not to endorse them, since the sparse evidence that some writers cite is only circumstantial. Recognizing the political context of first-century Galilee is necessary, though, to understand the gospel stories. What they tell hints at what the writers knew well: that everyday life in occupied Judea often included violence. Roman writers picture their empire as a civilizing force, but Josephus depicts first-century Judea as a land in turmoil. What has lent credence to stories of Pantera is what local people knew: that Roman soldiers brutally suppressed any hint of revolt, exploited subject people, and targeted local women with sexual violence.

The political context of Jesus's crucifixion is violence, as we shall see; at his birth, it surely contributed to the widespread and repeated rumors about his paternity, which clearly troubled some of his devoted early followers.

We've already noted that Mark's story includes startling contradictions. While proclaiming Jesus "Son of God" and "Messiah," Mark hints that he was born in rural Judea, apparently to local peasants, and regarded as possibly illegitimate. Matthew and Luke, Mark's revisers, working independently, took a different tack. Each decided to preface his narrative with an elaborate and detailed birth story. In the process, too, both writers challenged Jesus's detractors by offering an account that includes a father who could link Jesus to King David through his paternal line.

Matthew announces in his opening line what matters most to him: "An account of the genealogy of Jesus the Messiah, the son of David, the son of Abraham" (Matthew 1:1). From this beginning, he traces the lineage of "Jesus the Messiah" back to King David, and from David back to Abraham, in three sets of fourteen generations. As scholars have shown, however, this alleged genealogy is seriously flawed. The Roman Catholic scholar Brown points out a problem with Matthew's arithmetic: the last of the three sections traces only thirteen generations, not fourteen, not to mention the problems with Matthew's list of ancestors. Apart from other errors that Brown lists, we note only the most obvious: that Matthew's genealogy differs from Luke's in nearly every detail—starting with Jesus's paternal grandfather, whom Matthew names as Jacob, whereas Luke says his name was Eli (Matthew 1:16; Luke 3:24).

Most notably, of course, both set out to demonstrate that Jesus's seeming "irregular" birth was actually a miracle—one that utterly defies ordinary understanding. Immediately after Matthew sets forth a royal genealogy for Jesus, then, he turns to the question of how Jesus was conceived: "The birth of Jesus Christ happened like this. When his mother Mary was engaged to Joseph, but before they came together, she was found to be pregnant" (Matthew 1:18ff). Matthew acknowledges that Joseph, confronted with a pregnant fiancée, was shocked and deeply upset. What was he to do? Being "a righteous man"—that is, Torah-observant—he would have considered his legal options. At this point in the narrative, both Matthew and Luke allude to a section in the Deuteronomic legal code (Deuteronomy 22:23–24) that deals with the case of a man engaged to a young woman found to be pregnant, whose child he swears is not his. The law states that if she had sex with a man while in town, where she might have cried out for help, she is judged to have been complicit, and thus guilty of sexual immorality (Hebrew, *zenut*; Greek, *porneia*). In that case, she would be liable to the death penalty, along with her partner in crime.

The law goes on to state, however, that if the woman is in the countryside when a man rapes her, with no one else around, she is judged to be not guilty, since the court would assume that she was forced. In that case, because she has been violated, her fiancé would be advised to break the marriage contract. And as Matthew tells it, that is what Joseph decides to do. Instead of acting as if he thought his fiancée had betrayed him, Joseph responds as a man who assumes that she has been raped: he decides to break the marriage contract without disgracing her in public for what she would have been powerless to prevent.

Then, however, Matthew says that Joseph abruptly changes course and decides to marry her, making the magnanimous decision to adopt her child as his own. What changes his mind is a dream in which an "angel of the Lord" appears, ordering him not to be afraid to marry the woman, "for the child conceived in her is from the Holy Spirit. She will bear a son, and you are to name him Jesus" (Yehoshua; in English, Joshua: "deliverer" [Matthew 1:20–21]).

At this point, we may begin to guess what motivated Matthew to introduce a startling—and utterly unprecedented—innovation into what, at first glance, looks like a traditional Biblical genealogy. Such a genealogy ordinarily would list only patriarchs in the male line: "Abraham was the father of Isaac, and Isaac the father of Jacob, and Jacob the father of Judah and his brothers, and Judah the follower of Perez . . ." But, aware that people are slandering Jesus's mother, Matthew weaves into his genealogy something surprising—the names of four women: Tamar, Rahab, Ruth, and Bathsheba. Scholars have long debated Matthew's motives: *Why women?* And why *these* women, in particular? The Biblical stories told of each of these women have little in common, except this: each one includes hints of sexual scandal.

The first, Tamar, a childless young widow, disguises herself as a prostitute to trick Judah, her former father-in-law, into having intercourse with her. Discovered to be pregnant, she is sentenced to be burned to death for immorality. But then she reveals that Judah has failed to respect and support her as his daughter-in-law.

After Judah admits that he wronged her, he takes responsibility for the twins conceived through this incestuous match, and vindicates Tamar. He even declares, "She is more righteous than I," a judgment that a voice from heaven confirms (Genesis 38:26).

The second woman Matthew includes is Rahab, a prostitute living in Jericho. The book of Joshua tells how two men whom Joshua sent into Jericho as spies sneaked into the city and went to Rahab's house of prostitution. Surprisingly, this bold woman defied the king of Jericho by hiding the spies and sending their pursuers off on a false trail. And when they realize that she has saved their lives, Rahab asks in return that the Hebrew fugitives spare her and her family in the coming war, which they do. Jewish tradition suggests that she then married Joshua, becoming an unlikely member of Israel's royal dynasty—a claim that no other Biblical sources confirm.

The third woman Matthew weaves into his genealogy is Ruth, a childless widow, not even Jewish. She, too, has a tainted history, having deliberately seduced Boaz, a wealthy relative of her former mother-in-law, Naomi, and then pleaded with him to protect her by marrying her. He agrees, legitimizing the son whom she will bear, whom Matthew identifies as the grandfather of King David.

Finally, Matthew mentions Bathsheba, most notorious of all: a married woman, "very beautiful," whom King David, standing on the roof of his palace, saw bathing, and desired. The Bible bluntly tells what happened next. While Uriah, her husband, was away on military duty, "David sent messengers, and seized her; and she came to him, and lay with him"—a simple story of a king's lust, and a forced affair. Sometime later, with her husband still away, she sent word to the king: "I am pregnant" (2 Samuel 11:2–5).

Alarmed, David immediately recalled her husband from battle, hoping that he would sleep with his wife and make it look as though he himself had fathered her unborn child. When this plot failed, David, still hoping to keep his culpability secret, arranged to have Uriah murdered. Bathsheba grieved for her husband, but soon David sent for her again, and married her. The Biblical story goes on to say that what David did "displeased the Lord"; and even David recognized, on some level, that he himself deserved the death penalty for committing adultery and murder. But David did not die. Instead, "The Lord struck the child that Uriah's wife bore to David, and it became very ill, and died" (12 Samuel 12:15–18). Even after that, David went back to Bathsheba, "and lay with her," and she gave birth to a second child, the one they named Solomon, who would succeed his father as Israel's king.

Why, then, did Matthew include women—and *these* women—in his genealogy of Jesus? As we've seen, every one of them has a scandalous sexual history: incest, prostitution, rape, pregnancy before marriage. Furthermore, living in a patriarchal culture, none of these women would have any capacity to salvage her own reputation. Instead, each has to depend on a man whose social and legal status could save her from disgrace. But Matthew's genealogy shows that each one received that, and then far more: *a role in Israel's sacred history.* Now Matthew has prepared his reader for what he recounts next. Before mentioning Mary's premarital pregnancy, he has sought to soften the blow by preceding her story with those of other women suspected of *zenut*, yet later vindicated, even included in Israel's royal lineage.

In Matthew's story, Joseph makes the difficult and compassionate choice to proceed with the marriage, giving his name to her future child. In doing so, he not only legitimizes the child but also draws him into a traditionally Davidic ancestral line. Thus, like those of Tamar, Rahab, Ruth, and Bathsheba, Mary's sexual scandal was mitigated by the magnanimity of a socially powerful male protector. Yet, when telling this story, Matthew seems to ignore the most obvious objection, as does Luke: that neither of the two genealogies they offer could have anything to do with Jesus's biological ancestry, since both insist that Joseph had nothing to do with his conception, a point that Matthew emphasizes. Breaking the conventional pattern of genealogies, he lists "Matthan, the father of Jacob, and *Jacob the father of Joseph, the husband of Mary, of whom Jesus was born,* who is called the Messiah" (Matthew 1:15–16).

To deal with this complex situation, Matthew, himself immersed in the Hebrew Bible, follows Mark's lead by adding more passages from the classical prophets in order to validate his story, and to demonstrate its continuity with Israel's Scriptures. Some decades earlier, anonymous followers of Jesus may already have made this task easier. Convinced that Jesus must be Israel's Messiah, they went back and examined the prophecies of Isaiah, Jeremiah, Ezekiel, Hosea, and others, searching for passages that could be read as "testimonies" of him, confirming that many prophets had foreseen Jesus's coming.

Taking their clues from such lists, Matthew and Luke both claim that the prophet Isaiah, writing some six hundred years before Jesus's life, had predicted his miraculous birth. Above all, both draw upon Isaiah 7:14, in which Isaiah challenges skeptics who doubt God's power, declaring, *"The Lord himself will give you a sign. Behold, a virgin shall conceive, and bear a son; and shall call his name Immanu-el: 'God with us.'"* Invoking this oracle, both Matthew and Luke insist that what skeptics despise as an illegitimate birth is nothing less than a "sign," a divine miracle—signaling God's activity on earth.

Startling as it sounds, is this so different from what ancient authors claim for other remarkable men? At first glance, Jesus's birth story sounds like a familiar ancient trope—a story told to glorify a hero. For example, the Greek biographer Diogenes Laertius wrote in his *Life of Plato* that Plato's mother, Periktione, failed to conceive until her husband received a vision of Apollo. After that, Laertius writes, "he left her unmolested until her child was born . . . the same day on which the Delians say that Apollo himself was born." Similarly, the Roman historian Plutarch, when writing of Alexander the Great, tells how Alexander's mother, Olympias, as a bride, before she had sexual relations with her new husband, "dreamed . . . that a thunder-bolt fell upon her womb." Plutarch also tells how, on another occasion, "a serpent was once seen lying stretched out by the side of Olympias as she slept," indicating that "she was the partner of a superior being," as if "the god [Apollo], in the form of a serpent, [shared her] couch." Suetonius, a Roman court historian who wrote biographies of emperors, included a similar miracle story in his account of

Augustus's life. One night, when Augustus's mother was attending a midnight ritual at the temple of Apollo, "a serpent glided up to her and shortly went away." Suetonius's account suggests that Augustus, born nine months later, "was therefore regarded as the son of Apollo." When he became emperor, Roman coins hailed Augustus as "son of god."

An educated Christian like Justin, a philosopher converted from paganism, familiar with such stories, admits, "Our stories of Jesus often sound just like the myths often told of the gods." But, Justin insists, there's one enormous difference: those pagan stories are just myths invented to praise famous men, *but the stories of Jesus are actually true.* However, aware that Jewish and pagan critics ridiculed such claims, Justin writes an account of a debate in which he says he challenged Trypho, a Jewish philosopher, to explain Isaiah's prophecy of Jesus's "virgin birth."

During this debate, Trypho retorts that what Justin calls a miracle is based on nothing but ignorance—simple mistranslation. Pointing out that Justin is reading Isaiah's prophecy in Greek, in a version that translates the Hebrew word for "young woman" (*almah*) as "virgin" (*parthenos*, in Greek), Trypho declares that only someone ignorant of Hebrew could make such a mistake. Anyone reading Isaiah's prophecy in the original Hebrew would realize that the prophet was speaking simply of a "young woman" becoming pregnant and giving birth—something that happens every day. Read accurately, Trypho says, the Hebrew word Isaiah chooses, *almah*, does not connote sexual inexperience, as if the prophet were predicting something biologically impossible. Most likely, Trypho concludes, Isaiah was predicting the birth of a prince in the household of King Josiah, who was ruling Judea at the time, six hundred years before Jesus.

Although many of today's scholars of the Hebrew Bible would agree with Trypho, countless Christians have persisted in following Justin's interpretation of Isaiah 7:14. Matthew, who, like many educated Jews in the Roman Empire, spoke and wrote fluent Greek, and likely read the Jewish Scriptures in Greek translation, seems to read this passage as Justin did. About ten years after Justin's death, the Greek philosopher Celsus, writing his polemic against Christians called *On the True Doctrine*, echoed Trypho's argument, ridiculing believers who base their claim of "virgin birth" on a mistranslation. Yet many followers of Jesus, both Jewish and Gentile, still maintain their conviction that the prophet Isaiah predicted Jesus's "virgin birth." However unlikely, the idea stuck. And to this day, most English translations, from the King James Bible to contemporary versions, have translated *almah* as "virgin," erasing the suggestion of illegitimacy in favor of what countless Christians to this day celebrate as the Christmas miracle.

Some Roman Catholic scholars have characterized those who discuss the birth stories in the ways we are doing here as "hostile and negative" people intent on undermining church teaching. Yet many who share the Roman Catholic faith are simply seeking to understand, as far as possible, what motivated those who first told these stories and wrote them down. Even Raymond Brown, ordained as a Sulpician priest, a Catholic order dedicated to preserving "orthodoxy in religion," hedges his bets by saying that "virgin birth" is "a theological statement, not a biological one." What, I wonder, does he mean by that?

As I see it, Matthew did not intend to deceive people. Instead, being a devoted follower of Jesus, he had embraced Jesus's message as "good news"—even staked his life on it, in the face of intense hostility from leading members of Jewish communities as well as from Roman occupation forces. Convinced that Jesus was God's divinely chosen Messiah, he would have intently searched the Scriptures, seeking to understand how Jesus's questionable birth might have happened. Alighting on Isaiah 7:14, he, or others before him, may have experienced an "Aha!" moment, feeling that this must account for what the prophet meant when promising that the Lord would send a divine "sign" to challenge skeptics (Isaiah 7:11–14). And when he went on to investigate the Greek Bible in the light of Jesus's life and death, Matthew and others claimed that they continued to find more supporting clues.

Since Matthew believed that he had discovered the deeper meaning of Isaiah 7:14, he then modeled his narrative of Jesus's birth on the story of Moses. Anyone familiar with the great story, which Jews recall and reenact every year during Passover, might immediately recognize the analogies that Matthew found there. For, as we've seen, just as a violent, evil ruler threatened the life of the infant Moses, so King Herod sought to kill the infant Jesus. And just as Moses escaped death as an infant, so, Matthew says, the infant Jesus was saved when his parents fled into Egypt. Matthew also applies the prophet Hosea's oracle ("Out of Egypt I have called my son") to his birth story, suggesting that this oracle, like the others, bears a double meaning. While Hosea (11:1) obviously refers to God's people, Israel, as the Lord's "son," Matthew suggests that his oracle also refers to Jesus as God's "son," who embodies Israel's history—even recapitulates it—in his own life. And just as Israel's people then wandered in the desert for forty years, so, Matthew says, Jesus wandered in the wilderness for forty days (Matthew 4:2). When he emerged, just as Moses ascended Mount Sinai to receive the Torah, so, Matthew continues, Jesus ascended upon a mountain to announce a new version of Torah, his "Sermon on the Mount" (5:1ff).

Luke took a different approach to revising Mark's gospel. Instead of patterning his birth story only on Biblical stories familiar to Jews, Luke, the only Gentile among the New Testament gospel writers, adopts the style of a Greek historian. To establish his credentials, he opens by stating that, whereas "many people have tried to write down an orderly account of [these] events" (Luke 1:1), he himself has carefully checked out eyewitness accounts, and investigated everything he could find, before starting to write. Addressing a reader named Theophilus ("one who loves God"), most likely a prominent patron, or else his imagined reader, Luke promises to offer "an orderly account . . . so that you may know the truth" about the events he is about to relate (1:1–4).

But this does not mean that Luke simply intends to write a factual history. Instead, like Mark and Matthew, he writes to promote Jesus's message—"the good news." Since he has immersed himself in the Hebrew Scriptures, he opens his gospel with famous Biblical stories. Both involve married women blighted with infertility, which in their culture carried disappointment, failure, and disgrace. Then, surprisingly, the Lord blessed each of them with the birth of a son who becomes a great man. Luke first tells of a priest named Zechariah, and his wife, Elizabeth, who had no children; Elizabeth has been unable to conceive, and now she is far too old. But then an angel appears to Zechariah, terrifying and overwhelming him, announcing that his wife shall give birth to a son, who will become a great man. And when Elizabeth conceives the child who will become John the Baptist, she praises God "for taking away the disgrace I have endured among my people" (Luke 1:25). Although Luke does not name Israel's patriarch Abraham and his wife, Sarah, said to have given birth miraculously to Isaac when she was ninety years old (Genesis 17:17), he echoes their story in his account of Zechariah and Elizabeth.

Next Luke evokes the Biblical story of Hannah, a pious married woman who, like Sarah, fails to conceive, until, refusing to eat, weeping bitterly, she prays to the Lord, promising to dedicate any future son to serve in the Temple. Then Eli, the priest, hearing of her distress, blesses her; and after she returns to her husband, and he "knew his wife Hannah," she gives birth to a son, who will become the great prophet Samuel.

Luke prefaces his account of Jesus's conception, then, with these two stories of married women distressed by infertility. Unlike Matthew, Luke shows no sign of apologizing for an embarrassing pregnancy. Instead, he presents this as a joyful event, like the conception of Isaac or Samuel. Also unlike Matthew, Luke makes Mary, not Joseph, the star of his story—a fact that often prompts contemporary commentators to praise Luke's generously inclusive attitude toward women. But at the same time,

Luke ignores what he wants his audience to ignore: that Mary is not married—a point he leaves conspicuously absent. Nothing deters Luke from casting Mary in the role of Sarah or Hannah, as if her pregnancy, like theirs, were an answer to heartfelt prayer. But was it that, or a humiliating disgrace?

We've already noted Mary's ambivalent response to the angel's announcement. Cast into the role of God's slave, she speaks as if her only option is to submit. Yet when she visits her cousin, admitting that she is pregnant, Luke pictures Elizabeth responding with joy, encouraging his readers to do that as well. In this he has hugely succeeded. Ever since, countless Christians have echoed the joyful blessing Luke puts into the mouth of the angel, and then of Elizabeth: "Hail, Mary, full of grace; the Lord is with you. Blessed are you among women, and blessed is the fruit of your womb!" (Luke 1:26). Now Luke has Mary burst into song, praising God in words drawn from Hannah's song of praise, which Christians have enshrined in glorious music honoring Mary ever since: "My soul magnifies the Lord, and my spirit rejoices in God, my Savior; for he has looked with favor on the humiliation of his slave; surely, from now on, all generations shall call me blessed!" (1:46–55).

While announcing this miraculous pregnancy, neither Luke nor, for that matter, the angel says anything explicit about how it might have happened, leaving that question to the imagination of later artists and theologians. Yet historians like the Roman Catholic Jane Schaberg, sensing that a more troubling story lies hidden in the shadows, suggest what occurred to me when rereading these words. Mary's song opens with praise that God has relieved her distress over "the humiliation of his slave." Her words suggest that she has suffered shame, alleviated when her pregnancy is reinterpreted as a blessing. Schaberg agrees with other Christian historians that, before Luke and Matthew wrote these stories, each was informed by an earlier tradition in which "[Mary] had been violated and made pregnant, but . . . God had vindicated her, protecting her and her child, even recognizing . . . this child as God's Son and Messiah."

Luke's story raises further objections. Since he is revising Mark's narrative, which reports that Jesus had four other brothers and at least two sisters, how could he claim that Mary was a virgin? Luke dodges the issue by erasing Mark's words from his revision, and simply declaring that when Mary gave birth to Jesus he was her "firstborn" (Luke 2:7). Some Christians in later centuries came up with other suggestions: either that Jesus's other siblings must have been Joseph's children by a previous marriage, or that ancient writers used language loosely, and instead of being Jesus's actual siblings, those whom Mark names as his brothers—James, Joses, Judas, and Simon (Mark 6:3)—must have been his "cousins."

The questions keep coming. If Jesus actually was a member of the royal dynasty, housed in Bethlehem, why was he called "Jesus of Nazareth"? Since he was known to be from a humble family, how could he possibly qualify as Israel's Messiah? Had not Israel's prophets foretold the Messiah's birth in Bethlehem, as Matthew notes, and not in some relatively insignificant rural town? We've seen that Luke clearly considered such objections, and came up with a scenario to answer them, first declaring that Emperor

Augustus required "all the world" to be registered for taxation in their family's home city. And since he, too, insists that Joseph was descended from the royal family, Luke suggests that the family had to make a special trip to Bethlehem—just in time for Jesus's birth.

Was Joseph, then, Jesus's father? No, Luke says, clearly not. Instead, like Matthew, he pictures Joseph accepting the role of family protector and adoptive father, noting simply that Jesus "was the son, *so people thought*, of Joseph" (Luke 3:23). For millennia, many Christians have dismissed the discrepancies between the two genealogies by suggesting that Matthew traces Joseph's line, whereas Luke offers Mary's. But that does not work, either: both claim to trace Joseph's line, even while denying that he was Jesus's biological father.

Strikingly, too, Matthew and Luke offer radically different visions of the family's social status, perhaps intending to appeal to different audiences. Matthew situates his birth story in King Herod's royal palace, and populates it with "all the chief priests and scribes of the people" (Matthew 2:4), who share the king's concern, hearing of the birth of a rival prince. But Luke pointedly places Jesus among the working people. Since Luke is traditionally identified as a Gentile, whom many Jews would regard as their inferiors, he chose instead to picture Jesus speaking "good news to the poor"—to the oppressed and the needy, and to Gentiles and women. Consequently, Luke is the only writer to picture the stable, the animals, the infant cradled in a feeding trough, and angels appearing in the sky, announcing the good news "to people of good will"—not to kings, but to herdsmen working outdoors at night. He directs his story, so to speak, to the 99 percent.

Whereas Matthew traces Jesus's genealogy back to Abraham, Israel's great patriarch, Luke traces it all the way back *before* Abraham to Adam, whom Luke also calls "son of God." No wonder, then, that African American Christians, among countless others, often choose Luke's version of the gospel, which connects Jesus not only with Abraham, ancestor of the Jewish people, but with the whole human race.

Despite Luke's artful evasion of the question of Jesus's biological paternity, he concludes his narrative with a strong *symbolic* statement—the story of how, when Jesus was twelve, he traveled with his parents to the Jerusalem Temple to celebrate Passover. When Mary and Joseph set out to return home, they departed without checking that Jesus was with them—an unlikely story, except that it enables Luke to tell how they returned to find him discussing Torah with rabbis in the Temple, astonishing them with his precocious insight. Luke has Jesus himself deliver the punch line: "Why were you looking for me? *Did you not know that I must be in my Father's house?*" (Luke 2:49).

Although most scholars today regard all stories of Joseph as legends, when looking back at Mark's narrative, I realized that I was wrong to assume that he ignores the question of Jesus's paternity. For, like Luke in the previous scene, Mark deals with that unstated question in a far less literal way. To my surprise, I realized that he actually begins his gospel with a symbolic birth story! For in his first scene Mark pictures Jesus as a young man who hears John the Baptist preach, and goes forward with many others to accept baptism. Just then, Mark says:

> As he was coming up out of the water, he saw the heavens split apart, and the spirit descending upon him. And a voice came from heaven, *"You are my beloved son,* with whom I am well pleased." (Mark 1:10–11)

Here, Mark *does* declare that Jesus has a recognized father—the Lord God himself, speaking from heaven!

Though John, like Mark, says nothing about Jesus's birth in his gospel, he, too, makes his own view clear from the start. He acknowledges that some Jews hostile to Jesus insinuate that he was born illegitimate (John 8:41), but begins with a strong counterclaim. Responding to the question of where Jesus comes from, John opens his gospel declaring that he comes from God—from the divine Source of all creation, as Son of God, manifesting divine light in human form (1:1–18).

Finally, when I began to investigate the recently discovered secret gospels and "revelations," I was surprised to see that many of these, too, play on this theme of Jesus's heavenly father. Their authors, like Mark, interpret Jesus's "virgin birth" to mean that he has descended from God, to reveal God's glory. The Apocryphon [Secret Revelation] of John, for example, tells how, after Jesus's death, his disciple John, shamed and mocked for having followed a false messiah, and devastated with grief, turns away from the Temple to walk alone into the desert. Tormented with questions,

John says he suddenly saw the heavens open, the whole creation luminously bright, and felt the earth shake:

> I was afraid, and . . . I saw in the light . . . [someone with] multiple forms . . . [and] he said to me, "*John, John, why do you doubt, or why are you afraid? . . . I am [the] one who is with you always; I am the Father, I am the Mother, I am the Son.*"

Strikingly, here Jesus reveals himself as a luminous divine presence: a family trinity, simultaneously Father, Mother, and Son. Whom else but the Mother would we expect to see with the Father and Son? The Gospel of Truth, for example, when picturing Jesus as sent from the divine Source, speaks of how Jesus descends into the world to bring back all who are lost "into the Father, into the Mother, Jesus of the infinite sweetness." But when Christians in later centuries translated Aramaic and Hebrew sources into Greek and Latin, the gendered connotation of the word "spirit" was lost. Those translating various forms of *ruah*—the feminine term for "spirit" in Hebrew, Aramaic, and Syriac—into Latin translated it as *spiritus,* a word gendered masculine. Greek speakers translated it as *pneuma,* a word gendered neuter—effectively, however, erasing the vision of divine Mother, an interpretation of the Holy Spirit, whose presence resonates through many of the earliest sources.

I was intrigued to see that the Gospel of Philip offers a variation on this theme, suggesting that Jesus, like ourselves, was born of a human father and mother, Joseph and Mary. But when baptized, he was "born again," this time to spiritual parents—the Father in heaven, and divine Mother, the Spirit—just as we, when baptized, become reborn as children of God.

Seeking a single birth narrative, we find instead tapestries woven from disparate threads—some of them stories that seem primarily meant to claim that Jesus descends from Israel's royal dynasty, and so shall rightfully rule as God's Messiah. As for what actually happened—divine miracle, human dilemma, or both—who can say? As I see it, however these various writers interpret Jesus's origin, they all agree on the spiritual truth: that Jesus is "Son of God," and embodies God's presence on earth.

Now let's look at what matters most to all the gospel writers—Jesus's message, his "good news." What is it exactly? We do not need to go to the secret gospels to find depths of hidden meaning. We can turn to the earliest surviving gospel—Mark's—to ask what he might mean when speaking of "the mystery of God's kingdom."

2

Who Is Jesus? Miracles and Mysteries

WHO IS JESUS of Nazareth? This thematic question drives the Gospel of Mark, the earliest surviving account of Jesus's life. But instead of offering a simple answer, Mark shows that everyone who encounters Jesus asks this question: *Who is this man?* A healer empowered by God's spirit? Or a magician and fraud, as some of his enemies charge? Is he a prophet, as many of his contemporaries assume, or "out of his mind," as even his family members suspect? Or is he secretly "God's holy one," the "Son of the Most High God"—divine names that burst out of raving demoniacs? Could he possibly heal a dying child, even raise a dead one to life, as a grieving father desperately hopes?

The question should not be difficult to answer, since Mark announces in the opening line of his gospel, "This is the good news of Jesus, *Messiah, Son of God.*" Countless believers in later generations have taken this to mean that Jesus is some kind of supernatural being, unlike any other in the history of the human species—a kind of God/man, whose apparently hybrid nature theologians have sought to understand ever since.

But Mark, a devout Jew steeped in the Hebrew Scriptures, for whom there could be only one God, would know that these are traditional titles for a human being—specifically, titles of Israel's king, someone whom the Lord has "anointed" (*messiah*, in Hebrew) with his spirit, who thus is divinely chosen to rule over his holy people in Jerusalem, Israel's capital city. The great King David, who reigned a thousand years before Jesus's birth, received both titles during his coronation ceremony, when he was anointed with oil to signal the reception of God's spirit. This ancient ceremony, upon which the coronations of British monarchs are modeled to this day, signifies that God's sovereignty over the world is being delegated to his human servant, "Son of God," who represents the Lord on earth.

Anyone unfamiliar with the gospels might assume that starting with these titles means that Mark intends to relate the biography of a great ruler, as Plutarch, his near contemporary, does in his *Lives of the Noble Greeks and Romans*. But after exploring other biographies written around the same time, I've come to see that Mark's narrative is nothing like any first-century biography of emperors and statesmen. Then, as now, biographers well knew the conventions of their craft. Starting with stories of family and background, the writer would relate the hero's noble birth, youth, and achievements, then conclude with his death and legacy. Plutarch's biography of Julius Caesar, for example, includes all these themes, following his career and accomplishments to his bloody assassination on the Senate floor, and how his brilliant, ruthless eighteen-year-old protégé, Octavian, later named Augustus, fought for and grasped imperial power after him. (No one, as far as we know, wrote such biographies about women, except as they appear in men's lives. Plutarch, for example, in his biography of Mark Antony, pictures Egypt's Queen Cleopatra as the lover who ruined him.)

Mark starts in a very different way, leaving out the most obvious details. What, for example, did Jesus look like? Since the early accounts say nothing about this, artists, for centuries, have sought to fill in the gaps. So, when I was five and first heard of Jesus, I imagined that I knew what he looked like, having seen in a Methodist church a portrait of Jesus with long blond hair and blue eyes raised to the heavens. What complicated this impression, though, was what I saw in my best friend's nearby Catholic church, St. Aloysius. After pushing open the heavy wooden door and walking into dark halls lit by candlelight, I saw a tortured man beaten down, nearly naked, hung by nails through his hands and twisted feet. Another startling image showed Jesus pointing to his breast, carved open to expose what looked like a heart on fire. None of these images, though, has much to do with our earliest sources. And, recently, African American Christians, among others—like the poet Countee Cullen, author of the famous poem "The Black Christ"—have challenged such images, noting that Jesus likely had dark hair and eyes, and darker skin than many "white" Christians want to imagine.

Before anyone wrote about Jesus, though, people told stories about him, repeating what they heard him say, and what they'd heard from others. Papias, a Greek convert born a generation after Jesus, says that he tried to find out everything he could from those who had known him, "what Andrew or Peter or Philip or Thomas or James or John or Matthew, or any other of the Lord's disciples, had said," since he felt that the most authentic information was not anything written down but what he hoped to hear from "a living . . . voice." Papias and others then collected lists of Jesus's sayings, as followers of well-known teachers often did, in, for example, such collections as "The Wisdom of Jesus ben Sira," reputed to be the teachings of another famous rabbi, who lived about two hundred years earlier than Jesus, and the text called *Pirkei Avot* ("Sayings of the Fathers"), which contained sayings of well-known rabbis.

The writer we call Mark, reputed to be a younger follower of Jesus's disciple Peter, likely heard such stories, and drew upon an earlier narrative, now lost, that told only the most shocking part of the story: how Jesus was captured, arrested, and killed. Is this, as cognitive psychologists suggest, because when someone dies young and violently, those final events are what relatives and friends most vividly remember? However it happened, Mark focuses on Jesus's death. Drawing upon an anonymously written account of the crucifixion, Mark then prefaced and amplified it with a brief account of Jesus's public activity. What we call his "gospel" is less a biography than a passionate manifesto, showing how a young man from a rural background suddenly became a lightning rod for divine power. And although Mark's account ends in catastrophe—Jesus tortured, crucified, and buried, his friends discovering his body gone—Mark, surprisingly, calls it "good news."

To signal that this is no ordinary biography, Mark begins by depicting a clash of supernatural powers: God's spirit contending against Satan, in a world filled with demons. First he tells how, at Jesus's baptism, the "spirit of God" comes upon him, driving him into conflict with "the Satan," who embodies the evil forces ruling the world. This, then, is the "good news": that God is now acting on earth through Jesus, having charged him with divine power to overcome the evil energies that cause disease, oppression, and death. And although the gospels go on to show that these diabolic forces later catch up with Jesus and hound him to a hideous death, Mark insists that Jesus will reappear alive again, raised by God's power.

The baptism story, strikingly, appears right after Mark has introduced Jesus's royal titles. He tells of a young man from the rural town of Nazareth, in Judea, who walks into the desert near the river Jordan to join crowds of people listening to a wild-eyed prophet wearing a camel's-hair shift tied with a leather belt. The prophet, called John "the baptizer," who claims to speak for God, warns his listeners to get ready: the day of judgment is coming, and soon. Shaken by John's impassioned preaching, Jesus of Nazareth walks forward with others, and wades into the river to accept the baptism John offers to wash away sins. And as we've noted in Mark's story of Jesus's baptism, when he comes out of the water, Jesus is transfixed by a vision, seeing "the skies torn apart, and the Spirit of God descending" (Mark 1:10–11), and hears a heavenly voice identify him as God's beloved son.

Mark has no way of knowing, of course, that, centuries later, Jesus's followers would revere his narrative as Scripture. But since he—like Jesus himself, and other observant Jews of their time— reveres as "Scriptures" the writings included in the Hebrew Bible—which begin with creation stories and conclude with psalms and prophetic oracles—Mark intends to demonstrate the truth of what he writes by modeling his narrative on these sacred stories familiar to devout Jews. His first scene, then, suggests that just as Israel's first king, Saul, suddenly was seized with divine power when God's spirit descended upon him and "turned him into a different man," this is now happening to Jesus. For, Mark writes, "immediately the spirit drove him into the wilderness" to challenge Satan in single-handed combat. Caught in conflict with evil forces, Jesus struggles alone in the desert for forty days, as Israel's people had done for forty years. When he emerges from the desert, victorious, and hears the shocking news that King Herod has murdered John the Baptist, he boldly takes up John's message: "God's kingdom is coming soon!" (1:12–15).

But, again, who *is* this Jesus, and what does this message mean? Instead of explaining, Mark sets forth a brief, fast-paced narrative that requires the reader, like the bystanders he describes, to guess, or to infer, what it means from what Jesus *does*. First, while walking by the Sea of Galilee, seeing two men fishing, and two others mending their nets, he abruptly calls out and orders them to "Follow me!" (1:17). Immediately, Mark says, all four dropped their nets, left work and abandoned their families, and followed him. What does this suggest—that, even not knowing who he is, they sense some uncanny charismatic power in him?

What happens next confirms this impression. When Jesus enters a synagogue on Shabbat and announces the "good news" in public, a troubled man, possessed, suddenly bursts out, shouting at him: "*What do you have to do with us, Jesus of Nazareth? Have you come to destroy us? I know who you are: you are God's holy one!*" (1:24). Recognizing that demonic energies are speaking through the man, Jesus immediately shouts back, "*Be silent!*" The man goes into convulsions, screams, and collapses into silence. Shocked and amazed, the bystanders depart, to spread stories about what they have seen, exclaiming, "*What is this? New teaching—with power! He commands the unclean spirits, and they obey him!*" (1:21–28).

Next Jesus goes to the home of Peter, his disciple, and hears that Peter's mother-in-law is in bed with a fever. "He came and took her by the hand, and lifted her up; then the fever left her" (1:31). That evening, at sunset,

> they brought to him everyone who was sick or demon-possessed, and the whole city was gathered around the door. And he cured many who were sick with various diseases, and he cast out many demons. (Mark 1:32–34)

Mark packs all these actions into his first chapter, and concludes by saying that so many people were hearing of Jesus that "he could no longer go into a town openly, but stayed out in the country; and people came to him from everywhere" (1:45). Next, when he returned to Capernaum, "so many people gathered around that there was no longer room for them, even in front of the door" (2:2), impelling friends of a paralyzed man to climb onto the roof, tear open a large hole, and lower the sufferer down on ropes to the floor. After Jesus speaks to the man, suddenly he is healed; standing upright, he walks out, carrying his own stretcher, "so that," Mark says, "they were all amazed, saying, 'We have never seen anything like this!'" (2:12).

Like many readers influenced by rationalist assumptions, I once tended to skip over the miracle stories to focus instead on Jesus's teachings. But Mark's contemporaries would have recognized that the two are intimately linked. For, as he intends to show, when God's spirit descends upon Jesus, the spirit inspires him to speak in prophecy, and to perform acts of power. As Mark tells it, Jesus's power to heal is what demonstrates—and validates—his claim to speak for God.

Curing the paralyzed man, and many others, made Jesus famous—and notorious. As Mark reports, "a great multitude followed him" (3:7), so many that "he told his disciples to have a boat ready for him because of the crowd, so that they would not crush him . . . since all those who had diseases pressed upon him to touch him" (3:9–10). Mark often includes evil spirits among his cast of characters, since, as he tells it, performing healings requires Jesus to contend against these invisible energies that cause disease and suffering. Even today, of course, we learn as children that invisible agents, bacteria or viruses, can sicken or kill us. To protect ourselves, we use many of the same practices that Jewish teachers taught to avert danger from demons: washing hands; avoiding stagnant water or spoiled food; and touching sewage and decaying corpses.

All the gospel writers agree that Jesus first attracted public attention as a healer who could work miracles, since, as the historian Morton Smith notes, in ancient Palestine, as throughout the

Roman Empire, there were no hospitals. Doctors were rare and expensive, and even the best were often ineffective. Over a century after Jesus's death, Emperor Marcus Aurelius himself died of plague after his personal physician, Galen, the most famous doctor of his time, fled Rome to hide out from the plague at his country estate. Had Galen stayed, as he surely realized, he could have done nearly nothing against a disease that killed thousands in Rome, where piles of corpses were stacked in the streets, and many left there to rot. Those who could not afford doctors often resorted to practitioners of magic, many of whom invoked powerful spirits to perform spells, charms, and rituals, at a wide range of prices. A powerful healer, especially one who, like Jesus, charged no money, would have been in great demand.

Since exorcism involves a contest of powers, when Jesus commands demons to depart from their human prey, often they fiercely resist, threatening to "out" him, and to reveal the divine identity that he is keeping secret: "Whenever the unclean spirits saw him, they fell down before him and shouted, '*You are the Son of God!*' But he sternly ordered them not to make him known" (3:11–12).

Even though Jesus's healings amaze the crowds, they also alarm his family, as we've seen, and arouse fierce opposition in others. Mark says that when scribes, respected interpreters of the Scriptures, come down from Jerusalem to investigate Jesus's activities, they recognize that he has power, and immediately accuse him of practicing magic: "He is possessed by Beelzebub—he uses the ruler of demons to cast out demons!" (3:22). Accused of using demonic power, Jesus forcefully rejects the charge, insisting instead that his power comes from God: "How can Satan cast out Satan?" (3:23). Those making such accusations, he declares, are speaking blasphemy against the Spirit of God. Nevertheless, as Mark tells it, Jesus's public activity attracts powerful enemies who "immediately conspired . . . against him, how to kill him" (3:6).

Who *is* this man, both sought after and threatening? Nearly everyone who meets him, friendly or hostile, asks that question, with no answer in sight. When he speaks in parables to the crowds that surround him, what he says confounds his hearers as much as his miracles do. Finally, when his closest disciples are alone with Jesus, they ask him what his parables mean, wondering why he doesn't explain more clearly. And whereas Christian preachers nearly always say that Jesus teaches in parables in order to *clarify* what he means, Mark says the exact opposite. As Mark tells it, Jesus declares that he teaches that way in order to *hide* his meaning. Then he surprises his disciples even more, saying:

> *To you is given the secret* [or "the mystery"; in Greek, *myste-rion*] *of the kingdom of God—but to those outside, everything is in parables,* so that they may look, but not perceive; they may listen, but not understand, so that they may not repent and be forgiven! (Mark 4:11–12)

Startling words, since right before this, speaking to "a very large crowd" (4:1), Jesus offers what sounds like an open invitation for anyone to understand: "*Let anyone with ears to hear, listen!*" But here again Mark adds a contrary note, insisting that Jesus tells parables to *prevent* outsiders from understanding: "He did not speak [to outsiders] except in parables, but *he explained everything in private to his disciples"* (4:34).

Immediately after this, he astonishes his disciples again by enacting another miracle—one so unexpected that they admit that they still do not understand who he is. For when, terrified, they rouse him from sleep after a sudden storm swamps and nearly capsizes their boat on the Sea of Galilee, Jesus stands and rebukes the wind, and orders the sea to "Stop—be calm!" Seeing the wind cease, and a dead calm come over the sea, his followers stand for a moment in shocked silence, then say to each other, *"Who then is this, that even the wind and the sea obey him?"* (4:41).

As if Jesus hadn't already confounded them, Mark says that when their boat arrives near Gerasene territory, he steps out and encounters a naked man who lives in a graveyard, running wild, howling day and night, and cutting himself with stones. Seeing Jesus approaching, the man runs, shouting as loud as he can, *"What do you have to do with me, Jesus, Son of the Most High God?"* (5:7). Recognizing the man as demon-possessed, Jesus asks, *"What is your name?"* (5:9). For, like a physician diagnosing illness, an exorcist can heal only when knowing the name of the demon; as Smith notes, "It was thought that demons . . . obey when you call their names." Hearing the response—*"My name is Legion; there are many of us!"*—Jesus orders them to *"Come out of him!"* Although they do not have power to resist him, the demons cowering before him counter with a plea: seeing a herd of thousands of pigs on a nearby hillside, they beg Jesus, *"Send us into the swine; let us enter them!"* (5:12).

One of the strangest stories in Mark's gospel now follows:

"He gave them permission, and the unclean spirits came out and entered into the pigs; and the herd, numbering about two thousand, rushed down the steep bank into the sea and were drowned" (5:13). Shocked and horrified, the herders run away, telling everyone what they have seen. When people run back to see what actually happened, they see the formerly possessed man sitting and talking with Jesus, dressed, and in his right mind. Nevertheless, terrified by what they had seen and heard, "they began to beg Jesus to leave their neighborhood" (5:17).

In Mark's narrative, Jesus's *actions*, no less than the stories he tells, effectively serve as parables. His miracles, equally central to Mark's "good news," are events that, however shocking, are left for his disciples—and his readers—to decipher. For, next, Mark tells how Jesus heals a dead girl—or was she in a coma? The word "coma," in English, derives, after all, from *koimao*, the Greek verb that means "to sleep." In this case, though, perhaps to show that the girl actually had died, Mark says that, before Jesus responds to her father's plea for help, his servants come running to tell him that it is too late; she is dead. But Jesus, hearing this, orders her father, "Don't be afraid; just trust" (5:36). When he arrives at the house and hears mourners weeping and wailing, Jesus tells them to stop: "The child isn't dead, just sleeping" (5:39). The story is well known: when Jesus goes to the child and takes her hand, saying "*Talitha, cum*," which, in Aramaic, his native language, means, "Little girl, get up" (5:41), she immediately gets up and starts to walk.

Several other accounts credit Jesus with raising the dead—an astonishing feat, but one with precedents in the Jewish Scriptures, as well as in Greek literature. Luke tells of Jesus meeting a funeral procession, in which men are carrying a young man's corpse, followed by his widowed mother and a large crowd. Moved with compassion, Jesus tells her not to weep. After the pallbearers stop, he orders the dead man to arise: "The dead man sat up and began to speak, and Jesus gave him to his mother" (Luke 7:15), as the crowd, astounded, praises God for the presence of a "great prophet among us!" This episode echoes an account in 1 Kings 17:17–24, which tells how the prophet Elijah, encountering a widow devastated by her only son's death, raised him to life. Did Luke model his story on the previous one? Likely so, for this anecdote shows that Jesus wields great power—perhaps even greater than that of the prophet Elijah.

In graduate school, I was surprised to hear that the story of Jesus raising the dead girl resonates with a similar one told of another famous teacher and healer, Apollonius of Tyana, a near contemporary of Jesus. Apollonius was an itinerant holy man and miracle worker who gathered disciples and lived with them, while walking from temple to temple along the coasts of northern Syria and Greece, just as Jesus's apostle Paul, visiting synagogues along the same route, had done a few years earlier. Born to an affluent Greek family, Apollonius was a follower of the philosopher and teacher Pythagoras, who practiced vegetarianism and celibacy, wore his hair long, and dressed in white linen. After engaging for years in spiritual practice, he traveled to Babylonia to study with the *magi,* and then to India, to learn Hindu teachings from Brahman gurus. Later in his life, Apollonius traveled to Rome and to Egypt, visiting ascetics called "naked sages" who may have known and practiced Vedic or Buddhist teachings, and who were known to cultivate supernatural powers.

As in the case of Jesus, all these details were written down by the master's anonymous disciples. Reading *The Life of Apollonius* for the first time, I realized there must be a widespread fascination with miracles in the world of the ancient Mediterranean. Here is one from the *Life* very similar to the gospel story we noted:

There was a girl who appeared to have died just at the time of her wedding. The betrothed followed the bier, with all the lamentations of an unconsummated marriage, and Rome mourned with him, since the girl belonged to a consular family. Meeting with this scene of sorrow, Apollonius said, "Put the bier down, for I will end your crying over the girl." At the same time he asked her name . . . But Apollonius, after merely touching her and saying something secretly, woke the bride from her apparent death. The girl spoke, and went back to her father's house.

The Oxford historian Geza Vermes confirms in his influential book *Jesus the Jew* the sense that such miracle stories are far from unique. Vermes cites reports of other charismatic first-century rabbis, like Hanina ben Dosa, who, like Jesus, became famous for his power to heal disease, even at a distance. Such stories were not limited to Jews, either. Even the respected Roman senator Tacitus describes how Emperor Vespasian, to his own surprise, discovered that he was able to restore sight to a blind man, and to heal another man's paralyzed hand.

Mark emphasizes such stories to persuade people that Jesus's message is true, but it's not surprising that many outsiders insisted that they were tricks and accused Jesus of practicing magic. It's intriguing that, as we noted, when Mark tells the story of Jesus raising the dead girl, he breaks from his usual practice of writing in Greek to note carefully—and insert in his reports—the exact Aramaic words that Jesus had spoken on that occasion. Soon afterward, Mark also writes that, when healing a man who was deaf and had a speech impediment, Jesus put his fingers in the man's ears, then spat, and touched the man's tongue with his spittle, "saying, '*Ephphatha*,' which means [in Aramaic] 'be opened'" (7:31–37). Anyone familiar with magical practices would recognize that the "power words" and ritual acts reported here are similar to those found in ancient magical papyri, amulets, and inscriptions, which magicians in the ancient world used to invoke healing.

Why does Mark include such details? We can speculate that he realizes that Jesus's followers would want to know which words he had used in successful cases, and how to pronounce them in Aramaic: they, too, might find such information enormously useful. From the start of his public activity, Jesus orders his disciples to heal people and exorcise demons, too, giving them permission to use his own name to invoke God's power. And when Jesus's disciple John tells him, "Rabbi, we saw someone casting out demons in your name, and we tried to stop him, because he was not following us," Jesus replies, "Do not stop him," declaring that "whoever is not against us is for us" (Mark 9:38–40). In later generations, and ever since, followers of Jesus who practice healing have often used techniques similar to those that ancient magicians practiced, while invoking the power of his name, and of God's spirit.

Surprisingly, right after Mark tells of Jesus raising the dead girl, he follows with an anecdote in which Jesus tries to heal, but fails. As we noted, when Jesus returns to his hometown of Nazareth with his disciples, he stands up to speak in the local synagogue. But his former neighbors are shocked, asking, in effect, *Who does he think he is?* Met with suspicion and contempt from his former neighbors, Mark says, "he was not able to do any miracles there . . . and he was amazed at their lack of belief" (6:5–6).

None of Jesus's followers would have invented this report, as the historian Morton Smith observes. Not surprisingly, then, as we've noted, when Matthew revises Mark's story, he tries to make it less embarrassing, saying instead, "He could not do *many* miracles there" (Matthew 13:58); and when Luke revises it, he leaves this episode out. Smith notes, however, that Mark's version "fits the psychological facts," since "a faith healer cannot heal when he finds no faith." Often, throughout the gospels, Jesus tells his patient that "your faith has healed you." Is he acknowledging what medical people call the placebo effect? Whatever happened in Nazareth, Matthew rejects the suggestion that Jesus's power had limits, insisting that Jesus could heal anyone, anywhere:

> Jesus went throughout Galilee teaching in their synagogues, and proclaiming the good news of the kingdom and curing every disease and every sickness among the people. So his

fame spread throughout all Syria, and they brought him all the sick, those who were afflicted with various diseases and pains, demon-possessed people, epileptics, paralytics, and he cured them. And great crowds followed him from Galilee, the Decapolis, Jerusalem, Judea, and from beyond the Jordan river. (Matthew 4:23–25)

What are we to make of these stories? The answer you get depends on whom you ask. Rationalists who assume that miracles do not occur, and that such stories are simply legends, have long explained them as foolish misunderstandings, or else as exaggerations of natural events. Thomas Jefferson, for example, decided to "correct" the gospels by cutting these stories out of his own Bible with scissors, leaving intact only the teachings that he found rationally comprehensible and morally compelling. Retitling his abridged New Testament *The Life and Morals of the Great Prophet from Nazareth,* he created what others call *The Jefferson Bible,* a book with gaps visible in pages where he cut out the miracles, now on display at his plantation home in Monticello.

The historian John Dominic Crossan offers a different interpretation. Like Jefferson, Crossan declares, "I presume that Jesus . . . did not and could not cure [leprosy] or any other disease." Instead, the significance of these stories is that, although Jesus was not able to heal actual diseases—especially those that are incurable, like leprosy—he did reach out to lepers and other marginalized people. This, Crossan concludes, is what the healing stories convey: that Jesus's compassionate response helped sick people recover from "illness," which he defines as "the social isolation and rejection" that they often suffer, thus better enabling them to cope with disease, and perhaps find powers of self-healing.

Yet, many Christians believe that miracles can happen. From the first century to the twenty-first, many have claimed to heal the sick in Jesus's name; and to this day, the Catholic Church certifies genuine saints by investigating evidence of the healings attributed to them. Many other Christian churches also encourage the practice of healing. About a hundred years after Jefferson, Mary Baker Eddy, having suffered for decades from an apparently incurable disease, declared that Jesus had healed her through the power of prayer. In 1879, she founded the Church of Jesus Christ, Scientist, "to reinstate primitive Christianity and its lost practice of healing," a movement that now includes hundreds of thousands of members all over the world.

As is now well known, researchers have discovered that loss of speech, paralysis, mental illness, and even blindness, among other afflictions, can be psychosomatic. Such symptoms sometimes can resolve suddenly—if the intense distress underlying them is eased. And since certain individuals are adept at relieving such distress, some scholars believe that Jesus's exorcisms and cures "resulted from the sudden cessation of . . . psychological disorders." Stevan Davies interprets some of Jesus's miracles this way, challenging what his teacher, Morton Smith, had written in *Jesus the Magician*. In his book *Jesus the Healer,* Davies suggests that Jesus used techniques similar to those that shamans and healers practice in other cultures.

As for the gospel writers, though they surely intended to relate what Jesus actually did, stories like these confirm that they did not intend simply to write history. Instead, as we've noted, since they revered Jesus as a visionary and prophet, even the "Son of God," they were writing to promote his message, and encourage people to join their movement. But when we try to get "behind" these cryptic stories, and try to explain them, the first thing we learn is how much we do not, and likely cannot, know. Furthermore, the miracle stories, like so much else in the gospels, reflect an ancient cultural perspective that many people miss. As historian Dale Allison notes:

> Whatever else he may have done, Jesus did not celebrate rationality as a virtue. His tradition was not Greco Roman philosophy, but popular Galilean Judaism ... His mind ... was poetic, and his mental universe, filled as it was with invisible spirits, and informed by the cosmology of the Hebrew Scriptures, was mythological.

Many Christians, however, especially in America, tend to read the Bible with a perspective shaped by "fundamentalism," an early-twentieth-century movement started by a group of Protestant ministers who resolved to hold to the "fundamentals" of faith. Members of this group agreed that "Bible-believing Christians" must accept every word of the Bible as literally true—a perspective that often sets up irreconcilable conflict with people who accept scientific views.

People with a "fundamentalist" mindset often miss some of the most powerful messages encoded in the gospels. For, as we've seen, Mark carefully constructs his narrative, packing it with meanings not obvious on the surface. And that, Mark suggests, is how Jesus himself taught. Like the poet Emily Dickinson, who advised, "Tell all the truth but tell it slant—/ Success in Circuit lies," Jesus not only teaches in parables but also performs miracles that conceal—or reveal, to those who "have eyes to see" (Mark 8:18)—hidden meaning.

Who would be able to understand such meanings? How to decipher them? The gospel writers apparently assume that their anticipated audience of devout Jews—"those who have ears to hear"—would recognize how Jesus's teachings—and his actions—echo familiar Biblical stories. Many, no doubt, would note how Matthew patterns Jesus's birth story on that of Moses, his forty days in the desert on Israel's wanderings in the wilderness, and his ascent of a mountain to deliver his "Sermon on the Mount" on Moses's ascent of Mount Sinai. Did the gospel writers invent the idea of creating such resonances? My own guess is that Jesus himself taught that way. By echoing Biblical stories in both his words and actions, Jesus could effectively speak to his people "in code." For, just as people in colonized India and Africa often created ways of communicating that remained unintelligible to their European occupiers, so Jesus often hid from outsiders, especially from the Roman occupiers, what he wanted to reveal only to those who, he said, "had eyes to see, and ears to hear."

What meaning might hide in such strange stories? Let's consider the weirdest story of all—when Jesus encounters a naked man screaming in a graveyard and drives a horde of demons out of him into a herd of pigs, who stampede and drown in the sea. Who could possibly find meaning in that? Nearly no one, I suggest, except Galilean Jews, who, like Jesus, lived under harsh Roman occupation. The Romans exacted exorbitant taxes, crucified thousands of Jews, and wreaked havoc on defenseless people. Especially hated was Fretensis, the Tenth Legion, an elite military corps that Augustus had ordered into Judea circa 4 B.C.E. to put down a Jewish insurrection after Herod died. For decades afterward, as we noted, Roman soldiers were stationed throughout the Galilee and Judea to control the local people. Jews regarded Fretensis's banner, emblazoned with the image of a wild boar, as a further insult—the pig was an animal they regarded to be as filthy as the godless foreigners who proudly carried it.

By the time Mark writes, circa 70 C.E., he has lived through the Jewish war against Rome, seeing it end in disaster. After Roman soldiers desecrated Jerusalem's Temple of God and tore it down, they set it on fire. Roman commanders then turned the sacred Temple Mount into a military stronghold, garrisoning Fretensis on the site. From then on, and even more intensively after Jews attempted another revolution some fifty years later, in 135 C.E., Roman military forces sought to eradicate the Holy City, downgrading its status to that of a colony. Forced to submit, Jews bitterly recognized that, as one historian notes, "the emblem [of the wild boar] signified *Romanae potestati subiacere Iudaeos*"—that is, "Roman power to subdue Jews."

What could it mean, then, for Mark to tell how Jesus, Israel's Messiah, encountering a man driven mad by many demons, discovers their name: *"My name is Legion: for there are many of us"*? And when the Messiah forces them out in a powerful act of exorcism, inciting the horde to stampede and drown in the sea, who among the Jewish population could miss the allusion to the despised swarm of soldiers from the Tenth Legion? This dramatic scene anticipates how the Lord will drive out the Roman soldiers and destroy them, just as, in Moses's time, the Lord drove the Egyptian army into the Red Sea to drown. Anyone putting together these clues—the story of Israel's deliverance, and the facts on the ground in the first century—might read this scene as a "sign" promising that Israel's God is about to deliver his people once again.

Only Jews familiar with the Passover story, then, would understand this episode. For what Exodus says happened after the Lord drove Israel's enemies into the sea holds the key to what Mark will tell next. Before the Egyptian army drowned, Israel's people themselves had faced the dangerous waters of the Red Sea. The Lord told Moses to "lift up your staff, and stretch out your hand over the sea, and divide it" (Exodus 14:16), causing the turbulent waters to recede, and delivering Israel's people. So Mark, too, pairs his parable of the drowning Roman "legion" with the episode we noted earlier, when Jesus and his disciples are caught at sea in a violent windstorm, in danger of drowning. When, to their astonishment, Jesus commands the wind and sea to "Stop—be calm!" rescuing his followers from a watery grave, anyone familiar with the Exodus story might see what this means: that Jesus, like Moses before him, wields the power of God, who alone controls the wind and the sea.

Exodus next tells how Israel's people, having escaped death from the Egyptian army, and then from the raging sea, wander in the desert, hungry and fearing starvation, until the Lord miraculously provides manna for them to eat. Echoing that story, Mark now tells how Jesus and his followers "went away . . . to a desert place by themselves." But many people who saw them going, Mark says, "ran on foot from all the towns and arrived ahead of them" (Mark 6:32–33). Met by a huge crowd when he arrives in the desert, Jesus responds with compassion. By nightfall, realizing how hungry they are, with nothing to eat, he again astonishes his disciples by miraculously providing food for five thousand men, plus unnumbered women and children in the crowd (6:30–44).

When even his closest followers fail to see what this means—that Israel's deliverance is being reenacted right now before their eyes—Jesus acts again. Mark tells a similar story, of a second event, shortly afterward, in which Jesus provides food in the desert, this time for over four thousand people (8:1–21). Then Mark adds an ironic note. The Pharisees, members of a Jewish sect concerned with Torah interpretation, "began to argue with him, asking him for a sign from heaven, to test him" (8:11). Since they have completely failed to recognize the "sign" just given, Jesus, deeply disappointed, dismisses them with impatience: "No sign will be given to this generation!" And when even his own disciples fail to recognize the "sign," Mark again savors the irony. Right after this, Jesus boards a boat with his disciples, warning them to "beware of the yeast of the Pharisees"—the ingredient that spoils Passover bread. Hearing this, they exclaim, "We forgot to bring bread!" Shocked that even his closest followers take his words literally, Jesus bursts out in frustration: "Why are you talking about not having bread? Do you still perceive or understand? Have your hearts turned to stone? Having eyes, do you not see? Having ears, do you not hear?" (8:12–18).

As the poet William Blake recognized, "seeing" is the point. Contrasting Luke's focus on the "compassionate Jesus" with Mark's portrait of a fierce prophet, Blake wrote:

> The vision of Christ which thou dost see
> Is my vision's deepest enemy;
> Yours speaks of love to all mankind;
> Mine speaks in parables to the blind!

Compassionate Jesus, or fierce prophet, deliverer of inscrutable signs? Asking such questions, we find ourselves where we started, asking what everyone, admirers, enemies, crowds and disciples alike, keeps asking: *Who is this man?* Jesus is a man of many secrets, and one of the most closely held is the secret of his identity. At this climactic moment, then, Jesus challenges his disciples to answer that question: "Who do people say that I am?"

Before getting to this famous episode, though, Mark frames it with *another* miracle story, which serves as a metaphor for what follows. Unlike any other Biblical miracle story, this one proceeds in two stages. Seeking to heal a blind man, Jesus first puts saliva on his eyes, touches him, and asks, "Can you see anything?" Looking up, the man replies, "I can see people, but they look like trees walking." Since the man has recovered only partial vision, Jesus then tries again, touching his eyes. This time, the man opens his eyes, "and he saw everything clearly" (Mark 8:23–25).

With this anecdote, Mark prepares us to understand how

Peter, one of Jesus's first disciples, also comes to "see" in two stages. Startled by Jesus's first question ("Who do people say that I am?"), his disciples come up with tentative answers: "Some people say you are John the Baptist, back from the dead"; "the prophet Elijah"; "one of the prophets." Then Jesus challenges them more directly: "But who do you say that I am?" This time the others remain silent, until Peter finally dares answer, getting it right: "You are the Messiah." This, at least, *seems* to be right, since, of course, Mark has announced it in the first line of his gospel (*"This is the good news of Jesus, the Messiah, the Son of God"* [1:1]). But here, when Peter speaks this name, Jesus harshly stops him, saying, *"Don't tell anyone!"* and turns on Peter, calling him *Satan*.

For Peter's right answer is only half right. After allowing his disciples to glimpse him as *Messiah, Son of God,* Jesus immediately qualifies Peter's answer, warning, "The *Son of Man* must undergo great suffering." Throughout this narrative, then, Mark—or perhaps Jesus himself—*superimposes a second vision of his identity upon the first.* He is *Messiah,* yes; but he is also *Son of Man,* the term he most often uses to refer to himself. This latter term, though, is ambiguous. In some contexts, it simply means "a human being." But many of Jesus's Jewish contemporaries would recognize the "Son of Man" instead as a figure—human or supernatural—whom the prophet Daniel saw in a vision, standing in heaven before God's throne: someone whom the Lord himself appoints to rule the world, but who shall receive power only when he returns on "the clouds of heaven" (Daniel 7:13) after being rejected and killed on earth.

Now we see how subtly Mark constructs this climactic

moment, using the story of the blind man healed in two stages to show how Peter first partially "sees" who Jesus is, but only later—perhaps not until after the crucifixion—finally comes to understand fully the complexity of his hidden identity. Warning his disciples of suffering to come, Jesus declares that he, as Son of Man, would be killed, "and after three days rise again" (Mark 8:31). Only then, Mark suggests, would he come back to rule the world as Son of God.

Did Jesus actually foresee his own impending death, perhaps even a future resurrection? Or did Mark and other writers invent such "prophecies" after Jesus died, and write them as if he had predicted them? I tend to agree that, as many scholars suggest, Mark likely wrote some of these "prophecies" after Jesus died. What happens next, however, shows that from the start, Jesus was fully aware of the danger he was courting by announcing what he preached—that God's kingdom was about to burst in on the world—while hinting that he himself would have a major role to play.

After revealing his secret identity as God's Messiah to Peter, Jesus begins to act out certain scenes deliberately, as "signs." Preparing to enter Jerusalem, capital of the empire once ruled by King David, he dares act out a famous scene envisioned by the prophet Zechariah, who pictures God's designated Messiah arriving in Jerusalem riding not on a war chariot but on a donkey, "triumphant and victorious" (Zechariah 9:9), to initiate his reign.

As Mark tells it, Jesus heads straight toward Jerusalem, walking ahead of his disciples, who "were amazed, and those who followed were terrified" (Mark 10:32). Since James and John, his leading disciples, apparently assume that Jesus is about to seize power, they begin to jockey for prime positions in his coming administration (10:35–37). Approaching Jerusalem, he stops at a nearby village, ordering two of his men to go into town and find a donkey that had never been ridden, untie it, and bring it to him. After mounting the donkey, Jesus begins a procession into the Holy City, now crowded with Jews arriving to celebrate Passover. Seeing him, many others join his disciples, shouting praises to God, acclaiming him as Israel's king.

What did Jesus expect would happen? On this point, scholars disagree. Did anyone know what would happen next? Jesus's action suggests his confidence that the Lord would accomplish the rest—shatter the Roman world order, and inaugurate God's kingdom.

In any event, Jesus does what any devout Jewish pilgrim would do: he goes straight to the Temple of God, "look[s] around at everything." Then, as dark sets in, he departs to spend the night in the town of Bethany. The next morning, heading back to Jerusalem, "he was hungry. Seeing in the distance a fig tree in leaf, he went to see whether he might find anything on it. When he came to it, he found only leaves, for it was not the season for figs" (Mark 11:12–19). Then, Mark says, Jesus spoke to the tree, and cursed it: "*May no one ever eat fruit from you again!*" The following day, when passing the tree, his disciples were astonished to see that it had withered away to its roots. "Then Peter remembered, and said to him, 'Rabbi, look! The fig tree that you cursed has withered!'" (11:21).

What are we to make of this—a grown man cursing a tree when

he fails to find fruit out of season? While John Meier chooses to call this a "curse miracle," several European and American psychiatrists suggest that it is evidence of mental illness. Albert Schweitzer, the noted Biblical scholar and physician, having spent years sifting through historical studies for his classic *Quest of the Historical Jesus*, also wrote *The Psychiatric Study of Jesus*, summarizing a range of psychiatric opinions. The European analyst George de Loosten, noting Jesus's exalted view of himself, and his curt dismissal of his birth family even while claiming God as his father, offered a diagnosis of psychosis, with outbursts of depression, evinced by his "completely senseless cursing of a fig tree." The American psychiatrist William Hurst insisted instead, "Everything we know about him conforms . . . perfectly to the diagnosis of paranoia." Then, basing his evaluation on sayings that the Gospel of John attributes to Jesus—sayings that no reputable scholar would take as actual quotations—Hurst suggests that Jesus's illness had progressed to "megalomania." Noting that John's gospel says that Jesus, hearing thunder, interpreted it as God speaking to him (John 12:29), Hurst takes this as confirming his diagnosis. And the French psychiatrist Charles Binet-Sanglé, focusing on episodes like Jesus's encounter with Satan in the wilderness, which he sees as evidence of Jesus's "hallucinations," suggests a diagnosis of "religious paranoia."

As Schweitzer observes, however, many of the acts that these psychiatrists regard as abnormal, even psychotic, were elements of beliefs widespread among Jewish groups during Jesus's time, especially those engaged with apocalyptic thinking. We cannot take seriously "diagnoses" based on no personal interaction with the alleged "patient" and nearly no awareness of his cultural and historical context. What these comments show is how far misunderstanding can go when contemporary readers, like these learned psychiatrists, are ignorant of the symbolic language that Jesus's actions "speak."

For what they take as proof of insanity are "signs" that anyone immersed in the language of the Hebrew Bible might recognize. In the act of cursing the fig tree, Jesus is echoing oracles of the prophet Jeremiah (c. 600 B.C.E.), who pictures the Lord dividing Israel's people into two groups, like two groups of figs: a basket of ripe figs, good to eat; and a basket with rotten and inedible figs. The prophet Hosea, writing about a hundred years earlier, chooses the same metaphor, envisioning the Lord speaking to his people: "*I found Israel like the first fruit on the fig tree, in its first season; thus I saw your ancestors.*" But Hosea goes on to say that when certain people did evil, angering the Lord, he declared, "*I will drive them out of my house*"—that is, the Temple (popularly called the "house of the Lord")—and, moreover, "*their root is dried up; they shall bear no fruit*" (Hosea 9:10–16).

Jesus—or Mark, who tells this story—likely has such prophecies in mind. After picturing Jesus cursing the fig tree, Mark tells how Jesus returns to Jerusalem and enters the Temple. And, while loudly declaiming Isaiah's and Jeremiah's oracles of divine judgment,

> he began to drive out those who were selling and those who were buying in the Temple, throwing down the tables of the moneychangers, and those who sold doves, and he would not

allow anyone to carry anything through the Temple. (Mark 11:15–16)

Was he wielding a whip, as John's gospel reports? Whatever he did, his violent assault on the Temple's ordinary commercial activity ignited fierce opposition. Next time he dares return there, the Temple authorities amass in a body to confront him: "*By what authority are you doing these things? Who authorized you?*" But Jesus deflects their questions and refuses to answer, declaring, "*I will not tell you!*" (Mark 11:33).

Paula Fredriksen derisively calls this episode the "Temple Tantrum," insisting that it never happened. Instead, she suggests a simpler scenario: that the Jewish leaders charged with keeping the peace, recognizing that Jesus's presence in Jerusalem at Passover was drawing large and excitable crowds that could ignite a riot, decided to order his arrest as a preventive measure.

Yet Jesus's closest followers see even his outrageous behavior in the Temple as a "sign." This, in any case, is what Mark suggests. Mark is writing this episode several decades after Jesus has died, and shortly after Roman armies have attacked, desecrated, and torn down the Temple. He wants readers to see Jesus as acting out the Lord's anger against the Temple authorities—the very "rotten figs" destined to be driven out of the Temple, just as the prophet Jeremiah had warned centuries earlier.

As Mark tells it, Jesus, seized and arrested by the Temple police, is held that night in the courtyard of the high priests' residence, where the chief priests, the Jewish Council, and scribes quickly assemble for a nighttime trial, with the high priest presiding as judge. And although lesser charges against him could not be proved, when the chief priest asks, "Are you the Messiah, the Son of the Blessed One?" Jesus answers, *"Yes, I am; and you will see the Son of Man seated at the right hand of God . . . and coming with the clouds of heaven"* (Mark 14:62).

Mark intends this dramatic scene to show why Jesus demanded secrecy all along. The first time he publicly acknowledges his role as Messiah, he is sentenced to death, effectively accused of inciting revolution by claiming to be Israel's king. This likely is why, in Mark's narrative, Jesus almost always speaks of himself as "Son of Man," insisting on his dual identity—not only *Son of God* but also *Son of Man*. It is his cover, the Clark Kent to his Superman. Also, writing circa 70 C.E., Mark is intensely aware, as is his audience, that Jesus was captured and killed forty years earlier, and he has to qualify any expectations of Jesus's immediate victory. So, while insisting that Jesus's death as Son of Man "had to happen," Mark projects his anticipated reign as Son of God into an unknown future.

Is this, then, *"the secret of the kingdom of God"* (Mark 4:10–12)? When I first read and puzzled over these accounts, I was persuaded that historians like William Wrede had found the answer. Wrede, who published *The Messianic Secret in the Gospels* in 1901, suggested that the "secret" was what Peter had guessed: Jesus's hidden identity as Messiah. Now, however, having reflected on this question for some time, exploring various sources, I realize that Mark offers no simple answer.

What, then, is that other secret, which, Mark says, Jesus told privately to his disciples, but never revealed in public, one that might help Jesus's followers understand his role, and theirs, in the present time? What is the message that makes this story of his life, his death, and his miracles so compelling that we are still talking about them? What is meant by his promise of the coming "kingdom of God"? Again, we are left in the dark, and the sources offer little certainty. What we infer from the New Testament gospels depends on what we treat as valid evidence, and what we choose to ignore. Consequently, interpreters of the gospels run in wildly different directions, and that is what we need to explore next—the "secret of the kingdom of God."

3

What Is the "Good News"?

How the Message of "God's Kingdom"
Morphs into "Jesus Is God!"

OUR EARLIEST ACCOUNTS all agree: the "good news" Jesus announces is, "The kingdom of God is coming soon!" But what *is* "the kingdom of God"? This message focuses everything that Jesus says and does; but what does it actually mean? How would the people who heard him preach in Galilee, two thousand years ago, have heard this message, and what could it mean to his countless followers today?

As Mark tells it, this announcement electrifies Jesus's followers, who abruptly leave their homes and families, abandon their previous concerns and ambitions, and join his itinerant band. What are they expecting? Jesus begins his public activity by saying that announcing this message is "what I came to do" (Mark 1:38–39), and by offering miracles as "signs" of the kingdom's imminent arrival. Immediately after that, he sends out "the twelve" to announce "the good news of God" throughout all the towns of Israel (1:14; 6:7–13), apparently expecting an immediate response.

When I first realized that I didn't have a clear sense of what this message meant, I went back to the sources, looking for clues, but those that I found seemed to swerve in different directions. Is "the kingdom" an afterlife in God's presence, the opposite of being thrown into the fiery pit called "Gehenna"—that is, into "hell"? Is the present world about to be wrapped up and discarded, like an old scroll, or transformed to what it was in the beginning, restoring God's rule over a gloriously renewed earth? Or is it an earthly kingdom infused with divine values—perhaps even the future church, as some Christians today suggest?

Whatever it means, Jesus insists that he expects it to come within his own disciples' lifetime; Matthew and Luke hint that it has arrived. Both report Jesus's saying, "The kingdom of God has come upon you" (Luke 11:20; par.), but at other times Jesus seems to admit that it *hasn't* yet come. And Mark says that right before his death, Peter, James, John, and Andrew again "asked him privately, '*Tell us, when will this happen? What sign will show that all these things are about to happen?*'" (Mark 13:3–4).

As before, Jesus speaks of that "mystery" only secretly, with members of his inner circle. Responding to their urgent questions, he warns of danger: war coming, worsened by famine and earthquakes; a time when his followers shall be hunted down, betrayed by their families, attacked and killed. Even more shocking, when desperate people see foreigners desecrate and destroy the great Temple in Jerusalem, they will flee into the mountains, experiencing "such suffering as has not been from the beginning of creation ... until now" (Mark 13:19). Echoing the classical prophets, Jesus envisions cosmic catastrophe—sun and moon going dark, stars falling from heaven, signs portending the end of time.

Thus does Mark, writing around 70 C.E.—as we've seen, shortly after the disastrous Jewish war against Rome—picture Jesus, some forty years earlier, predicting the very "time of sufferings" that Mark and his contemporaries had just lived through, and would recognize *had* happened during their lifetimes. As Mark tells it, Jesus goes on to say that after these things happen, "*then* they will see the Son of Man coming . . . with great power and glory" to judge and transform the world (13:26).

Many of Jesus's Jewish contemporaries would recognize that he is echoing hopes that they share, recalling the glory of Israel's once-powerful empire. Since the reign of King David a thousand years before, their land had been invaded and conquered by successive foreign armies, first those of Babylon, then those of the Macedonian warrior Alexander the Great. Those conquerors had imposed crushing taxation and subjugated their people to be ruled forcibly by godless foreigners. And not long after Israel's leaders sought help by allying with Rome, the Roman Empire, with its far greater military power, had absorbed Israel, renaming it as their own Roman province, "Judea." So, although Jewish kings like Herod the Great nominally ruled Judea at the time of Jesus's birth, the rulers themselves, dominated by their Roman masters, consequently were despised by many Jews.

Those longing for Israel's deliverance refused to give up hope, encouraged by prophets like Isaiah, Ezekiel, Hosea, and Daniel. Throughout six long centuries darkened by war, such prophets continued to promise that the Lord would come to judge the world, destroy the foreign invaders, and restore Israel to its former glory. For on that day, the "day of the Lord," Israel's Messiah, God's chosen king, would convert, or else subjugate, all nations, and rule the world from Jerusalem. But how would this happen? On this question, those interpreting the oracles sharply disagreed. Were the prophets saying that when Israel gathered a militant army to fight and defeat the despised foreigners, the Lord would lead them to victory? Many devout Jews, especially in rural areas like Galilee, adopted this view, taking the prophecies as encouragement to stockpile weapons and secretly plan revolution. Others insisted that such hopes were mistaken. Instead, they declared, the prophecies offer an apocalyptic vision of the "day of the Lord." Rather than taking the initiative themselves and planning war, his people should wait for the moment when the Lord himself initiates the day of judgment, inaugurating the age to come in a cataclysmic apocalypse, shattering and re-creating the present world, as he did at creation.

When Jesus of Nazareth took up John the Baptist's message of the coming kingdom of God, many of his listeners, even among his closest followers, apparently found his message ambiguous. For, as we've seen, when his followers keep asking, "When will these things happen?" Jesus repeats what he had told them earlier: the kingdom is coming *soon*—within a generation, which some of them would live to see (Mark 9:1).

But by the time Mark wrote these words, even he might have found them hard to believe. More than one generation already had passed away since Jesus died; and by the time that Luke and Matthew revised his narrative—both repeating that same promise—more than *two* generations had come and gone. Furthermore, some forty years before Mark wrote, when Jesus's followers first heard the awful news that, a few days after he entered Jerusalem hailed as Israel's future king, he had been betrayed, captured, and crucified, many took this as proof that he had completely failed. And during the years of war since that time, anyone could see that the kingdom that had "come with power" was not God's. Instead, it was Rome's power, tightening its iron grip over Judea. Luke reports how some of Jesus's followers, disillusioned, quit the movement, saying, "We had hoped that he was the one to deliver Israel" (Luke 24:21), leaving unsaid what felt obvious—his failure. Meanwhile, outsiders, both Jews and Romans, mocked those who remained faithful to Jesus as traitors to Israel, or else as fools, deceived by a false prophet.

When I began to investigate the work of historians focused on the conditions of Jewish life under Roman domination, I found that many of them came to the same conclusion: that Jesus had failed. Samuel Reimarus, for example, writing circa 1744–48, dismissed what he saw as an elaborate frosting whipped up centuries later by Christian theologians—that is, the idea that Jesus envisioned "God's kingdom" merely as "the future church." In a book he dared not publish during his lifetime, Reimarus insisted that any serious historian must understand Jesus as a first-century Jewish prophet who sought to incite armed insurrection against Rome, convinced that God would grant his people victory.

As Reimarus reconstructs what happened, Jesus initially announced "God's kingdom, coming soon," hoping to arouse Jews all over Judea to unite under his leadership and fight to regain independence as a nation ruled by God alone, through his chosen Messiah. Consequently, he first told his followers to "go nowhere among the Gentiles" (Matthew 10:5), ordering them instead to spread the message to every town in Israel, expecting, Reimarus said, that "people would flock to him from every quarter, and immediately proclaim him Messiah." When that didn't happen, Jesus, disappointed, decided to defy the Roman occupiers by appealing directly to the Jewish crowds arriving in Jerusalem for Passover.

At first, as we noted, he seemed to succeed, having entered the city as excited crowds hailed him as "the prophet Jesus from Nazareth" (21:11), "Son of David," and chanting, "Blessed is the coming kingdom of our ancestor David!" (Mark 11:10). When Jesus headed for the Temple the next morning, igniting a second public demonstration, he openly defied the Temple authorities, scattering bystanders as he threw down tables and drove out commercial vendors, denouncing Temple practices in the name of the prophets. But, Reimarus says, "the people in Jerusalem did not rise up, any more than the Galileans had done earlier." Instead, after the momentary excitement his demonstration aroused, most people, acutely aware of the increased presence of Roman soldiers during Passover, opted for a safer course and dispersed.

What Mark wrote decades later suggests that by this time Jesus was aware of the danger he was in. Did he actually predict his own death? Here again, Reimarus dismisses such "prophecies," assuming instead that Jesus still expected some great divine intervention to promise him victory. What clinches his interpretation, Reimarus concludes, is the shock and terror that Jesus, captured the next night, expressed, above all, in his dying cry from the cross: *"My God! My God! Why have you abandoned me?"* (Mark 15:34). What else could this mean, Reimarus asks, if not that Jesus felt that he had failed to inaugurate God's earthly kingdom, and, in his final agony, cried out that God had failed him as well?

While many—likely, most—of his followers abandoned the movement, a stubborn few refused to give up the vision for which they had sacrificed their ordinary lives. Some dared claim that, after he died, Peter and others had seen him alive again, and announced that God had raised him from the dead. This unlikely claim, Reimarus concludes, ignited the movement that would become Christianity.

Is this an impossible scenario for the birth of a new religious movement? Anyone who imagines that it is might consider what many of us saw happen in New York City in the 1990s, when Rabbi Menachem Schneerson, the charismatic leader of the Hasidic Jewish community in Brooklyn, suffered a stroke at the age of ninety, and entered Beth Israel Medical Center. Nearly every day, *The New York Times* printed front-page news reporting that hundreds of his followers gathered outside and inside the hospital to support him in prayer. Some insisted, "He cannot die," believing him to be Israel's Messiah, who had come to his people at last. Supporters from New York to London circulated miracle stories to demonstrate the Rebbe's spiritual power, some covertly discussing his secret, divine identity as God's chosen king. Two years later, when, after a second stroke, he did die, many left the movement, as did most of Jesus's followers when their leader died.

A few, however, refused to give up, insisting instead that "he's coming back!" And since that time many researchers, historians, and psychiatrists have documented how the Chabad movement that grew up around Rabbi Schneerson continues to attract thousands more devoted followers. While driving into New York on the West Side Highway in the 1990s, I saw a giant billboard that pictured the Rebbe, without naming him, announcing, "Messiah has come!" A few years later, on a flight to Israel, I found myself surrounded by twenty women traveling together, singing songs of praise to their Messiah, whose return they expected. In addition, ever since the Rebbe died, his people say that many have seen or felt his presence working miracles and answering prayers, that he is even more alive now than ever. Fascinated to witness what looked something like Christianity being created all over again, I found his website, often updated, which to this day claims to document many recent miracles. Furthermore, since the movement first caught fire several decades ago among the Hasidic community in Brooklyn and in London, it has spread all over the world: today the movement embodied in Chabad Jewish groups worldwide numbers about a hundred thousand. And although this is one of the most recent stories of a Messianic movement that has survived the founder's death, it is by no means the only one.

Like other historians, including Dale Allison, I mention such events simply to show that Reimarus's scenario is far from impossible. Yet, as I see it, Reimarus's reconstruction of the early Jesus movement remains simplistic, since he refuses to consider anything that challenges a narrowly rationalistic perspective.

But, circling back to Mark and the other gospel accounts, how can we know which events actually happened, and which did not?

Most often, we have no way of knowing. For centuries, scholars have recognized that the gospels report historical events while interweaving them with parables, interpretations, and miraculous moments told in symbolic language. How, then, can we separate fact from what looks like fiction to get closer to Jesus's intentions? Did Jesus actually believe that the end of time was coming soon—God's victory over Satan—or was he far beyond beliefs that many people today consider absurdly naïve?

On this question, scholars sharply disagree. Those who see Jesus through the lens of Christian theology, as a divine being, or even as God incarnate, strenuously object to Reimarus's scenario. Surely, they say, Jesus did not share views common to other first-century Jews, as if he were thinking of "the kingdom of God" as an earthly territory ruled by a king from the Davidic dynasty. Instead, being divine, he would have been omniscient; or, at least, his vision would have penetrated far beyond that of his contemporaries. Like many raised in a culture infused with Christian beliefs, I once took such beliefs for granted—that Jesus was far more than human. Growing up, I seldom questioned such assumptions, or even gave them much thought.

But after investigating Mark, Matthew, and Luke more carefully, I've come to see that these early gospels, read in their first-century context, do not support the theological assumptions enshrined, for example, in the Nicene Creed, which declares, in effect, that Jesus is God incarnate—creeds that Christians wrote centuries after Jesus lived. Like other historians, I have come to acknowledge a basic truth in Reimarus's argument: that what these gospels report of Jesus's preaching offers overwhelming evidence that, like many of his contemporaries, apparently he *did* expect that God's kingdom would come during their lifetime. At the same time, though, I've come to see the limits of Reimarus's perspective. Read his way, Mark's account sounds like nothing but a fantasy spun around a failed Messiah, and the birth stories seem only elaborate attempts to cover up an illegitimate birth. Why bother with such stories, then? We can find many accounts of failed messiahs.

What we want to understand, though, is more intriguing— and far more helpful for understanding how Christianity began. Those who adopt a strictly rationalist approach miss, for example, what inspired Justin, a young philosopher living in Rome a hundred years after Jesus's death, to abandon his family's traditional gods, declaring that what he had heard of Jesus "lit a fire in my soul." When Justin began to read the gospels, he discovered Jesus's words "bursting with power"; they turned his values upside down and transformed his life. Later, accused in a Roman court of being a Christian, Justin famously spurned the judge's offer of a pardon if he would only agree to "deny Christ." Instead, he calmly accepted a death sentence, praising God for faith that enabled him to overcome the terror of death. Then he was marched out of the courtroom to be whipped and beheaded, as his five students were forced to watch. Even then, they managed to maintain their convictions, and followed him to their own deaths.

That is what I wanted to understand when I began these explorations. What makes the stories of Jesus so powerful that countless people, even thousands of years later, continue to read and engage them, even stake their lives on what they find in them?

Part of the answer is that Mark is *not* writing history; he has no intention of simply relating "facts on the ground." The story he calls "good news," as we've seen, mingles miracles, theophanies ("revelations of God"), and "wonders" (*thaumata*) into everyday scenes. So, for example, when telling how Peter, James, and John came to recognize Jesus's intimate relationship with God, Mark envisions him luminously transfigured before them; suddenly Moses and Elijah appear to be speaking with him. Elsewhere, we've seen that the gospels include stories in which Jesus miraculously feeds thousands of people in the desert, even raises the dead.

Whereas Reimarus's boldly revisionist account reminds us to interpret these stories in terms of their first-century Jewish context, historians committed to his rationalist approach tend to flatten them. Some suggest, for example, that the story of "transfiguration," which Mark sees as an epiphany, is only a mistaken account of an unusual weather phenomenon—sun shining through mist. Others seek to explain "the feeding of the five thousand" as nothing but a fanciful version of a rationally understandable event, in which one small boy takes out his lunch to share, prompting everyone else to bring food out of their knapsacks to share with their neighbors as well—a version of the story played out in a 1950s Bible movie called *The Robe*. Scholars like Reimarus seek to take the "historical kernel" from the imaginative husk that enwraps it. The result may help us understand something about what may have happened, but such narrow perspectives often strip the gospel narratives of meaning.

How, then, are those of us who take a historical approach sup-

posed to understand them? Can we find a delicate scalpel to separate what most likely happened historically—for example, Jesus's
crucifixion—from the miraculous events, like darkness falling at
noon, which Mark weaves into his story? How are we to discriminate between a story of Jesus healing a fever, and one in which he
raises a dead man being carried out for burial? Are we certain that
we know what is possible, or impossible?

Challenged by such questions, some scholars express a different concern. If we recognize any part of these stories as legends or
myth, would anything be left of the actual, human Jesus? In 1835,
David Strauss, a historian at the University of Tübingen, jettisoned the rationalists' approach for a different one. The bestseller
he wrote, *Das Leben Jesu, kritisch bearbeitet,* became a sensation.
After George Eliot translated it into English as *The Life of Jesus,
Critically Examined,* the earl of Shaftesbury attacked this kind of
Biblical criticism as "the most pestilential . . . ever vomited out of
the jaws of hell." For instead of trying to separate historical reality
from myth, Strauss urges his readers to admit that the gospels are
shot through with myth, legends, and imaginative storytelling.
Though they do, of course, mention actual events, such as Jesus's
baptism and crucifixion, they narrate these in ways intended to
convey spiritual meaning. Read this way, as Schweitzer also notes,
the gospel accounts "are not straightforward historical accounts
of miraculous [events]," nor are they "falsely interpreted [events
that] must be 'explained away'" historically.

Instead, Strauss suggests, the genius of the gospel writers is that
they deliberately weave myth and history together into a fabric of
meaning. What gives ongoing meaning to the events they relate

is precisely that they are told in the context of Biblical narratives, mythological themes, and poetic images. Their ambiguity—and complexity—opens the possibility of multiple interpretations.

But how could Jesus's message arouse faith, much less conviction, when its meaning is not clear? These earliest gospels offer a wide range of suggestions; no wonder the question of what "the kingdom" means divides readers to this day. And as we'll see, how anyone interprets "the kingdom" has a lot to do with which gospel—and which sayings—each interpreter chooses to prioritize.

For example, many Christians today are still waiting expectantly for the end time that Jesus promised was "coming soon!" So we can easily understand that many of his contemporaries shared that vision, one far more widespread among Jewish communities two thousand years ago than it is now. Even ten or fifteen years after Jesus's death, the apostle Paul, immersed in the prophecies of the Hebrew Bible, insists, "The appointed time has become very short" (1 Corinthians 7:29)—not enough time to get married, much less to have children—hardly even time to die.

But after more than two generations passed, as we've seen, some of Jesus's followers could no longer ignore the obvious questions. If he were a true prophet, why had his message failed? Why *hadn't* the kingdom yet come "with power"? By the time that Matthew and Luke, working independently, each set out to revise Mark's narrative, both were excited to have new clues to offer, and new information to include. For by this time, circa 80–90 C.E., each had gained access to at least one other early source apparently unknown to Mark—a cluster of Jesus's sayings and parables that scholars call Q (from *Quelle*, the German for "source")—which each treats as precious early tradition, and places at the heart of his narrative.

Surprisingly, perhaps, these teachings are shockingly radical, setting forth moral demands that sound nearly impossible to fulfill. And although Matthew carefully connects them with familiar Jewish tradition, picturing Jesus going up on a mountain to announce his "Sermon on the Mount" just as Moses had received the Torah on Mount Sinai, his Jesus claims authority to challenge—even revise—the Ten Commandments. Instead of prescribing ethics for ordinary life, Jesus escalates the demands of the Torah to a fever pitch. So, he declares, if "you heard it said to those in ancient times, *'Do not kill,'* and *'Whoever kills shall be liable to judgment'"*; now *"I say to you"* that anyone who bursts out in anger against his brother, insulting him, will face judgment, even the fires of hell (Matthew 5:21–22). Then he goes on to say:

> You have heard the ancient command, *"Do not commit adultery."* But I say to you that everyone who looks at a woman with desire has already committed adultery with her in his heart. If your eye causes you to sin, tear it out, and throw it away! (Matthew 5:27–29)

Are these precepts for our lives now? Taken literally, they might look like insanity—like something that actually happened at the university where I teach, when a student newly converted to Christianity, and passionately intent on fulfilling Jesus's teaching, blinded himself in one eye before being rushed to a mental hospital for a year of treatment. Far more often, of course, people either ignore such radical teaching or challenge it. Is Jesus saying that God punishes not only wrong actions but even normal emotional impulses? Aren't these teachings contrary to human nature—counterintuitive, or, at least, wildly impractical?

What about the famously radical demands that follow:

Love your enemies, do good to those who hate you . . . If anyone hits you on the cheek, offer the other one too; if anyone steals your coat, give him your shirt as well; give to everyone who asks something from you; and if anyone takes what belongs to you, do not ask for it back. (Luke 6:27–30)

How could anyone accept, even invite, evil treatment in a world as cruel and crushing as first-century Judea was then—and as so much of the world has always been—especially for people impoverished, abused, and exploited? Matthew goes on to say that Jesus concluded these sayings with an even more startling demand: *"Be perfect, even as your Father in heaven is perfect"* (Matthew 5:48).

Extreme as these teachings sound, people who share Jesus's apocalyptic vision might find nothing masochistic about them. Instead, those persuaded that "the time is very short" might rush to adopt these practices. Is this "sermon," then, meant as a prescription for daily life, as many believers assume? Or did Jesus intend it instead as an "interim ethic" that requires radically escalated moral action only for the brief time remaining before God's kingdom arrives? Christians have debated this question for centuries—even millennia. Some, including Catholic and

Orthodox monastics, interpret these teachings as "counsels of perfection" intended for especially devout believers, who reject the ordinary business of life, including marriage, in order to live on earth "like angels" (Luke 20:36).

My own guess, exploring the sources, is that Jesus saw himself on the cusp of a transformation that demanded no less than total commitment. For aren't his commands not to feel anger, much less express it, or ever to experience desire for someone else's partner, nearly impossible to fulfill, unless, perhaps, in the short time left before end-time catastrophes shatter the world? Once we recognize the apocalyptic context in which Jesus speaks, these teachings take on new meaning—and a sense of urgency—that we hadn't noticed before. This perspective may help us to make sense of his paradoxical blessings, too, the "beatitudes" and "woes":

> Blessed are you who are hungry now, for you will be filled.
>
> Blessed are you who weep now, for you shall laugh.
>
> Blessed are you when people hate you, exclude you, despise you . . . Rejoice, then, and leap for joy; for surely your reward is great in heaven.
>
> But woe to you who are rich; you have received your consolation.
>
> Woe to you who are full now; you shall be hungry.
>
> Woe to you who now are laughing, for you shall mourn and weep." (Luke 6:12–25)

Strange as these sayings are, they offer clues to understand Jesus's message. In them, far from describing the world in which we now live, Jesus envisions this world turned upside down, its values shattered, the status quo abruptly reversed. Those who now are "first" in this world, prominent and powerful, suddenly, and soon—he warns—may find themselves last in God's kingdom, when "the last shall be first" (Matthew 20:16). And since judgment day is nearly here, Jesus says, watch out! Now you must prepare to survive "the great and terrible day of the Lord" (Joel 2:31, Malachi 4:5; also alluded to in Revelation 6:12).

Here again, Jesus's message hinges on his vision of the kingdom, and on the day of judgment that precedes it. How will God judge? Speaking to those who soon—and very soon—expect to face that "day," Jesus reveals the principle of divine judgment: "*What you give*"—to others now—"*will be what you get*" from God then (Luke 6:38). In anticipation of that "day," we are to act *toward other people* now precisely as we hope God may act *toward us* then. So, Jesus says, "Do not judge" others, and "you will not be judged" harshly, either; "Do not condemn, and you will not be condemned." For, Matthew adds, "If you forgive others their sins, your heavenly Father also will forgive you; but if you do not forgive others, neither will your Father forgive your trespasses" (Matthew 6:14). So Jesus urges us to "*give*"—nothing stingy, with huge generosity, "*and the measure you give will be what you get back; a good measure, pressed down, and running over*" (Luke 6:37–38).

This, Jesus declares, is all that matters now. Since that day is coming fast, you must act with no regard for your ordinary welfare. What's at stake is whether the Lord will invite you into his kingdom, or turn you away to depart into outer darkness. So, when his disciples ask how to pray, Jesus says to pray for what you are hoping to see happen. Teaching his followers "the Lord's Prayer," he says, pray like this: "May your kingdom come, your will be done, on earth, as it is in heaven!" (Matthew 6:10–11). Next, aware that judgment day is near, forgive others, so that you may receive God's forgiveness ("forgive us our debts, as we also have forgiven those who have sinned against us" [6:12]). And finally, pray to be spared the terrible sufferings that precede the end of time: "Lead us not into temptation" (*peirasmon:* "the time of testing" [6:13]). So although followers of Jesus have invoked "the Lord's Prayer" for over two thousand years in every situation imaginable, when Jesus first prescribed it, these words eagerly anticipated the apocalypse, which, he proclaimed, was nearly here.

Even while placing this radical teaching at the heart of his gospel, however, Matthew is aware of doubts that trouble many believers. Above all, it's late—much later than Jesus has warned anyone to expect. Why, then, *hasn't* the end time come? Why the delay? Has his prophecy failed, or was it simply wrong? Noting the lapse of time since Jesus's death, Matthew piles on multiple warnings not to give up: "Watch, then; for you do not know on what day your Lord is coming" (24:42). "Watch, then; for you do not know the day or hour" (25:13). Apparently concerned that these warnings may not be enough, Matthew urges believers to remember the flood that drowned everyone but Noah. Consequently, he says, stay awake—not like people caught by surprise when thieves break in at night (24:43).

More warnings follow, told in parables. First, if the master of a household returns unexpectedly and finds a slave manager abusing his position, he will "cut him in pieces" and throw him out (24:45–51). Second, if bridesmaids waiting for the bridegroom's arrival are not prepared for a delay, they will be shut out of the wedding feast (25:1–13). Third, if a slave entrusted with his master's resources fails to work hard during his absence, when his master returns he will order other slaves to "throw this worthless slave into the outer darkness, where there will be weeping and gnashing of teeth" (25:14–30).

Suddenly, though, Matthew stops this barrage of threats, and offers a different picture. Instead of parables drawn from everyday life, he offers a parable that projects God's kingdom into a future beyond this world. "When the Son of Man comes in his glory, and all the angels with him, then he will sit on the throne of his glory," requiring all the nations to stand before him for judgment, separating them to his right and left, "as a shepherd separates the sheep from the goats" (25:31–32). By contrast with his harsh and rigorous "sermon," now Matthew pictures the heavenly Son of Man making one far simpler demand: *Act with compassion toward those in need*. In this parable, he, as divine judge, graciously welcomes everyone who does this into his kingdom:

Come, you blessed ones . . . and inherit the kingdom . . . for I was hungry, and you gave me food; I was thirsty and you gave me something to drink; I was a stranger, and you welcomed me; I was naked, and you clothed me; I was sick and you took care of me; I was in prison, and you visited me. (Matthew 25:34–36)

When his hearers, astonished, insist that they never saw him in need, much less took care of him, he offers the famous reply: *"Whatever you did for one of the least of these, my brothers, you did for me."* Then, turning to those on his left, he castigates them for having ignored those in need, harshly ordering them, "You who are accursed, depart from me into the eternal fire prepared for the devil and his angels" (25:40–41).

Does Matthew conjure this vision to suggest an alternative to the nearly impossible demands of that earlier "sermon"? I suspect that he does. Or, as other scholars suggest, is he addressing this parable to Gentiles whom he hopes to see joining Jesus's followers—people who may not be able to observe the strict demands of Torah, but who might embrace a simpler practice? If so, it's no wonder that many people today find this parable especially appealing, as I do. And since this transcendent scene bypasses the question of when—or whether—the kingdom is actually coming on earth, it speaks to countless people who have lived centuries, even millennia, after Jesus's lifetime—effectively transforming "the kingdom of God" into a reward for the righteous after death. At the same time, Matthew also pictures the Son of Man cursing the damned, threatening them with eternal suffering—visions that would inspire Christians like Dante, over a thousand years later, to create an elaborate multichambered architecture of hell, purgatory, and heaven.

Luke, who also struggles with questions of the kingdom's timing, tends to leave out sayings that refer to the future, in order to emphasize instead the sayings that hint that the kingdom is already present on earth, at least partially—its power now transforming the world. So, after Luke pictures Jesus reading Isaiah's prophecy of "good news" in his hometown synagogue, he has Jesus conclude by announcing, "*Today* this [good news] is fulfilled in your hearing!" (Luke 4:21). Surprisingly, Luke pictures Jesus criticizing people who "assumed that the kingdom of God was to appear immediately" (19:11), and telling them to *stop* looking for signs:

> Once, when Jesus was asked by the Pharisees when the kingdom of God was coming, he answered, "The kingdom of God is not coming with signs that can be observed, nor will they say, 'Look, it's here!' or 'Look, it's there!'" (Luke 17:20–21)

Now Luke seems to take a giant leap. The next thing he reports is Jesus saying that the kingdom is already here: "*for the kingdom of God is within you!*" (17:21). Does this mean that Luke is reinterpreting the kingdom as a *present* reality, instead of a cataclysmic event at the end of time? Some scholars say yes, adding that surely this is what Jesus must have meant all along—and that Luke got it right.

The theologian Marcus Borg, for example, declares that, although Schweitzer and others argue that Jesus was an apocalyptic prophet, he actually intended to transform apocalyptic tradition, envisioning God's kingdom as an *inner* reality. Rather than expecting the world to end, Borg says, when Jesus urged people to "seek the kingdom of God" he was using the term as a metaphor to encourage them to envision "a different vision of life now"— a vision of life "centered in God." As a Bible scholar and teacher, Borg clearly wants to emphasize the contemporary relevance of Jesus's message. So, rather than responding with platitudes to believers who are waiting for the end of time, as preachers often do, paraphrasing the Biblical saying that "a thousand years in your (the Lord's) sight, is like an evening gone," he focuses on Luke's sense of the kingdom as a present reality. And though I appreciate his insight, I suggest that his enthusiasm for this message leads him to overlook the complexity we find in Luke's gospel.

For, when Luke constructs his gospel, gathering sayings from various sources, he often includes mixed messages; and, unlike Borg, Luke doesn't avoid paradox. Instead, he includes sayings that directly contradict each other. For example, shortly after Jesus rebukes people who are looking for signs and expecting the kingdom's imminent arrival (19:11), Luke pictures him ordering his disciples to watch for signs (21:25–27). Furthermore, Luke, like Matthew, sometimes projects the kingdom into an unknown future, after death. When he narrates the crucifixion scene, for example, Luke—and only Luke—includes an anecdote of a man crucified and dying next to Jesus, who pleads with him, "Remember me, Lord, when you come into your kingdom!" Then, as Luke tells it, Jesus answers, "Truly, I tell you, *today* you shall be with me in Paradise" (23:43).

So, whereas some theologians claim to show "what Jesus really meant," as if he always spoke consistently, we've noted that Luke avoids offering any single identification of God's kingdom; instead, he throws out a scattershot of hints. Is it here now? Coming soon, in future time? Or in the afterlife? I agree with the literary critic Frank Kermode that this very ambiguity—or shall we call it multivalence?—has opened up the imaginations of believers for millennia, and still does. Since, as we've seen, Luke admits that many people, disillusioned by what they saw as failed prophecy, had left the movement, we may speculate that he, like others seeking to hold on to the "good news," may have wondered whether he might have misunderstood what Jesus meant. He often seeks to salvage Jesus's prophecy by reinterpreting it—a strategy that followers of spiritual leaders often use when prophecy fails.

This process of revision, of course, does not stop with Luke. For thousands of years since then, countless believers have wrestled to understand Jesus's teaching, as many still do: this is how ancient traditions are renewed and reinterpreted to survive through time. What amazes me is that so much energy shines through these stories of Jesus that his movement, instead of trailing off into a dead end, has forged unexpected new paths. And around the same time that Matthew and Luke were writing, or perhaps shortly afterward, others took up the same challenge. Two of these produced what we might call "dueling gospels"— the Gospel of Thomas and the Gospel of John. Each of these goes beyond its predecessors, to stake out opposite claims—and each, as we'll see, becomes enormously consequential.

The first of these, the Gospel of Thomas, takes a further interpretive leap beyond where Luke landed. Opening with the words "These are the secret sayings which the living Jesus spoke and which Didymos Judas Thomas wrote down" (Thomas 1), this gospel's anonymous writer, claiming the authority of Jesus's disciple Thomas, offers to reveal what Mark refuses to tell: *the secret of the kingdom of God*" (Mark 4:11). At the same time, though, Thomas confirms what Mark reports: that, although Jesus speaks to the crowds in apocalyptic language, preaching about judgment

and the coming kingdom, he privately reveals the deeper meaning hidden in these words. In Thomas's gospel, then, Jesus speaks
with irony to set his closest disciples straight:

> Jesus said: "If those who lead you say to you, 'See, the king-
> dom is in the sky,' then the birds of the sky will precede you.
> If they say to you, 'It is in the sea,' then the fish will precede
> you. *Rather, the kingdom is inside of you, and it is outside of you.*
> *When you come to know yourselves, then ... you will realize that*
> *it is you who are the [children] of the living Father."* (Thomas 3)

After echoing what Luke reports ("the kingdom of God is within
you" [Luke 17:21]), here Jesus goes on to explain that God's kingdom is not a *place* in space—not, as often imagined, in the sky,
or in "heaven." Nor is it an *event* in time, coming at the end of the
world. Instead, it's a state of spiritual awareness—illuminating
who we truly are, and who we always have been, even before the
world was created.

When our team of graduate students and faculty at Harvard
first opened the Gospel of Thomas, we knew that, although widely
read in antiquity, it had remained almost completely unknown
for some two thousand years. Consequently, we expected to find
what our professors warned us to expect—bizarre mythology and
garbled magical incantations. Instead, we were amazed; about
half of the "sayings of Jesus" in Thomas were already familiar from
the New Testament: the "parable of the mustard seed," "love your
brother," "blessed are you poor." Whoever wrote these into the list
of sayings found in Thomas, we realized, likely drew upon some

of the same, or similar, sources as Matthew and Luke. We were even more surprised, though, to find *other* sayings—more than fifty—that were entirely new. When I first read through this list of Jesus's "sayings," this one stopped me: "Jesus said, '*If you bring forth what is within you, what you bring forth will save you. If you do not bring forth what is within you, what you do not bring forth will destroy you.*'" Stunned by this insight, so similar to the insights of psychotherapy, I thought, "You don't have to *believe* this—it just happens to be true!" Eagerly reading more, I was fascinated by the challenges these sayings present, and I love to reflect on them.

Then, of course, we began to ask questions: What *is* this gospel? Is it a genuine list of Jesus's sayings, unknown because they were told in secret? Again, as so often, we do not know. Having discussed these questions elsewhere, as many other scholars have as well, I cannot go into them in detail here. What seems likely, though, is that whoever wrote Thomas, as with Matthew and Luke, edited and reinterpreted sayings that he received. Furthermore, since such teachings were often communicated through oral tradition, those listening may have heard variant versions. Possibly, too, what Mark and Thomas both suggest may be right: that Jesus taught in different ways, depending on his audience and on the time and place. So there's still much that we don't know, even now, more than seventy years after Thomas has been translated into many languages; scholars throughout the world continue to debate questions like these, often in heated arguments—with no resolution in sight.

For our present purpose, let's simply note that many of these newly discovered sayings sound plausibly like those of a first- or second-century rabbi. As some scholars of Jewish tradition suggest, some of the sayings in Thomas seem to correlate with ancient Jewish mystical teachings, long hidden from outsiders, who only heard of such teachings more than a thousand years later, after certain collections of esoteric Jewish teachings, often called *kabbalah* ("tradition"), were published in Spain, circa 1300–1600. In Thomas, for example, Jesus explains that "the kingdom" refers to the primordial energy called into being when God first declared, "Let there be light" (Genesis 1:3, cited in Thomas 50), a passage often interpreted mystically in Kabbalah. Since Genesis had not yet gone on to tell of the world's creation, this could not refer to ordinary light, like that of the sun or moon. Instead, here Jesus speaks of "light" as a metaphor for the divine energy that brings forth everything that exists—the world, with its skies and seas, forests and deserts, reptiles, birds, and animals, including ourselves.

In Thomas's Saying 77, Jesus speaks as a voice from that primordial light, blazing through everything that exists: not only ourselves but also through sun, stars, trees, and stones, and all living creatures:

> Jesus said, "It is I who am the light which is above them all; It is I who am the all. From me did the all come forth, and unto me did the all extend. Split a piece of wood, and I am there. Lift up the stone, and you will find me there."

When reflecting on what it means that we are created in the image of God, Thomas, like the prophet Ezekiel, envisions God's image, hidden deep within us, through the metaphor of light. In

Saying 24 in the Gospel of Thomas, Jesus goes on to say, "*There is light within a [person] of light, and he lights up the whole world. If [the person] does not shine, [everything is dark].*"

Here Jesus teaches that, once we recognize that we all come forth from the same divine source, we may come to understand who we are, spiritually speaking. For, although we ordinarily identify ourselves as separate individuals, differentiated in obvious ways—by name, gender, race, ethnicity, age, family background—Jesus challenges us to seek a new level of insight, recognizing the more essential ways in which we are, spiritually speaking, the same, and part of the same family: God's family, as Thomas teaches. Here "the living Jesus" sets forth questions and responses for a *further* baptismal ritual that offers spiritual rebirth: "Jesus said, 'If they say to you, "Where did you come from?" say, "We come from the light—where the light first came into being, which shines through the image of God in us." ' " Next, Jesus says, "If they ask, 'Who are you?' Say, 'We are children of the light . . . children of the living Father' " (Thomas 50–51).

Now we've returned to the theme that Jesus announced at the start of this gospel:

Jesus said . . . "the kingdom [of God] is inside of you, and it is outside of you. When you come to know yourselves, then you will become known [by the Father] and you will realize that it is you who are the [children] of the living Father." (Thomas 3)

Having come to know Thomas's gospel, we begin to understand why certain leaders calling themselves "orthodox" (literally,

111

"straight-thinking") found its message dangerous, and rejected it as diabolic blasphemy. For, instead of revering Jesus as the *only* Son of God, as later Christian tradition would insist, Thomas teaches that *everyone* is potentially a child of God—just like Jesus! So, in Saying 13, when Thomas addresses Jesus as "master" (often translated in the New Testament as "Lord"), Jesus refuses the title, declaring, "No; I am not your master!" Later, he explains to Thomas that whoever understands his secret teaching *"will become like me; and I will become that person, and the mysteries will be revealed to him"* (Thomas 108).

Once we see Jesus as a member of our spiritual family, we come to recognize everyone else as potentially our relatives. This insight transforms relationships, requiring us to treat everyone we see as family members:

> Say, then, from the heart, that you are the perfect day and in you dwells the light that does not fail. Speak of the truth with those who search for it . . . Make firm the foot of those who have stumbled and stretch out your hands to those who are ill. Feed those who are hungry and give repose to those who are weary, and raise up those who wish to rise, and awaken those who sleep . . . [In this way,] you do the will of your Father, for you are from him. (Gospel of Truth I 32–33)

Having extended the vision of the "kingdom of God" even further than Luke, Thomas focuses on its presence right now, in this world:

His disciples said to him, "When will the kingdom come?" Jesus said, "It will not come by waiting for it. It will not be a matter of saying, 'Here it is,' or 'There it is.' Rather, the kingdom of the Father is spread out upon the earth, and [people] do not see it." (Thomas 113)

We can trace a pattern, then, from Mark's gospel to those of Matthew and Luke, and from theirs to Thomas, as each gospel writer successively interprets "the good news of the kingdom" in ways that speak powerfully to him, and to the listeners he addresses.

So far, though, we've left out another gospel—the New Testament Gospel of John, which many Christians today regard as the most familiar of all. Although John's gospel has become enormously influential, I've left it for last because it sharply deviates from the pattern we have seen in Mark, Matthew, and Luke. Ironically, the anonymous author who calls himself "the beloved disciple" is by far the most radical revisionist among the New Testament gospel writers. As the prominent Bible scholar Rudolph Bultmann noted long ago, "John" actually *leaves out* what every one of the other evangelists sees as "the gospel"—the *message,* the "good news of the kingdom"—to focus instead on the *messenger*—Jesus himself.

For Mark, Matthew, Luke, and Thomas all picture Jesus proclaiming "the kingdom," but John rewrites Jesus's words to speak instead of *himself.* John opens his gospel with a poem that echoes Genesis 1: "In the beginning was the word," the divine "Word" through which God created the world (John 1:1). In the next few lines, John implicitly identifies this "Word," which, he says, "became flesh" in human form, like "a father's only son," with Jesus of Nazareth (1:14, 18). Then, throughout his gospel, in a series of sayings that scholars aptly have named the "I am" sayings, John pictures Jesus continually insisting on what he says "*I am*": the "water of life," "the bread that comes down from heaven," "the door," "the way," "the vine," "the resurrection and the life." All these and more are metaphors for the divine being that John declares not only created the world but also became incarnated as Jesus.

And whereas Mark, Luke, Matthew, and Thomas all focus primarily on God's *kingdom*, John almost never mentions it. At the start of his gospel, he speaks of it only once, and then only as a spiritual state that only baptized people may "see" (3:3). And when John's Jesus *does* speak of the kingdom, he radically changes the required criteria for "entering" it. Instead of calling for repentance to change how we live, John's Jesus insists above all that we "must" believe—not in the message of the kingdom but in Jesus himself—and to seal this belief by accepting baptism. This alone, John's Jesus insists, enables those who are baptized to "*see the kingdom of God*" (3:3).

What is it, then, that John says we "must believe" about Jesus? As his narrative progresses, John leaves no doubt. He actually has Jesus declare, "You will die in your sins *unless you believe that I am He*" (8:24). Who *is* he, then? Next John pictures Jesus claiming for himself the divine name God gave to Moses ("before Abraham existed, *I AM*" [8:58])—a claim that arouses other devout Jews to pick up stones to kill him for blasphemy (8:59). Shortly after this, when again they threaten to stone him, John's Jesus provokes them again, insisting, *"The Father and I are one"* (10:30). John so radically escalates Jesus's status that, in his gospel, the *messenger* who has now become the *message* is no longer merely a prophet, or only Messiah. Instead, John coins a new term, declaring that Jesus is God's *"only begotten Son"*—nothing less than God incarnated in human form.

At the same time, John reinterprets the meaning of Jesus's life and death, picturing him as the "Lamb of God" (1:29) who descends from heaven in order to die a sacrificial death for "the sin of the world." In the most frequently quoted line of his gospel, John declares that this shows God's surpassing love: *"God so loved the world, that he gave his only begotten Son, so that everyone who believes in him, may not die, but have eternal life"* (3:16). The line that follows, though, is quoted far less often: John warns, *"Those who do not believe are already condemned"* to *"die in [their] sins"* for the mortal sin of rejecting what his gospel demands (3:18).

Having mentioned "the kingdom" at the start of his gospel to say that only those who are baptized shall "see the kingdom of God" (3:3), John mentions it a second time near the end, when recounting the scene of Jesus's trial before the Roman governor. Here Pilate, who clearly assumes that talk of a kingdom means that Jesus is plotting insurrection, demands to know, "Are you the King of the Jews?" (18:33). In response, John has Jesus dismiss both literal and apocalyptic connotations of the term, and reply, *"My kingdom is not of this world"* (18:36). Here, then, as John's Jesus earlier explains to his disciples (14:1–6), he speaks of his "kingdom" as a supernatural realm *beyond* this world, to which he shall return after his death, inviting only those who believe "in him" to join him there.

What can we make of the astonishing turn into which John takes his gospel—suggesting that "the gospel," Jesus's primary message, no longer focuses on *God's kingdom coming* but upon the messenger himself, that, in effect, Jesus "*is God*" (1:1–2, 8:24)? This question has intrigued—and troubled—me for decades. Ever since John's revisionist message ("*Jesus is God*") was written into the Nicene Creed that both Catholics and Protestants use to this day, declaring that Jesus is "*God from God, light from true light, true God from true God, begotten, not created, of one being with the Father,*" countless Christians have come to revere John's gospel as the "most spiritual" of all. And when I realized that this same gospel has inspired Christian mystics and poets—from the sixteenth-century Catholic mystic who named himself "John of the Cross," to the Anglican poets John Donne and T. S. Eliot—initially I was reluctant to admit what an outlier John's gospel is. Having struggled to understand what motivates John to write as he does, and having discussed it in detail elsewhere, I can only make what seems to me like the simplest suggestion.

I suggest that the writer who calls himself "the beloved disciple" has encountered followers of Jesus who offer teaching like what we find in Thomas—namely, that every human being, created in God's image, is potentially a child of God. But John, who focuses his own devotion entirely on Jesus, whom he reveres as God's *only* son, finds such views not only wrong but deserving of eternal damnation—and so, I suggest, he writes the Gospel of

John to make that point as clearly and forcefully as he can. And, as anyone raised in the Christian tradition knows, this gospel enormously influenced the shape that orthodox Christianity would take in the future.

This, then, raises a basic question: who chose the four gospels now included in the New Testament—Mark, Matthew, Luke, and then, surprisingly, John—but excluded sources like Thomas as "heresy"? That question will come up again later, as we proceed. For now, however, two more immediate questions arise. If "the secret" at the heart of Jesus's message involved an apocalyptic vision that many people today no longer share, what continues to make his story so compelling? And if Jesus was an apocalyptic prophet whose prophecy failed, why was he crucified? These are the questions we turn to next.

4

The Crucifixion: What Happened, and What Could It Mean?

M ARK BEGAN HIS fast-paced narrative with Jesus announcing "good news" and performing healings and exorcisms, interspersing it with episodes of challenge, miracle, and suspense as Jesus encourages his disciples' hopes for a future kingdom. But as his narrative darkens toward its conclusion, Mark reports that, when Jesus begins walking on the road toward Jerusalem, "he was walking ahead of them, and they were amazed, and those who followed were terrified" (Mark 10:32). What Jesus tells them on the way would terrify them even more: he expects to be betrayed, arrested, put on trial, condemned, mocked, and killed. I agree with most scholars that his followers added detailed predictions like these after his death. Nevertheless, Mark shows that, like other courageous people who have dared to risk death when acting out of moral conviction—Martin Luther King Jr., Alexei Navalny—Jesus was fully aware of danger.

What he did next enormously intensified that danger. Like King and Navalny, he set up public demonstrations. Jesus and his followers ignited Passover crowds packed into the city to shout and acclaim him as "Son of David," Israel's king. If that "triumphal entry" was anything like what Mark describes, it surely would have alerted Roman soldiers stationed in the Holy City to expect trouble. The following morning, rather than retreating, Jesus walked back into Jerusalem and headed straight for the Temple of God. Shouting words from Israel's prophets, while throwing down tables and scattering their contents, "he would not allow anyone to carry anything through the temple" (11:16). When enraged Temple authorities and chief priests accosted him, demanding to know "by what authority" he dared do such things, he refused even to answer (11:27–33).

Now the action moves fast, infused with a sense of impending disaster. Immediately before starting these demonstrations, Mark says, Jesus had spoken confidently with his closest disciples, as if anticipating that success would soon follow, promising that God's kingdom would come within their lifetime (9:1). Yet only a day or two later, while sharing with them his final Passover meal, he speaks of impending betrayal, and acts out a "sign." Handing bread and wine to his disciples, he speaks as if he were giving them his own body and blood to eat and drink. Is he feeling conflicted, anxious about what would happen next? On that night, Mark says, he speaks as if expecting the kingdom to come very soon: "*I will not drink wine with you again until I drink it again with you in the kingdom of God!*" (14:25). Or did he mean something else: that he expects to celebrate with them only after his death, when judgment day would have shattered the world and brought in the new age?

After dinner, Mark says, Jesus and his closest disciples walk outside the walls of Jerusalem to the Mount of Olives, overlooking the city. When they arrive, he ominously warns: "You are all going to be horrified and run away; for, as the scriptures say, '*I shall strike the shepherd, and the sheep shall be scattered*' [Zechariah 13:7]; but after I rise up again, I will go before you to Galilee" (Mark 14:27–28).

Writing this scene in retrospect, of course, Mark likely intends it as readers today most often take it, as prophesying Jesus's death and resurrection. But if Jesus actually spoke such words on that night, the outcome yet unknown, might he or his disciples have taken Zechariah's oracle as prophesying victory? Zechariah's prophecy goes on to say that, after an initial setback, God's Messiah would conquer "all the nations," and then "command peace" and rule the world "from sea to sea . . . to the ends of the earth" (Zechariah 9:10).

At this crucial moment, however, Mark reports that Jesus, having anticipated that his followers would abandon him, leads them to the olive grove called Gethsemane. Telling them to stay behind as he walks on farther, and taking only Peter, James, and John with him, "he began to be deeply distressed, and agitated." He allows them to see his vulnerability: "I am terribly grieved, even to death; stay here—and keep awake!" (Mark 14:33–34). Then, "throwing himself on the ground," Mark says, he desperately prays to be spared the horror he feels is imminent, even while struggling to accept that God's will may differ from his own.

Later that night, sharply rebuking Peter and the others for having fallen asleep, Jesus suddenly sees a crowd of men armed "with swords and clubs," led by Judas, who "immediately went up to him and said, 'Rabbi!' and kissed him" (14:43–45). Then, as Mark tells it, Jesus is seized and arrested, while one of his disciples, desperate to defend him, draws a sword and attacks, clumsily injuring the chief priest's slave. But the moment his followers see him captured, likely to be tortured and crucified, they bolt and run for their lives.

The arresting mob then delivers Jesus to the chief priest's residence, where "all the chief priests, elders, and scribes were assembled," to hold a full-scale trial before the entire Jewish Council. Charged with making threats against the Temple and challenged to answer whether he sees himself as Messiah, Jesus boldly replies, "*I am*" (14:62). Here Mark shows why Jesus needed to keep his divine identity secret: the first time he admits it in public, "all of them condemned him as deserving death" for blasphemy (14:64). The next morning, Mark says, after a night of abuse, mockery, and beatings, the chief priests and "the whole council" hand the prisoner over to the Roman governor, Pilate, accusing him of insurrection ("He said he was King of the Jews").

What happens then? Strangely, as Mark tells it, Pilate seems unconcerned about the charge, even unconvinced. Adopting the role of omniscient narrator, Mark claims to know the governor's inner thoughts: "He realized that it was out of jealousy that the chief priests had handed him over" (15:10). A story familiar to Christians follows: Pilate, recognizing that Jesus is not guilty of sedition, refuses to pass sentence. Instead, he actually defends him. But after timidly trying three times to release him, Pilate, "wishing to satisfy the crowd" clamoring for the death sentence, reluctantly submits to the demands of a shouting mob and "hand[s] him over to be crucified" (15:15).

Is this what actually happened? No one doubts that Jesus was crucified; everyone from his devoted followers to their harshest critics agree on this. As the British military historian S. G. F. Brandon writes, "Ironic though it be, the most certain thing known about Jesus of Nazareth is that *he was crucified by the Romans as a rebel against their government in Judea.*" Yet historians raise serious questions about *how* it happened; this is a crucial—and problematic—moment in Mark's story.

What Brandon states as obvious includes an embarrassing fact that the gospel writers want to suppress: namely, that Pontius Pilate, the Roman governor of Judea, judged Jesus guilty, and sentenced him to the standard penalty for treason against Rome. And as we'll see, the gospel writers work hard to mitigate the negative impact of his verdict, since people who knew nearly nothing else about their Messiah often knew this. Tacitus, a Roman senator who despised Jesus's followers as "a class of people hated for their superstitions," mentions only that Pilate (whom he calls "prefect") had sentenced Jesus to this "despicable death," a statement that the Jewish historian Josephus, writing independently, confirms. And when Justin "the philosopher," himself a convert, dares defend his fellow believers, petitioning the future emperor Marcus Aurelius to stop Roman magistrates from torturing and killing them, he admits, "This, they insist, is our insanity: that we worship a crucified man along with the eternal God."

The reality of crucifixion is horrifying, and raw. Roman military men, famous for inventing what Cicero called the "cruelest and most horrible" forms of torture, reserved this, the worst of all, for insubordinate slaves and insurrectionists. Roman magistrates ordering crucifixions often placed them on well-traveled roads as "a billboard" to deter others, displaying naked men groaning and writhing in agony that could go on for days. Jesus's followers, shocked to hear of his sudden arrest and execution, later heard stories of how he had been whipped, mocked, and paraded through the streets before his hands and feet were torn through with nails, which forced him into an upright position, trying to raise himself up on broken feet to gasp for breath.

When setting out to write, then, Mark faces an enormous challenge. While claiming to announce "good news of Jesus, Messiah, Son of God," he has to answer overwhelming objections. If Jesus really were God's anointed king, how could he have failed so miserably? How could his followers have abandoned him and gone into hiding, while enemy soldiers captured, tortured, and crucified him as a common criminal? And wasn't he widely known as a seditionist, tainted by association with the since-failed war?

Contending with questions like these, Mark, as we've seen, chooses to set his story of Jesus not simply within the context of the war against Rome but within the cosmic war between good and evil. As he tells it, the stark events of Jesus's life and death could not be understood apart from the clash of supernatural forces playing out on earth, with Jesus a lightning rod for their conflict. Rather than simply writing a history, then, Mark intends to tell his story in terms of its hidden dynamics—to tell it, in effect, from *God's* point of view.

After beginning his gospel with the story of how God's spirit descends on Jesus at his baptism, driving him to contend against Satan, Mark pictures him engaging in conflict with evil forces at every turn, first against demonic powers tormenting people who are possessed, raving, and diseased; then against the Jewish leaders who, early on, "conspired to kill him" (Mark 3:6); and later against his own disciple Peter, whom he denounces as "Satan." Harshly rejecting Peter's well-intentioned protests, Jesus recognizes that he must fight to the death (8:33). So, as we've seen from the start, each of the New Testament gospels pictures Jesus's crucifixion as the culmination of the struggle between good and evil initiated at his baptism.

Although Satan seldom appears onstage in these gospel accounts, he plays a central role in the divine drama. After all, the story the gospel writers tell would make little sense *without* Satan. How could anyone claim that a man betrayed by one of his own followers, then brutally killed on charges of treason against Rome, not only *was*, but still *is*, God's appointed Messiah— unless his capture and death were not a final defeat but only a preliminary skirmish in a vast cosmic conflict now enveloping the universe? Sustained by this conviction, Mark sets forth his stark, unvarnished narrative.

But even after placing his narrative in the context of cosmic war, Mark has to deal with the most explosive question. If Jesus was innocent, why was he sentenced to death? And since he was convicted of inciting insurrection, how could his followers possibly claim that he was not guilty? As prefect of Judea, Pilate was the only man authorized to order crucifixion; and only Roman soldiers had the equipment, experience, and manpower to carry it out. Inevitably, as everyone knew, Pilate gave the order. There is no other way it could have happened. At this crucial moment, Mark dodges the question. Refusing to state plainly that Pilate ordered the death penalty, he offers instead his alternative scenario, the scene of the "Trial Before the High Priest." And as we'll see, Matthew, Luke, and John each will go to even greater lengths to obscure the same point.

Scholars investigating Jewish judicial procedure have shown that what Mark reports of the "Trial Before the High Priest" likely did not happen. Paul Winter, for example, points out that, as far as we can tell, the Jewish Council never met at night during the first century. Even had it done so, the charge Mark mentions did not carry a capital sentence: claiming to be Messiah is not blasphemy, since the term "Messiah" refers not to the Lord but to the human ruler who represents him. Furthermore, in cases when the Jewish Council did meet and order a death sentence, Jewish law required a twenty-four-hour delay before it was carried out, and it would have been death by stoning—not by the method Roman forces used against insubordinate slaves and provincial insurrectionists.

Fergus Millar, Oxford's historian of classical Rome, agrees. In an influential article, he suggests that the far simpler story told in John's gospel offers a much more likely scenario. Members of the Jewish Council, concerned that Jesus's public activities during Passover could cause riots and provoke Roman reprisals, followed a more usual procedure: they ordered his arrest, and sent him to Pilate for judgment.

Can we know what actually happened when Jesus was crucified? Some historians, like Crossan, noting that Jesus's disciples fled when he was arrested, insist that we know nearly nothing. Pointing out that the gospel writers use oracles from Israel's prophets and psalms to fill in the gaps when writing about the crucifixion, Crossan implies that they do so because they knew nearly nothing of what actually happened. But Crossan seems overly skeptical. As Allison notes, Mark may have heard reports from some of Jesus's women followers, including Mary Magdalene; Mary, the mother of James and Joseph; and Salome, who, he says, were "watching from afar" (Mark 15:40–41), after the male disciples had gone into hiding. And since crucifixions were public events, often with crowds of onlookers, "it makes . . . historical sense to believe that some people—some sympathetic, some hostile, some undecided, shared with others what they had seen and heard."

Allison also noted that when someone dies suddenly, "people in all cultures typically respond to death by seeking out and telling stories about a deceased friend or relative . . . Further, memories and imaginations, shortly after a death, often converge on . . . the events leading up to the loss." Especially when a death is premature, violent, and cruel, "the story of the dying may become preoccupying," so that it "eclipses the retelling of their living; the way they died takes precedence over the way they lived." That seems to have happened initially, at least, in the case of Jesus. Many scholars agree that, even before Mark wrote, some of Jesus's anonymous followers, shocked and grieving, had composed an early account of his death drawn from stories that apparently circulated widely. When Mark set out to write, then, he likely had in hand not only a list of Jesus's teachings but also an earlier "passion narrative"—a story that begins with the arrest and ends after his burial.

Throughout Jesus's lifetime, as we've seen, devout and militant Jews fighting to free Judea from Roman occupation had faced continual failure. Around 4 C.E., the revolutionary leader Judas the Galilean had been captured and crucified after he led a surprise attack on a Roman fort in Galilee. Roman magistrates responded to outbursts of protest and violence with increasing force, until, in 66 C.E., even the Jewish leaders ended their collaboration with Rome, igniting a war of revolution "in the name of God and our common liberty."

Although Jesus had been killed some thirty years earlier, his contemporaries who wrote about him and the movement he started, whether allies or enemies, placed them in the context of the troubles in Judea in general. For, when priests at the Jerusalem Temple suddenly stopped offering the daily sacrifices for the emperor's welfare that Rome required, effectively declaring war, the Roman general Titus marched sixty thousand soldiers into Jerusalem to besiege the city, cutting off supply lines to surround and starve the inhabitants, while soldiers stormed the militants and roamed the streets, setting off countless reports of robbery, rape, and slaughter. After four agonizing years, as battles raged throughout the city, the Romans finally overpowered the last Jewish holdouts, who had barricaded themselves within the Temple walls. Roman soldiers desecrated the Temple by offering sacrifice to Jupiter within the inmost sanctuary. Then they tore down the Temple's huge stones and set fire to what remained, turning the center of the Holy City into piles of broken stones, trash, and charred rubble.

Since Mark began writing about Jesus during the final years of the war, or a few years later, around 68–70 c.e., we cannot understand his gospel, or those of Matthew and Luke, until we recognize that they are, in effect, *wartime literature.* Like other Jews, Jesus's followers were shaken by these world-shattering events. Yet some, like Mark, seemed to find in them a gleam of hope. Hadn't Jesus himself predicted that the Holy City would be "surrounded with armies" (Luke 21:20), the Temple desecrated and destroyed? Hadn't he warned that "signs of the end" (Mark 13:22–30) would precipitate the "worst suffering since the creation of the world" (13:19), before the world would be shattered and transformed?

> As he came out of the Temple, one of his disciples said to him, "Look, Rabbi, what wonderful stones, and what wonderful buildings!" And Jesus said to him, "Do you see these great buildings? There will not be one stone on another, that will not be thrown down . . . But when you see the abominable sacrilege set up where it ought not to be—then let those in Judea flee into the mountains." (Mark 13:1–14)

Even as they lived through these terrible years, Mark and some others tenaciously held on to the hope that what Jesus had prophesied would happen next: "*Then* they will see the Son of Man coming in clouds and great glory . . . so when you see these things happen, you know that he is near, at the very gates" (13:26–29).

At the same time, Mark and others loyal to Jesus were intensely aware that many other Jews despised them for championing someone who looked like so many other failed insurrectionists and false messiahs, perhaps even like Judas the Galilean himself, who was crucified on the same charge along with thousands of his men some sixty years earlier. The philosopher Celsus, writing circa 170 C.E., claims to report how Jewish critics mocked Jesus's followers:

> You have been deceived! . . . *Would a god—a savior, as you say, and Son of the Most High God—be betrayed by . . . those closest to him . . .* [and be] arrested and executed in the most humiliating of circumstances[?] . . . Let us disregard . . . the nonsensical idea that Jesus foresaw everything that was to happen to him (an obvious attempt to conceal the humiliating facts) . . . A fine god indeed . . . who could not . . . avoid the disaster that ended his life in disgrace . . . [In any case, they say] he had told his robber band beforehand that he would come to no good end, and wind up a dead man.

In the aftermath of his death, some of Jesus's most devoted followers, aware of such attacks and desperate to prove that their Messiah had not failed, pored over the Jewish Scriptures, especially the prophetic oracles and the psalms, searching for hints that even the worst that had happened—Judas's betrayal and Jesus's crucifixion—might hold deeper meaning. As in the case of the birth stories, they found many passages that they felt might be relevant.

Yet how could devout Jews possibly imagine Jesus as the triumphant warrior and Messiah whom the prophets envision? Astonishingly, even before the gospels were written, some of

Jesus's followers began to read certain psalms attributed to King David—psalms speaking in the voice of a righteous king who suffers unjustly, lamenting and pleading for help, while anticipating God's deliverance—as prophesying what had happened to their Messiah. The plot of these psalms (Psalms 18, 22, 31, 40, 42, and 69), as the Biblical scholar Richard Hays points out, typically moves from humiliation and danger to praise of God's deliverance. No wonder, then, that Jesus's followers took these to suggest that, in times of extremity, "Jesus prayed the Psalms":

> Many devout Jews interpreted these laments and prayers as if they embodied the experience of King David himself, or even of Israel's people, so often defeated and crushed, yet who hoped, even insisted, that their God surely would deliver them. *When Jews who revered Jesus read these "royal psalms" after hearing of his terrible death, they felt that they could hear Jesus' voice speaking through them.*

Paul himself, writing decades before Mark, Matthew, or Luke, reads Psalm 69:9 as if Jesus himself were speaking ("The insults of those who insult you have fallen upon me"). Mark and Matthew make similar claims, suggesting that Jesus prayed the opening line of Psalm 22 as his dying words (*"My God; my God; why have you abandoned me?"*). Luke, though, refuses to include that embarrassing cry in his gospel. Instead, he replaces it with a humble, trusting prayer found in another psalm attributed to David ("Father, '*into Your hands I commend my spirit*'" (Psalm 31:5).

King David's lament over a friend who had turned against him also struck a chord. Some believers decided that, read prophetically, what he wrote could account for Judas's betrayal: *"My own familiar friend, whom I trusted, who ate bread with me, lifted his heel against me"* (Psalm 41:9). Even this shocking event, then, could be part of the divine plan. Mark, noting the same passage, traces a similar interpretive path, saying that Jesus identifies Judas as betrayer by giving him a piece of bread, declaring that the traitor is "one of the twelve, *who is dipping bread in the same bowl with me."* John's gospel takes this identification even further, saying that immediately *"after [Judas] received the piece of bread,"* Satan entered into him, precipitating the betrayal (John 13:26). Might this exonerate Judas, if his role in Jesus's crucifixion were divinely preordained? Apparently troubled by this question, the gospel writers chose to emphatically answer *no*. Both Mark and Luke declare, *"The Son of Man goes as it has been written of him, but woe to the one by whom he is betrayed!* It would be better for that one not to have been born" (Matthew 26:24).

Furthermore, when reading Psalm 22 as prophecy, Jesus's followers felt that it corresponds so strikingly to crucifixion that they went on to write many of its details into their narratives of Jesus's death. In passages where the Hebrew original of this psalm seemed less apt for this purpose than the Greek translation more accessible to them, the evangelists, writing in Greek, adopted the latter—a practice that English translators followed, over a thousand years later, when translating the following passage from the Greek:

I am poured out like water, all my bones out of joint ... they have pierced my hands and feet; I can count all my bones; they stare and gloat over me; they divide my clothes among them, and they gamble for my cloak. (Psalm 22:14–18)

One phrase of the original Hebrew text is uncertain, perhaps suggesting instead that the sufferer's hands and feet have shriveled (Hebrew: *ka'aru*). Christian translators nearly always choose to follow the Greek translation (*ōruxan*), which more aptly suggests a Roman form of crucifixion—a practice likely unknown to Jews in David's time.

When Matthew revises Mark's narrative, especially concerned to counter criticism from fellow Jews who despise his Messiah, he focuses even more intensely on prophetic oracles. We've seen how, in his birth narrative, Matthew uses a Greek translation of Isaiah's prophecies to validate his account of Jesus's birth: "a virgin" (*parthenos*, in Greek, instead of the Hebrew *almah*, "young woman") "shall conceive and bear a son" (Isaiah 7:14). So, too, when narrating Jesus's death, though Matthew closely follows Mark's account, he sometimes changes words and adds new episodes, to demonstrate his conviction that the crucifixion, far from being a total catastrophe, is part of a deeply hidden divine plan.

Mark already had adopted this strategy, adding details found in psalms and prophecies to his narrative of Jesus's death. Even while saying that Jesus burst out crying, in the words of Psalm 22, that God had abandoned him, Mark may have meant to weave a note of hope into the crucifixion scene, since Psalm 22 ends on a note of trust and praise. When Matthew revises Mark's account, he omits details that show Jesus's vulnerability, choosing instead to emphasize that Jesus not only understands his imminent death as God's will but confidently embraces it. So, while acknowledging that Jesus is agitated in Gethsemane, Matthew avoids saying that he was "distressed and agitated," admitting only that he was "grieved" (Matthew 26:37). Next, he writes that when Judas arrives to kiss him, Jesus challenges him, showing that he is fully aware of what is going on. Finally, instead of the chaotic scene Mark reports, Matthew pictures Jesus completely in charge, harshly rebuking the disciple who fights to defend him:

> Then Jesus said to [the disciple], "Put your sword back in its place! Everyone who wields a sword will die by the sword. *Do you not know that I could appeal to my Father, who would immediately send me more than twelve legions of angels? But then, how would the scriptures be fulfilled, [which say] that this must happen?*" (Matthew 26:52–54)

Even in this moment of crisis, Matthew pictures Jesus giving orders, teaching nonviolence, and informing his terrified disciples that his sufferings are necessary "to fulfill the Scriptures." And when Matthew tells how Jesus, bound and beaten, is sentenced to death by the chief priest, then delivered to Pilate for judgment, he adds an episode to show Judas's remorse and his suicide. As he tells it, when Judas hears that Jesus has been sentenced to death, he repents and goes back to the Temple to return the blood money to the authorities. Spurned, he throws the money down on the floor, "and went and hanged himself" (Matthew 27:5).

Here again, Matthew alludes to oracles from Jeremiah and Zechariah to show that even Judas's fate fulfills the scriptures (Matthew 27:9; see Zechariah 11:12–13 and Jeremiah 18–19).

Matthew still has to deal with the most challenging question: how to claim that Pilate never pronounced Jesus guilty. Here again, he follows Mark's lead, expanding his narrative to show that Jesus was *not* a militant. Mark already has given the clue to the question *If not, how could he have been crucified?* by picturing Jesus sentenced to death—but not by Pilate. Both Mark and Matthew make this point when staging that dramatic "Trial Before the High Priest," in which Caiaphas, the Jewish high priest, interrogates Jesus, and tears his own clothes while sentencing him to death for blasphemy. Then, they say, the Jewish authorities deliver him to Pilate's judgment hall, falsely accusing him of sedition. Even there, these writers claim, "all the chief priests and the elders of the people" go on to dupe and pressure Pilate into "handing Jesus over" to be killed (Mark 15:1; Matthew 27:1).

Continuing to follow Mark's lead, Matthew pictures Pilate haplessly asking the noisy and frenzied crowd what he should do with Jesus, while repeatedly trying to defend a man he sees as innocent ("Why? What has he done wrong?" [Matthew 27:23]). In the tense moments before Pilate gives in to crowd pressure, Matthew adds two episodes that enormously intensify the governor's hesitation and the crowd's culpability. First, while Pilate sits in judgment, his wife sends him an urgent message, pleading with him to "have nothing to do with that righteous man" (Matthew 27:19). Second, "when he saw that he was gaining nothing, and a riot was starting, he took water and washed his hands" before the crowd, declaring himself innocent "of this man's blood," telling them, in effect, *You do it!* (27:24).

In response, Matthew declares, they do just that: *"The whole people"* shout a terrifying reply: *"His blood be upon us, and upon our children!"* (27:25). As Matthew tells it, this works. Moments later, Pilate releases a notorious insurrectionist named Barabbas to the crowd, and, after having Jesus whipped, he *"handed him over to be crucified"*—without, Matthew carefully implies, having ever pronounced sentence. As historians of Rome note, this story, too, is wildly unlikely: voluntarily releasing a known insurrectionist would endanger the governor's own position, and even his life.

When Luke independently revises Mark's narrative, addressing a predominantly Gentile audience, he seems even more determined to show that, whatever happened in court, Jesus was innocent. To make this point, he tells a far more unlikely story— one that, like Matthew's version, implicates only Jesus's *Jewish* enemies. First, Luke actually conjures an extremely unlikely story: "The chief priests, the officers of the Temple police, and the elders" arriving at Gethsemane in person instead of the armed posse Mark mentions, to arrest Jesus late at night. Next, as Luke tells it, Jesus stops Judas before he even gets close enough to kiss him, and defiantly challenges the chief priests and Temple police, denouncing them to their face as agents of Satan, "the power of darkness" (Luke 22:53).

As Luke tells it, the next morning the entire Jewish Council puts Jesus on trial, and unanimously sentences him to death. Then, handing him over to Pilate, Luke suggests that the council members invented more false charges: "We found this man perverting our nation, forbidding us to pay taxes to the emperor, and saying that he himself is Messiah, a king" (23:2).

In Luke's account, as in Mark's, Pilate ignores these accusations, and simply asks Jesus whether the charges are true. Here, as in Mark's account, Jesus deflects the question, and Pilate accepts this, declaring, "*I find no basis for accusing this man!*" (23:4). But when the chief priests continue to press charges forcefully, Luke, and only Luke, adds that Pilate sends Jesus to Herod, suggesting—counterfactually—that the Jewish king has authority in this matter. And although Herod was eager to see Jesus, Luke says, he was disappointed when the prisoner refused to answer his questions or do any miracles, and sent him back to Pilate. At this point, Pilate again tells the angry Jewish mob, "*I have not found this man guilty of any of your charges against him . . . He has done nothing to deserve death. So I will . . . release him*" (23:14–15). As the crowd shouts even louder, Pilate pronounces Jesus innocent for the third time: "*I found in him no basis for the death sentence; so I will . . . release him!*" "But," Luke says, "the chief priests, the leaders, and the people" kept urgently demanding with loud shouts . . . " 'Crucify! Crucify him!' . . . and their voices prevailed" (23:13–23).

Here, then, even more explicitly than Mark and Matthew, Luke insists that Pilate never sentenced Jesus. Instead, he writes, Pilate finally "decided . . . in favor of their demand," and "handed Jesus over for what they wanted. And as they led him away, they seized a man passing by, Simon of Cyrene, and forced him to carry the cross behind Jesus" (23:23–26). Shockingly, in a passage in which Luke chooses his words with extreme care, he implies something impossible: that "they"—*the Jews, not the Romans*—

led Jesus away and crucified him. Here again, in Luke's account, Pilate three times pronounces Jesus innocent, and never actually orders crucifixion!

And Luke doesn't stop there. After picturing Jesus crucified between two other Jews charged with insurrection, Luke, and only Luke, has one of them confess his own guilt and pronounce Jesus innocent: "We, here, are condemned justly, getting what we deserve . . . but *this man has done nothing wrong!*" (23:41). Luke ends this episode as the Roman centurion standing guard repeats the same refrain: "*Certainly this man was innocent!*" (23:47). How could anyone find this credible? As Luke tells it, the chief priests and the Jewish Council, joined by the Jewish crowd, unanimously accuse Jesus of sedition, whereas Romans, from Pilate himself down to members of the execution squad, *defend* him. Writing the book of Acts as a sequel to his gospel, Luke re-emphasizes the same point: here, too, whenever Luke pictures Roman magistrates interrogating Jesus's followers, the Romans invariably declare them innocent.

To make his case that the Romans did not condemn Jesus to death, Luke and other followers of Jesus effectively had to invent a new Pilate—and they did. In order to indict the Jewish leaders and exonerate the Romans, they replaced Pilate with a durable caricature—that of a well-meaning weakling solicitous of justice, intimidated within his own council chamber by local crowds shouting outside until, unable to withstand the pressure, he gives in and executes a man he knows is innocent.

Others among Jesus's contemporaries, both Jewish and Roman, describe a very different man. Even Josephus, the Jewish general who fought against Rome and later wrote about his people's history in a way calculated to gain respect for them, reports that Pilate displayed contempt for his Jewish subjects, illegally appropriated funds from the Temple treasury, and flagrantly violated their religious sensibilities. Josephus also reports how Pilate dealt with crowds of Jews shouting protests against his policies: how, for example, he ordered his soldiers to conceal their weapons while surrounding a crowd of protesters, and then, at a signal, to attack and kill those who refused to disperse. Philo of Alexandria, an influential member of the Alexandrian Jewish community, entrusted to lead a delegation to negotiate with Emperor Gaius in Rome, offers a blunt and forceful indictment, describing Pilate as a man of "inflexible, stubborn, and cruel disposition," infamous for "greed, violence, robbery, assault, *frequent executions without trial,* and endless savage ferocity."

What motivates the gospel writers, then, to characterize Pilate as they do? I find no simple answer. Obviously, they meant to clear the reputation of their beloved teacher, who, as far as we can tell, *was* innocent of sedition. But, after struggling to understand why they spun their various stories as they did, I came to see that these writers also shared an urgent practical concern: *to save their own lives, and those of their fellow believers.* Hoping to attract newcomers to their movement, they were also intensely aware that their continuing loyalty to a man crucified for insurrection was placing them, as his followers, in serious danger of suffering the same fate.

Especially after the war, the Roman magistrates and soldiers occupying Judea were wary of any hint of renewed sedition.

Rumors spread that Jesus's relatives had been arrested in Jerusalem and charged with plotting insurrection. Reports sent from regions as far away as Gaul—today's France—and Rome, Spain, and North Africa, attest that Jesus's followers were popularly regarded with suspicion and contempt. Roman aristocrats like Tacitus regarded them like Jews, only worse: "[For] those who are converted . . . the earliest lesson they receive is to despise the gods, to disown their country, and to regard their parents, children and brothers as of little account." They "regard as profane all that we hold sacred." Tacitus also reports that, because of public animosity against them, Emperor Nero used them as scapegoats for civil disturbance. Accusing them of having set fires in Rome that damaged much of the city, Tacitus says, Nero had some of them arrested, hung up on posts, and burned alive in his own gardens as a public spectacle, to deter others from arson.

At the same time, stories of how their most respected leaders were targeted and killed circulated quickly among Jesus's followers throughout the empire. In 62 C.E., a lynch mob in Jerusalem seized Jesus's brother James and publicly stoned him to death near the Temple; some said that the chief priest, Ananus, had ordered his execution. About two years later, a Roman magistrate ordered the arrest of the apostle Paul, then had him whipped and beheaded. Shortly after that, Jesus's disciple Peter, then leader of a group based in Rome, was arrested, tortured, and savagely mocked while being crucified.

To deflect such danger, Jesus's followers chose to spin the story of Jesus's execution as if "the Jews" had engineered his death, amplifying the role of prominent Jewish leaders who, as the Jewish historian Josephus confirms, did indeed initiate the charges presented to Pilate (Acts 2; 1 Thessalonians 2:14–15). Those who wrote gospels after Mark began to depict Pilate in an increasingly favorable light. As the historian Paul Winter notes in his analysis of *The Trial of Jesus:*

> The stern Pilate grows more mellow from gospel to gospel [from Mark to Matthew, from Matthew and Luke to John] . . . the more removed from history, the more sympathetic a character he becomes.

At the same time, as I've shown elsewhere, when characterizing Jesus's *Jewish* enemies, the gospel writers do the same in reverse. We've seen how each of the later gospel writers, Matthew, followed by Luke, pictures "the Jews" as increasingly hostile, ferociously intent on engineering Jesus's death. Though Mark often notes that the Temple leaders chose to restrain their hostility toward Jesus because of his popularity among "the people," Matthew and Luke both end their accounts of the trial picturing "the crowds" shouting demands for his crucifixion. Mark notes some antagonism between Jesus and the Pharisees, but Matthew actually pictures Jesus himself hurling hateful accusations against them, attacking them as "hypocrites . . . snakes, and vipers" who deserve to be "sentenced to hell" (Luke 13:31; Matthew 23:13–33). As Mark's narrative is told and retold, what he implies—that Jesus's opponents are energized by Satan—Matthew, Luke, and John state far more explicitly.

So let's glance, finally, at how, in the Gospel of John—written some ten to twenty years after the others (c. 90–110 C.E.), at a time when some groups of Jews were challenging Jesus's followers—the writer who calls himself "the beloved disciple" suggests that from the start of Jesus's public activity, some of the Jews began "seeking to kill him" (John 5:16–18). John repeats this charge throughout his narrative, even having Jesus himself accuse "the Jews" of "trying to kill me" (7:19; 8:40), as if he were not one of them! John agrees that they accuse Jesus of blasphemy, but not for claiming to be Messiah, a king. Instead, John's version enormously escalates the charge: here "the Jews" accuse Jesus of "making himself equal with God" (5:18)—a claim that, in Jewish tradition, obviously *is* blasphemy.

So, whereas Mark, Matthew, and Luke all picture Jesus much more believably as a devout, more traditionally minded Jew who rejects any equation between God and any human being (Mark 10:18, Matthew 19:16–17, Luke 18:19), much less between God and himself, John wants to persuade the reader that the opposite is true: that Jesus actually *is* God in human form. John goes so far as to imagine Jesus claiming for himself the divine name (*"I am"*) that the Lord revealed to Moses; and when he does, John says that "the Jews" picked up stones to kill him (John 8:58–59).

Finally, as John's Jesus anticipates his death, he displays no hint of hesitation or grief, much less terror. Instead, John's account challenges—and directly contradicts—what Mark and Matthew had reported. In Gethsemane, John's Jesus acknowledges only that "my soul is troubled." But then he asks rhetorically, *"What shall I say, 'Father, save me from this hour'? No: it is for this reason that I have come!"* (12:27). Here again, John goes much further than the others. Whereas Matthew shows Jesus in complete control during his arrest, John pictures him actually orchestrating his own arrest, trial, and execution.

As John tells it, Jesus not only identifies Judas as his betrayer but effectively orders him to carry it out ("Do quickly what you are going to do" [13:27]). Next, leaving out the Passover meal as Jesus's last supper, John tells how Jesus leads his disciples to Gethsemane, "knowing everything that was going to happen to him" (18:4). Consequently, when Judas arrives in Gethsemane leading an armed posse, Jesus steps forward and demands to know, "Whom are you seeking?" When the soldiers and the police reply, he volunteers, "I am he"—at which, John says, "they stepped back and fell to the ground." Seeing the posse of armed men on the ground, now helpless, Jesus again demands to know whom they are seeking; then he gives them his orders: *"I told you that I am he. So if you are looking for me, let these men go"* (18:4–8). When Peter tries to defend him, attacking the chief priest's slave and cutting off his ear, Jesus rebukes him: "Put your sword back in its sheath!" (18:11). Next, countering the episode in which Jesus pleads with God to spare him ("remove this cup from me" [Mark 14:36, Luke 22:42, Matthew 26:39]), John pictures Jesus announcing his willingness "to drink the cup that the Father has given me" (John 18:11).

When put on trial and questioned by Pilate, John's Jesus questions him back. And when Pilate asserts his own power ("I have power to release or crucify you" [19:10]), Jesus corrects him, declaring that all power belongs to God. Standing in court, Jesus himself pronounces sentence—not upon himself but upon "the

Jews," who, he declares, are "more guilty" of manipulating his unjust death than the clueless governor: *"The one who handed me over to you is guilty of a greater sin"* (19:11). And when Jesus declares, "Everyone who belongs to the truth listens to my voice" (18:37), Pilate ends up asking him, "What is truth?" Even at the last, when Jesus declares from the cross, with his final breath, that "it is accomplished"—that is, his voluntary and necessary death— John shows that no one could kill him. Instead, John says, at that very moment, "he bowed his head, and gave up his spirit" (19:30).

During the late second century, as Jesus's followers continued to preach and publicize these stories, their increasing success and popularity, especially among working people and those enslaved in the cities, began to alarm prominent men among Marcus Aurelius's imperial circle. The Neoplatonic philosopher Celsus, for example, seeing them readily gaining new converts, went on the attack. He realized that insults alone were no longer enough to stop the movement's growth, so he carefully studied what Christians wrote, along with what Jewish critics were saying. Then he began to write his widely read and influential polemic *On the True Doctrine*. Intending to take down each of their talking points in turn, Celsus marshals cogent arguments, taking special aim at the "virgin birth" and the crucifixion. He despises Jesus for having been betrayed by one of his own men, and ridicules his followers for having come up with "the idea of saying that he foreknew everything."

Celsus concludes that Jesus's disciples invented the stories they wrote about him; and even though they were lying, their stories weren't constructed well enough to hide this monstrous fiction (II.26)! Often claiming to echo what Jewish critics are saying, Celsus adds that, although they quote the prophets, these "prophecies could be applied to thousands of others far more plausibly than to Jesus" (II.28), whom he dismisses as a fraud and a magician (I.5–6). He often challenges gospel stories, demanding to know why, for example, if Jesus died voluntarily, "does he utter loud laments and wailings, and pray that he may avoid the fear of death"? Astutely noting how later gospel writers change and revise Mark's narrative, Celsus notes that "some believers" blatantly contradict themselves, and "alter the original text of the gospel three or four or several times over, and they change its character to enable them to deny difficulties in face of criticism."

Finally, dismissing the movement as a cult, a "secret society" "whose members huddle together in corners," Celsus declares that they are fully aware of "the death penalty that hangs over them" (I.3). He endorses the capital charges against them, since they refuse to swear an oath of loyalty to the emperor.

Celsus apparently realizes that the Christians' primary motive for picturing the "trial before Pilate" as a travesty was defensive, motivated by concern to show that Jesus was falsely charged, and thus that they, too, are innocent of sedition. Nevertheless, spinning the story as they did gave rise to enormous unanticipated consequences. When I began to consider the crucifixion stories with these concerns in mind, I was startled and distressed by things I had never noticed before.

How had I failed to see that the way Jesus's followers shaped these stories—casting "the Jews" as agents of Satan—opened the way for Christians to demonize Jews outside their movement in ways that have ignited turbulence, violence, even state-sponsored mass murder, throughout Christianity's two-thousand-year history? When I asked our professors at Harvard about this, several, including a distinguished professor of New Testament, who was also a German Lutheran minister, vehemently denied that the gospels could possibly communicate anti-Jewish messages, much less messages that fueled anti-Semitism. Obviously, though, they often do, since, for centuries, countless people, both Christians and Jews, have taken for granted that *the Jews killed Jesus*. Many have even gone on to take Matthew at his word, believing that what he accuses "the whole [Jewish] people" (Matthew 27:25) of doing implicates all their descendants in evil—a crime that Christians in later generations called "deicide," "killing God."

How could I, and countless others raised within Christian tradition, have missed seeing—consciously, at least—the insidious implications woven into these stories? Troubled by this question, I went back to trace what happened. After Emperor Constantine suddenly took Christ as his divine patron in 312 C.E., ordering the end of state persecution of Christians, their status began to reverse. Within decades, members of this formerly endangered minority gained social and political power and were now regarded as the emperor's allies. Throughout the later fourth century, as Constantine's successors reshaped Roman legal codes in order to "Christianize" the empire, they not only outlawed crucifixion and declared rape a capital crime but also decreed harsh penalties against Jews, creating precedents that have lasted for centuries, even millennia. In the process, as the historian Timothy Barnes notes, "Christian prejudices against the Jews became legal disabilities."

Furthermore, since religious convictions arouse strong emotion, people seeking power have used versions of Christianity ever since to promote their social and political agendas. King Louis IX of France, for example, called upon his Catholic subjects to fight and kill Muslim "infidels" during the First Crusade; later, as is well known, Catholic and Protestant Christians engaged in mutual slaughter during three decades of "religious war" in Europe. And when European Christians encountered indigenous people in what they called the New World, many assumed that those they "discovered" in the Americas could not have descended from Adam, and so must be less than human, likely descended from animal species, to become "Satan worshippers." European colonial leaders in such places as India and Africa also adopted dehumanizing views to enforce their rule, as slave traders and owners have done for some three centuries in the Americas. Especially since the seventh century, Christians participating in the African slave trade have claimed that Black Africans are the "sons of Ham," whom the Biblical Noah cursed into perpetual enslavement—a view that white supremacist Christians maintain to this day. Ironically, as Sylvester Johnson has shown, some African American Christians actually endorsed that view, hoping it would show that Black people *did* descend from Adam, and so, indeed, are human.

When mentioning this history, my intent is neither to deprecate nor to defend the gospel writers, who were struggling to survive in a precarious time, but simply to speak openly of what

The variety of gospel stories, none describing how Jesus looked, has given visual artists a free hand in depicting him. American artist Warner Sallman claimed that he painted *Head of Christ* (1940) in response to a vision. Adopted primarily by Protestants, this image is said to have been reproduced more than a billion times during the twentieth century.

Guido Reni, a prolific Italian artist, painted *Head of Christ Crowned with Thorns* (c. 1636), widely reproduced, copied, and displayed in Catholic churches throughout the world.

The Dutch painter Rembrandt van Rijn (1606–1669) chose to illustrate Luke's birth story, picturing Jesus at his birth and in other scenes of his life as a humble man who lived among the poor. This sharply contrasts with Lochner's Nativity scene, below, which pictures Jesus born as a royal prince, soon to become king of the world.

Stefan Lochner (c. 1410–1451), although less well known than other artists of his day, was revered during his lifetime. In this magisterial *Adoration of the Magi*, originally painted for the council-chapel St. Maria in Jerusalem in Cologne, Germany, and then moved to Cologne Cathedral in 1810, he chose to illustrate Matthew's birth story, picturing the infant Jesus as a divine king, receiving homage from kings all over the world.

In his *Adoration of the Magi,* Italian painter Gentile da Fabriano (c. 1370–1427) chose, like countless other artists, to combine Luke and Matthew's birth stories, picturing Jesus born in a stable yet receiving kings adoring him. This masterpiece, commissioned for the *Strozzi Altarpiece,* is in the Uffizi Gallery in Florence.

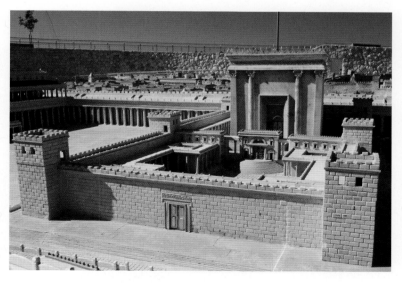

People often ask if Jesus was a real person; the historical record supports that he was. This is a model of the Temple of God in Jerusalem as it was in the time of Jesus before Roman soldiers destroyed it during war in 66 C.E. It is displayed in the Israel Museum in Jerusalem.

Matthias Grünewald (c. 1470–1528), a German Renaissance painter, depicted the agonies of crucifixion in his most famous painting, the *Isenheim Altarpiece,* now in Colmar, France.

Raffaello Sanzio da Urbino, also known as Raphael (1483–1520), commissioned by Pope Julius II, chose not to picture the human agony of crucifixion. Instead he depicted the scene as John's gospel tells it, as if Jesus were offering his body as bread, his blood as wine for angels to collect, originating the ritual of the eucharist, also called the Mass (literally, "table").

Italian artist Piero della Francesca (c. 1415–1492) painted this scene to illustrate the New Testament gospels' story of Jesus raised bodily from the grave, the wounds of torture and crucifixion visible on his body.

In this painting, English poet and artist William Blake (1757–1827) illustrated a story told in the gospels of Luke and John, picturing Jesus appearing to his disciples after his death in a luminous body, fully alive.

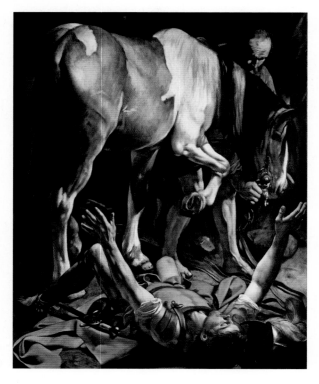

Rather than portraying Jesus raised bodily from the dead, Italian master Caravaggio (1517–1610) chose to illustrate what the apostle Paul reports: that he "saw" Christ in the form of a brilliant light in the heavens that first blinded Paul and then illuminated him.

Belarusian-French artist Marc Chagall (1887–1985) obsessively painted crucifixion scenes during the years of Nazi occupation of Europe (1938–1945) until his escape from France, pointing to the irony of Hitler's attempt to exterminate the Jewish people in the name of the Jewish rabbi Jesus. His *White Crucifixion,* the most famous in this series, is now shown in the Art Institute of Chicago.

Marc Chagall titled this painting *Exodus 1952–66*, honoring Jews leaving Europe to seek a safer homeland in the state of Israel (founded 1948), depicting himself in the bottom right corner carrying the Torah that Moses was said to have received from the hand of God.

Here again Chagall links the suffering of Jesus to that of European Jews, often falsely accused of being "Christ killers," after the New Testament writers (see Matthew 25) spun the story of Jesus's crucifixion to suggest that it happened only after "the Jews" overcame the Roman governor's reluctance, and even his explicit refusal, to order the execution.

In *The Crucified,* Chagall echoed themes from paintings and gospel narratives of Jesus's crucifixion, juxtaposing them with scenes of the torture and execution of millions of Jews in Eastern Europe during World War II.

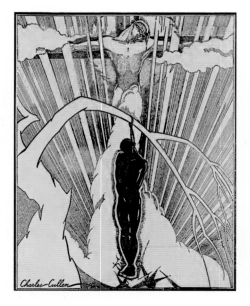

Countee Cullen, an influential poet of the Harlem Renaissance, created this image of a lynched Black man superimposed over the crucified Christ as the frontispiece for his famous poem "The Black Christ" (1929).

This is a photograph of the same window after the (white) face of Jesus was blown out by a Ku Klux Klan bomb that killed four young Black girls attending Sunday school at the church in 1963.

This stained-glass window shows Jesus standing at the door of the heart and knocking, a subject often reproduced and shown in American Protestant churches. This window was installed in the Sixteenth Street Baptist Church in Birmingham, Alabama, during its founding in 1911.

After the earlier window was blown out in the 1963 bombing attack, Welsh artist John Petts created this window to replace it. It pictures a crucified Black Christ and is inscribed with Jesus saying, "You do it to me," echoing the verse from Matthew 25:40: "Truly I tell you, whatever you do to the least of my brethren, you have done to me."

Spanish artist Salvador Dalí (1904–1989), named, like his deceased brother, "Savior" to echo a title of Jesus, painted *Christ of Saint John of the Cross* in 1951, picturing a strong, unblemished young man poised between earth and heaven, its title referring to the sixteenth-century Spanish Catholic mystic.

By contrast with Dalí, whose crucifixion painting implicitly identifies
Christ with himself and his deceased brother, Titus Kaphar, in his painting
Holy Absence II (2014), erases the images of St. John the Evangelist, Mary
Magdalene, and Mary, mother of Jesus, from Frans Pourbus's crucifixion
painting (c. 1569–1577) and replaces them with the image of a young Black man.
As the artist declares, "If we don't amend history by making new images and
new representations, we are always going to be excluding ourselves."

FROM THE MAKERS OF U-CARMEN EKHAYELITSHA, WINNER OF "THE GOLDEN BEAR" 2005

WINNER
"BEST FEATURE"
L.A. PAN AFRICAN
FILM FESTIVAL

GRAND JURY PRIZE
NOMINATED
"WORLD CINEMA"
SUNDANCE
FILM FESTIVAL

OFFICIAL SELECTION
BFI LONDON
FILM FESTIVAL

A SPIER FILMS PRODUCTION
PAULINE MALEFANE AND ANDILE KOSI
SON OF MAN

"One of the most **extraordinary and powerful** films at Sundance"
-Roger Ebert

"*Son of Man* **could hardly be bettered**"
-Variety

The film *Son of Man* (2006), directed by South African director Mark Dornford-May, retells the story of Jesus in the context of South African politics. The film's depiction of Jesus's death recalls Michelangelo's *Pietà*, as well as the death of Stephen Biko, who was tortured and killed for openly opposing the former Afrikaner regime.

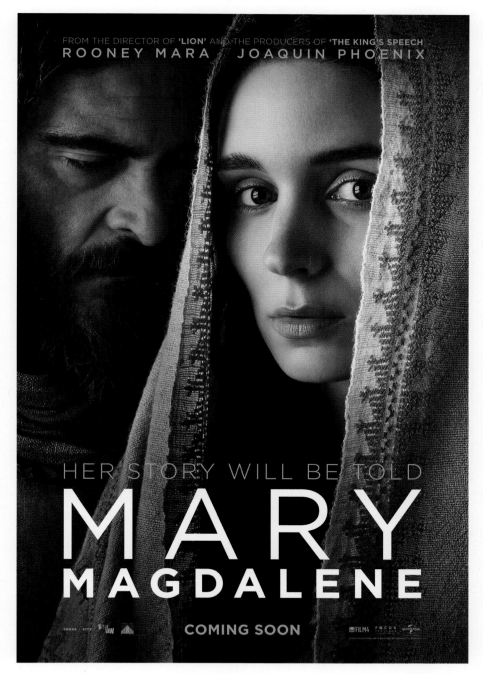

The film *Mary Magdalene* (2018), written by British screenwriter Helen Edmundson and directed by Garth Davis, offers a different version of the Jesus story, focused on Mary Magdalene. It challenges the popular stereotype of Mary as a prostitute, picturing her instead as the disciple who best understands Jesus's spiritual message.

Adapting Nikos Kazantzakis's novel, American director Martin Scorsese produced and directed *The Last Temptation of Christ* (1988), a powerful retelling of the life of Jesus as a struggle between the flesh and the spirit.

Christians often choose not to notice. One friend, raised Catholic, objected, asking, "But isn't Christianity all about love?" At its best, of course, it is; and later I hope to show that this has given Christianity its staying power. But these complex stories simultaneously transmit an undercurrent that may incite hate. And since Christians often identify with Jesus's disciples as they read the gospels, for some two thousand years many have associated their opponents—whether Jews, or those they later targeted as "pagans" or "heretics"—with forces of evil, and thus with Satan. A centuries-old tradition requires Christians attending church on Palm Sunday, a week before Easter, to play the part of Jews, shouting "Crucify him! Crucify him!" Responding to this practice, Jews throughout Europe often stayed out of town on Easter Sunday, fearing that mobs might come out of churches to insult and attack them.

Extreme as John's version is, it culminates the gospel writers' attempts to address the most challenging question they confronted: how to maintain hope when facing horrendous loss, especially when such loss is intentionally inflicted. This question, so often asked, was never raised more urgently, or more cogently, than by Viktor Frankl, a Jewish psychiatrist reflecting on his experience as a prisoner in Auschwitz. Living through unimaginable violence, Frankl focused his energy on asking how he, or anyone else, could possibly survive when everything around him—the stench of smoke from the crematoria, stacks of tortured and starved bodies, guards with guns, some obviously enjoying their power to rape, torment, and kill—pointed toward despair? Though not himself a participant in religious tradition,

Frankl recognized finding meaning as an essential human need. What's original—and illuminating—is his insight that such meaning must be more than some generalized cliché. Instead, Frankl insists, the meaning that any of us finds must engage our own situation—a specific meaning found in each person's life. And when there's none to "find," Frankl shows how we can, and often must, *create* meaning.

What meaning, then, is there to be found in Jesus's death? Throughout the New Testament gospels, when Jesus speaks in awareness that he might be killed, the words attributed to him seldom indicate what his death might mean—perhaps, as one historian suggests, because he didn't yet know the outcome of his mission. But as we noted at the start, right after he died, those of his followers who refused to give up hope, like Peter and Jesus's brother James, gathered together in shock and grief, sharing stories of what had happened. The apostle Paul, who joined their movement a few years later, says they told him how they had begun to shape these stories into the form of a ritual, which they acted out "in memory of him." Meeting together to reenact his "last supper," Jesus's followers sought to strengthen their conviction that what had happened *did* have meaning, as part of a pre-ordained divine plan.

Strikingly, in writings even earlier than the gospels—in Paul's letters—we find his most explicit suggestion of what Jesus's death might mean. Since worship in the Jerusalem Temple required animal sacrifice, often for atonement, anyone desperately seeking meaning in the crucifixion might suggest that Jesus died as a *human* sacrifice, atoning for sin. Indeed, Paul says, "the most important thing" that he heard from Peter and James was that Jesus *"died for our sins, according to the Scriptures"* (1 Corinthians 15:3). Recalling that Jesus's death happened at the time of Passover, Paul declares, "Christ, our Passover [lamb] is sacrificed for us; therefore, let us keep the feast!" (1 Corinthians 5:7).

Astonishingly, Paul insists that Jesus's death, far from being something to hide, is instead something to "proclaim"—to hold up and to act out. Declaring that he "received from the Lord" what he came to see as its meaning, he offers this script for the drama:

> On the night that the Lord Jesus was betrayed, he took a loaf of bread; and having given thanks, he broke it, and said, "This is my body, for you; do this to remember me." In the same way, he took the cup, saying, "This cup is my new covenant, in my blood. Do this, whenever you drink it, in memory of me." *And whenever you eat this bread and drink this cup, you proclaim the death of the Lord, until he comes.* (1 Corinthians 11:23–26)

Practicing this ritual meal, in varying forms, became widespread among groups ranging from Jerusalem to Syria, Africa, Greece, and Rome. As we've seen, Mark, Matthew, and Luke all include the scene of Jesus's "last supper," using similar words set in ritual form, envisioning Jesus's death as a voluntary sacrifice, given, as Matthew says explicitly, "for many, for the forgiveness of sins" (Matthew 26:28).

And, finally, John's gospel escalates Paul's image of Jesus as Passover lamb to a fever pitch. In the very first scene in which Jesus appears, John the Baptist announces: *"Behold—the Lamb of*

God, who takes away the sin of the world!" (John 1:29). Like Paul, John insists that Jesus's death reveals the meaning of his entire life. Unlike Mark, then, who says that Jesus came "to proclaim the kingdom of God," John agrees with Paul that he came into the world "to die for the sin of the world"—a mission only "accomplished" with his last breath.

John is so intent on this theme that he offers a different chronology of the passion narrative. Matthew, Mark, and Luke all agree that Jesus died late on Friday, having celebrated a Passover meal on the previous night. But John *omits* that ritual meal, and places Jesus's last night on Thursday instead. Only in that way can John picture *Jesus himself* as the Passover lamb. Declaring that "the Jews" handed Jesus over to Pilate on a Friday morning, John creates the following picture: Jesus, standing in Pilate's judgment hall, is sentenced to death "on the day for preparing for Passover, about noon" (John 19:14)—which, as John notes, is precisely the time when lambs were being slaughtered for the evening's Passover meal.

John then inserts another episode to make sure that anyone familiar with the Passover ritual would recognize his meaning. Claiming that "the Jews" did not want corpses left exposed "because it was Passover," he says that they persuaded Pilate to order soldiers to break the legs of the crucified men to hasten their deaths. But as John tells it, when soldiers sent to dispatch the dying "saw that Jesus was already dead," they did not break his legs. John declares that he himself personally had witnessed this—an event that, he insists, "happened so that the Scripture might be fulfilled, 'you shall not break any of its bones'" (19:36)—lifting this passage from a traditional instruction for cooks preparing the Passover lamb (Exodus 12:46) as if it were prophecy.

There we end our brief review of the sources included in the New Testament, having discovered the lengths to which Jesus's followers would go to find meaning in his death, interpreting it in the context of atonement and sacrifice for sin. Had they failed to do so, the movement he started likely would not have survived. And we see more of the same effort in sources beyond the familiar ones, in the Gospel of Truth, the Gospel of Philip, the Gospel of Mary Magdalene, and the Round Dance of the Cross. Like Paul, the anonymous authors of these esoteric sources sought to plunge into deeper meanings of the gospel stories, opening up a wider range of insights into the meaning of Jesus's life and death.

One that I find hauntingly beautiful is the Round Dance of the Cross—a mystical song, chant, and ritual liturgy found in the Acts of John, a collection of ancient traditions that may date back to 100–300 C.E., having remained mostly buried in monastic libraries ever since. Some anonymous poet, or perhaps some group, apparently composed the Round Dance to fill in the gap we noted in John's gospel, where John omits mention of a final Passover meal. Instead, the Round Dance suggests that, after Judas went out at night to initiate the betrayal, Jesus spoke intensely with the others, and then led them into the garden of Gethsemane. There he invited them to join with him in a mystical dance, circling around him as he began to chant and sing. And although it is written anonymously, the Round Dance, like the Gospel of John, is told as if the disciple John himself were telling the story. What follows are selections from a much longer song, chant, and ritual:

[Jesus] told us to form a circle holding one another's hands, and himself stood in the middle, and said, "Answer Amen to me."

So he began to sing a hymn, and to say,
"Glory be to thee, Father."
And we circled round him and answered him, "Amen."
"Glory be to thee, Logos: Glory be to thee, Grace."—
"Amen . . ."
"We Praise thee, Father:
We thank thee, Light;
In whom darkness dwelleth not . . ."

As Jesus continues to chant, his disciples encircle him, responding "Amen" in the rhythm of an ancient circle dance:

"I will be saved, And I will save."—"Amen."
"I will be loosed, And I will loose."—"Amen . . ."
"I will eat, And I will be eaten."—"Amen . . ."

Then, as a woman disciple enters the dance, embodying Grace, the chant continues:

"I will pipe, Dance, all of you."—"Amen . . ."
"To the All it belongs to dance in the height"—"Amen . . ."
"Whoever does not dance does not know what happens."—
"Amen . . ."
"I am a lamp to you who see me."—"Amen."
"I am a mirror to you who know me."—"Amen."

"I am a door to you [who] knock on me."—"Amen."

"I am a way to you [the] traveler."—"Amen . . ."

Circle dance is traditional in Roman Asia Minor—today's Israel, Lebanon, Syria, Turkey—and often central to celebration. To perform it, a leader, standing in the center, would chant and sing the words attributed to Jesus, perhaps also playing the flute, as the other participants whirled around him, chanting and singing responses in words drawn primarily from the Gospel of John. Here, as in John's gospel, Jesus speaks of himself as "the way," "the door," and "the light"; then as a mirror to all who participate, who "see themselves in him," envisioning the entire universe joining them in this sacred dance. What follows, presented as Jesus's words, would be spoken aloud, or chanted:

Now if you follow my dance, see yourself in Me who am speaking, and when you have seen what I do, keep silence about my mysteries.

You who dance, consider what I do, for yours is this passion of Man which I am to suffer.

For you could by no means have understood what you suffer, unless to you as Logos I had been sent by the Father . . . Learn how to suffer and you shall be able not to suffer . . .

During the dance ritual, the celebrant speaks words attributed to Jesus, just as Catholic and Orthodox priests do when celebrating mass. But unlike the usual interpretation of the eucharist as enacting Jesus's sacrifice, the Round Dance interprets Jesus's suffering and death as manifesting the suffering experienced by every human being. At the same time, the Round Dance encourages the participants to transcend their suffering. For, as Jesus here concludes:

> I will that holy souls be made in harmony with me . . . I made a jest of everything and was not made a jest at all. I leaped . . . When you have understood it, say, "Glory be to thee, Father."—"Amen."

Reflecting on the Round Dance, I have come to agree with others who see it as an early form of a eucharistic ritual ("I will eat, And I will be eaten") that followers of Jesus created and enacted during those early centuries. Although it was startlingly different from the mass that Catholic and Orthodox churches later would celebrate, countless Christians in ancient times, perhaps most likely in Syria and Egypt, participated in this early liturgy, chanting, singing, and dancing "in memory of him."

The intimate connection between Jesus and his followers that the Round Dance celebrates as the meaning in Jesus's death resonates with what we find in other recently discovered gospels. The Gospel of Philip, found at Nag Hammadi, offers another interpretation of eucharist, the sacred meal that, as Paul famously said, "proclaims [Christ's] death." Philip's gospel declares that "the eucharist is Jesus" (Gospel of Philip II 63.21), noting that his name, translated into Syriac, suggests that Jesus is *"the one who extends himself"* (II 63.22), perhaps evoking an image of him stretched out on the cross. When it is consecrated through prayer, Philip continues, "the cup . . . contains wine and water" (II 75.14–15), symbolizing Jesus's blood. And although this sacred "mystery" (*mysterion,* a Greek term that may refer to the ritual itself) communicates through symbolic language, the Gospel of Philip insists that it is by no means nothing but words. On the contrary, the cup offered in eucharist "is full of the holy spirit . . . and when we drink this, we shall receive for ourselves" the living spirit of Christ (II 75.15ff).

The Gospel of Truth, written by an anonymous follower of Jesus (some say by Valentinus, a poet and preacher later called "heretical"), offers to reveal the secret teaching of the apostle Paul. Its author notes that Paul, like Jesus, taught in two different ways: publicly, proclaiming "Christ crucified," a simplified message condensed into a slogan ("Christ died for your sins"), while privately revealing "divine mysteries" to a chosen few. Writing to believers in Greece, Paul explains that when he first came to them, he offered them only the simpler message (1 Corinthians 2:1–5). Although he wanted to teach them much more, he says that he was disappointed to see that they were only beginners, "babies in Christ," so immature that they could only digest "milk," not "meat," the solid food of adults (3:1–2). Paul hastens to add, though, that whenever he finds people who are spiritually mature, "among [them], we do speak wisdom . . . God's wisdom, secret and hidden"—mysteries that, he says, God's spirit taught him directly (2:6–13).

Having been taught by the spirit, this writer continues, he offers to reveal those hidden secrets in the Gospel of Truth—*"the true gospel,"* which, he says, *"is joy"* (Gospel of Truth I 16.31). This secret text tells the entire gospel story in a new key, so to speak, in order to open up deeper insights. This story begins even before the world's creation, saying that when "all beings" first came into existence, they were terrified, being cast into utter darkness, feeling abandoned, like children wandering in the dark, searching for their lost parents. But when the divine Source of all being saw his offspring suffering from fear and ignorance, not knowing where they came from, or who they were, he was moved with compassion, and sent his Son, "the hidden mystery, Jesus the Christ" (I 18.15–16), to show them—that is, to show us—who we really are. So, the story continues, Jesus descended into the world to "show . . . [us] a way"(I 18.19), and to reveal "the true gospel"— the joyful news that we belong to the family of God, having all come forth from the same divine Source.

The story then goes on to tell how, through Jesus, the Father calls each one by name, sending his Spirit to run after us, extending her hand to raise each one from the ground, bringing us back "into the Father, into the Mother, Jesus of the infinite sweetness" (I 24.7–9). Here, acknowledging that "Father" is an anthropomorphic metaphor, this writer uses both feminine and masculine epithets for the divine Source, envisioning a divine Mother embodying Spirit and Wisdom (both feminine terms in Hebrew: *ruah*/spirit; *hokhmah*/wisdom).

At every turn of the story, this writer takes cues from Paul, interpreting his mysterious comment that "the rulers of this world . . . crucified the Lord of glory" (1 Corinthians 2:6–8) to mean that when Jesus came into the world, "the rulers," those who seek to dominate humankind through fear, became angry. Since he threatened their power, these hostile rulers pursued him and hounded him to his death, "nailing him to a tree" (an early image of the cross). Then, adapting this image, the Gospel of Truth pictures the crucified Jesus as "fruit" on that tree, which blossoms into a new "tree of knowledge." For, unlike the tree in Paradise that brought death to Adam, the cross, seen as the tree of "*true knowledge,*" enables us to come to know God through Christ.

In what is here called the "true gospel," Jesus's death is not seen primarily as atonement for sin, as if a loving Father could not, or would not, forgive human sin "apart from shedding of blood" (Hebrews 9:22), as many Christians insist. This gospel challenges that idea, insisting instead that the Father is not "small, nor envious" (Gospel of Truth I 42.5); on the contrary, he overflows with compassionate love. Here, then, Jesus's suffering and death, like our own, are no longer seen as punishment for sin. Instead, they are simply the necessary cost of entering into human life, motivated by love. "O such great teaching!" this author exclaims, marveling that Jesus willingly descended into the world to deliver us from terror and ignorance, even knowing that doing so would cost him great agony, "since he knows that his death is life for many" (I 20.13–14). Thus this gospel teaches that Jesus came into the world to reveal "what is written on our hearts," bringing joy by showing us who we are.

Like other sources found with it at Nag Hammadi, the Gospel of Truth suggests that when we come to know ourselves, we simultaneously come to know God, as the source of our being. Instead of being *intellectual* knowledge, this is *heart* knowledge, intuitive recognition of deeper, hidden aspects of ourselves, and of each other. Furthermore, this kind of knowing (*gnosis*, in Greek) involves paradox. And its secret is this: First, we need to know that we cannot "*know God*" in the sense of *comprehending* the Source of all being, since that Source far transcends our understanding. At the same time, what we need to know, and what we *can* know, is that we are intimately connected with that Source. To put it in words that Luke attributes to Paul, "in him we live and move and have our being" (Acts 17:28).

When first exploring this "gospel," filled with poetic images and musical resonances, I realized that it was meant to be spoken, even preached. I imagine that when it was written, and long afterward, someone may have told this story to men and women fasting and staying awake all night in darkness on the night Christians call Holy Saturday, as they waited to be baptized into "the family of God" on Easter morning—the day when ancient Christians traditionally baptized new believers—telling them, in effect, *This is your story, and mine.* Even though Bishop Irenaeus ridicules "heretics" for telling mythical stories, this is myth as Plato understood it: a poetic story meant to reveal the deeper truth of human experience.

Whether or not we recognize such experiences as our own, the speaker concludes, this mythical story has real consequences. Those who fail to recognize its truth, who lack any sense of connection with the Father, with the Mother who is the Spirit, and with all beings, live as in a nightmare:

As if we were asleep, deep in disturbing dreams; either running in terror, or as if we are striking out at others, or receiving blows, or falling from high places, or as if someone were murdering them, or they themselves are killing their neighbors, stained with their blood . . . (Gospel of Truth I 29.9–25)

For, as we know, people who are ignorant of spiritual connection, their lives dominated by a sense of isolation and terror, can, and often do, turn such nightmares into horrific reality. But those who recognize their connection with all beings are impelled to act in ways that demonstrate that we all are members of the same family:

Speak the truth to those who seek it; stretch out your hands to those who are ill; feed those who are hungry; give rest to the weary . . . and give a hand to those who wish to rise . . . If, then, these things have happened to each one of us, let us remain silent, in holiness. (Gospel of Truth I 32.35–33.6)

Could this be Paul's secret teaching? Here, again, we don't know. As Paul himself says, he only told it privately to certain people, and did not write it down (1 Corinthians 2:1–16). What we can say, at least, is that this gospel offers another example of how Jesus's followers dealt with the fact of his crucifixion—finding meaning in his death, as many people still do.

What I find most astonishing about the gospel stories is that Jesus's followers managed to take what their critics saw as the most damning evidence against their Messiah—his crucifixion—and transform it into evidence of his divine mission. So powerfully were they able to reimagine it that, to this day, countless Christians all over the world—Roman Catholic, Orthodox, Protestant, and many others—have turned their ritual enactment of his crucifixion into the centerpiece of worship: the "mass," "the Lord's supper," "holy communion," often called "eucharist," from the Greek word for "thanksgiving."

Surely, this could not have happened except for the conviction that seized some of them, then many more, shortly after his death, that he was alive again, resurrected. In the flesh? His scarred body, raised to new and glorious life? As a spiritual presence? What can we make of that, except to turn next to the stories of his resurrection?

5

Resurrection: What Did People Say Happened—and What Can Be Known?

JESUS'S PUBLIC DEMONSTRATIONS excited his followers, raising their expectations, and his sudden death left them shocked and disillusioned. Luke pictures them grieving, venting disappointment: "We thought he was the one to deliver Israel" (Luke 24:21). The gospel accounts suggest that the movement that started with Jesus was already unraveling, his disciples having gone into hiding to save their lives, their followers dispersing, and, no doubt, hundreds of others drifting away. The few who remained, especially the men, surely knew that maintaining allegiance to their crucified leader would invite suspicion and endanger their lives.

Then something happened—but what? Resurrection? We do not know. Dale Allison, having devoted decades to this question, calls it the "primary puzzle of New Testament research." The reports we have are brief, and often conflicting. Some followers thought that they had seen Jesus's ghost; others, as we shall see, vehemently insisted that what they had seen "was *not* a ghost" (Luke 24:39). And all these stories speak of events not susceptible to historical documentation: visions of Jesus after he died, restored back to life.

The gospel accounts agree that when Peter and other disciples first heard such rumors, they dismissed them as nonsense, an "idle tale" (24:11) told by people assumed to lack rational judgment—women. Yet the rumors circulated, and persisted, that "the Lord has risen, and appeared to Peter" (24:34), then to several other men, including Jesus's brother James. For Jesus's followers, who saw his life and death in the context of Jewish apocalyptic traditions, these claims of resurrection had special meaning—raising hope that his "gospel" *was not wrong*. Perhaps, as they once believed, he actually *was* God's anointed Messiah, who arrived to initiate the end of time, bringing in judgment day and the sufferings that would signal the approach of God's kingdom.

For nearly two millennia, countless Christians have accepted their claims that Jesus's resurrection was an event unique in the history of the world. As Luke tells it, Peter told crowds in Jerusalem that after Jesus died he came back to life, his body raised from the grave (Acts 2:29–36). Until the European Enlightenment, as Allison notes, "Orthodox, Roman Catholic, and Protestant Christians accepted the New Testament accounts of Jesus' resurrection as historically accurate down to their details, and interpreted these details literally." Since that time, however, many Christians have come to think of these stories only as myth masquerading as fact. For over a hundred years, historians and scholars have filled thousands of books and articles debating a wide range of suggestions: Were these reports based on hallucinations, or on projection, born of grief? Did Jesus's disciples remove his body from his grave in order to fake a resurrection? Did someone else steal it, or, as a few historians suggest, was his corpse thrown out, never buried at all? Or were some reports claiming to document his resurrection telling of actual encounters with the risen Jesus, alive again after his death?

Here again, as I see it, we do not know. Yet some people say that they *do* know—among them the conservative Anglican bishop Tom Wright, who insists that he can prove that Jesus's "bodily resurrection" is historical fact: that after Jesus died and was buried, he emerged, fully restored to life, and appeared to many people, before ascending physically into heaven. Wright often sets up speaking engagements to publicize his views, as he did recently, sending an advance team to Princeton and asking me to engage with him in a public debate. His invitation clearly implied the role in which he intended to cast me: that of an East Coast "liberal" who, he assumed, could be counted on to argue that Jesus was *not* physically resurrected. Knowing that situations like this are often staged to ridicule those who question the literal view that Wright sees as the basic premise of Christian faith, I declined. Instead, I suggested that he invite a member of Princeton's History Department to debate with him, a suggestion he rejected; even Tom Wright realized that historians would dismiss his topic as one that has nothing to do with history.

When saying this, I do not intend to imply that reports of resurrection are false. Instead, as I see it, historical evidence can neither *prove nor disprove* the reality that gave rise to such experiences. What we *can* verify historically, though, is that after Jesus died, many people claimed to have seen him alive. What fascinates me, and many others, is how their various reports of visions and appearances catalyzed the explosion of activity that led to the spread of Christianity all over the world; even now it attracts new converts.

How did that happen? Since our earliest sources include only *one* firsthand report, written by someone who claims to have "seen the Lord"—a report likely composed within five years of Jesus's death—let's start with that. Paul of Tarsus, a contemporary of Jesus who had neither seen nor met him during his lifetime, but who, infuriated by what he had heard, resolved to "destroy" Jesus's followers, tells us in his own words, but leaves them terse and sparse. The whiplash events of his story are well known:

> You have heard of my earlier life in Judaism; I was violently
> persecuting God's assembly, trying to destroy it. I advanced
> in Judaism beyond many of my people of my own age, for
> I was far more zealous for the traditions of my ancestors.
> (Galatians 1:13–14)

Driven by passionate commitment to traditional Torah practice, Paul says his life was shattered when "God revealed his son in me" (Galatians 1:15–16), an event so unexpected and shocking that it left him stunned, reduced to a state of helplessness and, as the book of Acts tells it, temporary blindness. And although he often tells how his experience of that vision changed him completely—the ferocious enemy of Jesus's followers becoming their most enthusiastic missionary—Paul's surviving letters offer nearly no details.

Stories of what happened did circulate, though, likely drawn and amplified from what he told other people. Luke's book of Acts includes three versions, one telling in Paul's voice how, "when I was on my way to Damascus," suddenly he was stopped, seeing a brilliant light flashing around him and hearing a heavenly voice. Yet Paul insists that the person whom he saw in that vision was not simply Jesus of Nazareth, teacher and prophet, as most people had known him. Instead, Paul says, he saw him as a divine being, "the Christ" (the anointed one), transfigured in dazzling light— alive, powerful, and commanding. And after coming to recognize Jesus's presence in this glorified form, Paul declares that, beyond any possible doubt, he had *"seen Jesus our Lord!"* (1 Corinthians 9:1).

What Paul saw, apparently, was someone enveloped in light, somewhat like what the prophet Ezekiel reported having seen hundreds of years earlier when claiming to have received "visions of God" (Ezekiel 1:1). Perhaps to avoid an overly anthropomorphic account, Ezekiel cautiously writes that he saw "something that looked like a human form," obscured by "something that looked like fire, with splendor all around," a vision of what he calls "the glory [in Hebrew, *kavod*] of the Lord." "When I saw it," he writes, "I fell on my face" (1:26–28), as Luke says Paul did, and heard someone speaking (Acts 9:4–7). Similarly, some forty years after Paul, John of Patmos opens his own account of prophetic visions, telling how he had seen a glorious and terrifying vision of the risen Jesus, "his eyes like flaming fire, his face like the sun shining with full force," who announced, "I was dead, and now I am alive forever more" (Revelation 1:12–18). Struggling to describe what happened, John, too, echoes language from the Hebrew Bible, in this case from the prophet Daniel's account of a heavenly vision (Daniel 10:5–9). As Daniel says he trembled, turned deathly pale, and fell down, so John says that when he saw this vision of "someone like a Son of Man," he fell down at his feet "as if dead" (Revelation 1:13, 17).

Like Daniel and John of Patmos, Paul was amazed, overwhelmed. And although, as we noted, his letters say little about that experience, what he does write resonates with its aftershocks. This encounter with "Jesus Christ, our Lord" initiated his transformation from an angry, conservative Pharisee intent on destroying Jews who deviated from traditional practice into a man who was not only willing to interact with Gentiles but who, seeing himself as Christ's chosen spokesman ("apostle") to them, would devote the rest of his life to their spiritual welfare.

Surely, this could only happen through God's power. So, he later wrote, God has sent the spirit of his Son into our hearts, crying, "*Abba*"—"Father!" (Galatians 4:6). And as the Bible reports of his famous namesake, Israel's first king, Saul, when the Spirit of God came upon him, charging him with energy, this second Saul, also known as Paul, speaks of God's Spirit "turning him into a new man" (1 Samuel 10:6). Later, at a loss to describe an ineffable experience, Paul again draws on Scriptural precedent, declaring that what happened must be his destiny, preordained by God, who "set me apart before I was born, and called me" (Galatians 1:15), just as he had called the prophet Jeremiah.

What Christians often call Paul's "conversion," however, was not simply a matter of what Paul *believed*. Instead, as Alan Segal notes in his book *Paul the Convert,* what changed him was this experience, which, in Segal's words, involved "something deeply mysterious." Segal reminds us, too, that while Paul experienced a conversion, it did not draw him into "Christianity," since the traditions we call by that name had not yet been invented. Instead, Segal writes, Paul was "converted to a new, apocalyptic, mystical, and—to many of his contemporaries—a suspiciously heretical form of Judaism."

After this wrenching experience precipitated him into an unexpected new life, Paul wrestled to understand what Christ demanded of him: how to spread "his gospel" to everyone, especially to Gentiles. Convinced that his experience had transformed him, Paul envisioned it as a paradigm for everyone: "*anyone in Christ is a new creation*" (2 Corinthians 5:17). Struggling to articulate a deeply felt paradox, he declares that the person he used to be is dead: "*I died . . . so that I might live to God.* I have been crucified with Christ; while living, it is no longer I who lives, but Christ lives in me" (Galatians 2:19–20). He does not suggest that this happened instantly, like a bolt of lightning, as Martin Luther imagined it had, or as the Catholic poet Gerard Manley Hopkins pictured it, "once at a crash." After the initial shock, Paul realized that his initial vision had catalyzed a process that would continue throughout his whole lifetime, and beyond this life.

How, then, to bring others "into Christ"? Paul wants far more for his listeners than that they believe what he preaches. Instead, he passionately longs for them, too, to "*be transformed.*" Writing to people in Rome, he promises that this may happen to anyone initiated "into Jesus Christ" through baptism:

> *Do you not know that all of us who have been baptized into Jesus Christ were baptized into his death?* Therefore we have been buried with him in baptism into death, so that just as Christ was raised from the dead . . . we too might walk in newness of life, *being joined in a resurrection like his.* (Romans 6:3–5)

So, Paul declares, whoever descends into the baptismal water, often by being submerged in a river, is "baptized into Christ's death," and "buried with him." Emerging dripping wet, and receiving new clothes, the baptized person is being "clothed with Christ." And when this happens, baptism erases the initiate's previous identity markers, including those on which Paul had most prided himself—being Jewish, male, and freeborn. Anyone baptized into God's family, Paul declares, is now equal in status to everyone else:

> You are all children of God through faith. Whoever among you were baptized into Christ have clothed yourself with Christ. *There is no longer Jew or Gentile, slave or free, male and female: you are all one, in Christ Jesus.* (Galatians 3:26–28)

Once we are baptized, infused with God's spirit, Paul says, our faces increasingly radiate divine light, since "we are being transformed . . . from one degree of glory to another, through the Holy Spirit" (2 Corinthians 3:18).

Following this impassioned, deeply felt passage, Paul brings his hearers back down to earth, reminding them that "this amazing power" comes only from God, not from ourselves. As long as we live on earth, we remain embroiled in struggle and suffering. Although some of his enthusiastic admirers later insisted that, being baptized, they already were living a resurrection life (Ephesians 2:6), Paul himself stops short of making such a claim. Instead, intensely aware of challenges he faces every day, he warns that being "transformed into the image of Christ" takes time, and continual striving. Before experiencing resurrection, he says, we, like Jesus, must suffer and die. Only then can our earthly bodies be "conformed into his glorious body" (Philippians 3:21); that is, transformed, like the glorious presence Paul saw in his vision. Written decades before the gospels, Paul's letters celebrate the resurrection as their central theme, one essential to what would become Christianity.

What Paul experienced resonates especially in what he says about the finality of death. When asked, *Was Christ actually raised from the dead? Can we actually hope to be raised after we die?* Paul says, *Yes; everything depends on this.* For if not, he declares,

> our preaching is empty, and your faith is empty . . . we would be found to be lying about God . . . for if the dead are not raised, then Christ is not raised, your faith is futile, and you are still in your sins. Then those who have died in Christ have perished. *If we have hoped in Christ only for this life, we are of all people the most pitiable.* (1 Corinthians 15:12–19)

"But someone will ask, 'How are the dead raised? With what body do they come?'" (1 Corinthians 15:35). Asked these obvious questions, Paul engages what would become a central debate, and he goes to great lengths to respond. First, using the metaphor of a seed buried in the ground, as Jews traditionally wrap corpses in shrouds and bury them, he notes that every kind of seed "has its own body," just as there are many different kinds of flesh: human, animal, bird, and fish. Resurrection, Paul says, is like that: "what is sown," that is, buried, like a seed or a corpse, is perishable; but "what is raised is imperishable," no longer earthly, but heavenly (15:42): *"What is sown is a physical body; what is raised is a spiritual body"* (15:44).

When carefully rereading this passage, especially when reading it in Greek, as Paul wrote it, I was astonished to see that the Christians who taught me in Sunday school, and some even in graduate school, along with many presiding in churches, often scrambled what Paul here works so hard to clarify. We've seen that a surprising number of commentators, like Wright, insist that when Paul writes the letter we call 1 Corinthians, he teaches "the resurrection of the *physical* body"—but Paul says the exact opposite. What may confuse some readers is that he speaks of two different kinds of "body." The first, our present, earthly bodies, he says, are "from earth . . . made of dust," like the "first human, Adam." What comes after the physical body dies, then, is what Paul calls the "psychic body," that is, a being that consists not of flesh but of *psyche*, the Greek term for soul. That is what Paul calls the "second Adam," "the image of the heavenly one, Christ" (48–49).

Speaking with increasing intensity, Paul continues: "What I am saying, brothers, is this: *flesh and blood cannot inherit the kingdom of God, nor can what is perishable inherit what is imperishable*" (15:50). Pausing for emphasis, he declares, *"Listen: I will tell you a mystery"*—something that we can neither fully understand nor adequately describe in words. For when "the Lord himself . . . will descend from heaven," and angels trumpet the end of time, those who are still alive on earth, along with those who have already died (1 Thessalonians 4:16–17), "shall be raised, imperishable," since *"this perishable body must put on imperishability, and this mortal body must put on immortality"* (1 Corinthians 15:50–53). Only then will those "in Christ" experience the joy of seeing "death . . . swallowed up in victory" (15:554).

I find it striking that when Mark and other gospel writers report resurrection experiences, they offer quite different impressions. Instead of envisioning a heavenly presence, as Paul claims to have done, each of the New Testament evangelists features Jesus's grave unexpectedly open and empty, suggesting that the physical body has been raised. Most likely, Paul had heard rumors of such accounts. Yet, after his initial vision, rather than seeking out Jesus's closest followers to learn more, Paul says he kept his distance from them, insisting on his own fierce independence. Writing to believers in Galatia, he declares:

I want you to know that *the gospel I proclaimed did not come from any human source* . . . I received it in a revelation from Jesus Christ . . . When God was pleased to reveal his Son to me, . . . *I did not confer with any human being, nor did I go up to Jerusalem, to those who were apostles before me*; instead, I went immediately into Arabia, and later returned to Damascus, in Syria. (Galatians 1:11–12, 15–17)

He may have avoided Jesus's closest followers for a more practical reason: because they suspected his motives. A sworn enemy suddenly claiming to be "one of them" could be trying to infiltrate the group. Luke writes in the book of Acts that when Paul first tried to join Jesus's disciples, they avoided him, since "they were all afraid of him, for they did not believe that he was a disciple" (Acts 9:20–26).

Only after he had worked as a missionary for three years for what he called "my gospel" does Paul say, "I did go up to Jerusalem," apparently with trepidation, "to visit Peter" (Galatians 1:18), where he also met Jesus's brother James, who by then had become a leader among Jesus's followers in the Holy City. Suspicious or not, Peter allowed the visit to continue for two weeks, during which he and James, along with others, may have talked with Paul into the night, telling him anecdotes and details of Jesus's life, arrest, and crucifixion. Paul makes a point of saying that before he departed they shook hands with him, acknowledging his missionary work. Certainly, Peter and James would have told him, perhaps to dampen his obvious pride, that both of them, whom he calls the movement's "recognized pillars," had *also* "seen the Lord." Not only that: Paul admits that they taught him a preaching formula, saying that *hundreds* of people had received such appearances:

> Christ died for our sins according to the Scriptures; . . . he was raised on the third day . . . and he appeared to Peter, then to the twelve, then to five hundred brothers at one time, . . .

and then appeared to James, and then to all the apostles.
(1 Corinthians 15:3–7)

Repeating this list in a letter, Paul immediately adds himself, with a show of modesty that he quickly retracts:

Last of all . . . he appeared to me. For *I am the least of the apostles, . . . because I persecuted the church of God . . . but I worked harder than any of them*—well, not I, but God's grace in me.
(1 Corinthians 15:8–10)

Perhaps it's no surprise that decades later, when Mark, Matthew, Luke, and John write their gospels, every one of them ends with a scene at the empty grave, and with hope of resurrection. For, given the shame of Jesus's execution, what else but an enormous, miraculous reversal could validate their claim to tell "good news"? Similarly, when Luke writes the book of Acts as a sequel to his gospel, he first pictures Peter addressing crowds in Jerusalem announcing that the same man who died and was buried, "God has raised up," his body having vanished from the grave. Peter now declares that he has been taken into heaven, and "made . . . both Lord and Messiah—this Jesus whom you crucified" (Acts 2:32–36).

Mark concludes his original narrative with only a hint of future sightings, as a young man standing in the tomb promises the startled women that "you will see him" (Mark 16:5–7). What Mark *does* include, however, is an account of Jesus's burial, likely

intended to refute rumors that hostile critics were circulating—
that Jesus's followers had taken him down from the cross before
he died and revived him, later faking his resurrection. So Mark
makes a point of saying that Jesus died on the same day he was
crucified, and that Joseph of Arimathea, a member of the Jewish Council, went to Pilate "and asked for Jesus's body" (15:43).
Only after Pilate checked with soldiers to make sure that Jesus
was dead, Mark says, did he grant permission. Joseph then bought
a shroud, had the body wrapped and buried in a tomb carved out
of rock, and sealed the opening of the tomb with a large rock. We
noted earlier Mark's famously abrupt conclusion, which tells of
women going to the grave, shocked to find it open, and who, overwhelmed with fear, "said nothing to anyone, because they were
terrified" (16:4–8).

This ending prompted some of Mark's early listeners to object.
How could he end what he calls "good news" on a note of stark
terror? And if the women had never told anyone, how could the
story have spread? When Matthew revises Mark's narrative, he
apparently finds the last line too problematic. He simply drops
it, and rewrites the episode, changing both tone and motive. As
Matthew now tells it, the women "quickly left the tomb, *with fear
and great joy, and ran to tell his disciples*" (Matthew 28:8). Even
before they could depart, Matthew adds, Jesus himself appeared
to the women, and they "came to him, *took hold of his feet,* and
worshipped him" (28:8–9). Since ghosts often are assumed to
have no feet, this detail matters: Matthew intends to show that
the risen Jesus was not a ghost. Unlike Paul, he envisions Jesus
raised from death *bodily*.

Like Mark, Matthew narrates Jesus's death as a huge cosmic drama, and adds even more vivid details. Mark had already told how, as Jesus was dying, the sun went into eclipse, darkness descended at noon, and the Temple curtain split, portending divine judgment. Matthew shared with many other Jews the conviction that when "the end of the ages" comes, all the righteous dead would be raised from their graves. Paul, too, had declared that Jesus's resurrection was only the "first fruit" of God's final harvest, the glorious consummation for which devout Jews pray to this day: "Blessed are you, Lord God of Israel, who gives life to the dead." Now Matthew escalates the drama to create an astounding scene. Perhaps alluding to the graveyards seen to this day on the Mount of Olives, overlooking Jerusalem, he says that immediately after Jesus died:

> The earth shook, splitting the rocks; and the tombs were opened, *and many bodies of the righteous ones who had died were raised. After his resurrection, they came out of the tombs, and entered the Holy City, and appeared to many people.* (Matthew 27:51–53)

By the time Matthew writes, some ten to twenty years after Mark, he seems acutely aware that outsiders accused Jesus's followers of fraud. Here he counterattacks, charging that "the chief priests and Pharisees" invented lies, spreading stories that Jesus's followers had stolen his body in order to fake the resurrection that he had predicted (27:62). To bolster what Mark wrote, Matthew adds that the Jewish leaders, anticipating such deception, persuaded Pilate to send Roman soldiers to seal and secure the tomb, and then to stand guard there. But, Matthew says, as the women set out for the tomb at dawn,

> suddenly there was a great earthquake; for an angel of the Lord, descending from heaven, came and rolled back the stone and sat on it. His appearance was like lightning, and his clothing white as snow. For fear of him, the guards were shaking, and became like dead men. (Matthew 28:2–4)

When the women arrive, Matthew pictures this terrifying angel telling them an amplified version of the message that Mark says they'd heard from a young man: Jesus "has been raised" (28:6). Then, Matthew says, when the soldiers went back and told the chief priests of this astounding theophany, the priests conspired to bribe them, offering them a lot of money to lie and to say instead that "his disciples came at night, and stole him away while we were sleeping"—a story that, Matthew admits, "is still told among Jews to this day" (28:11–15).

Some historians today challenge the entire premise of this story. The Episcopal bishop John Spong, citing other scholars, declares that, since Jesus was tortured and killed as an enemy of Rome, most likely he was never buried. Instead, like countless insubordinate slaves and insurrectionists, "Jesus' body most likely was dumped into a common grave." Crossan makes the same point, suggesting that what happened was even worse. Alluding to an extensive catalogue of Greek and Roman authors writing about crucifixion, Crossan notes that victims, either fastened or nailed to crossbeams, most often were left hanging, naked and unburied. Crossan declares that since "Roman crucifixion was state terrorism . . . its function . . . was to deter resistance or revolt . . . The body was usually left on the cross to be consumed by wild beasts," such as hawks, vultures, or wild dogs: *denial of burial was the final horror.*

As evidence, Crossan points out that, although many thousands of Jews died by crucifixion, archeological excavations in Israel so far have yielded only one (now two) that were given a decent burial, each of them the corpse of a young man in his twenties. Crossan is well aware that the Jewish historian Josephus reports a rare exception: after he himself fought against Rome and was captured (later cooperating with Roman leaders), he once saw "many prisoners who had been crucified; and when I recognized three of my acquaintances among them, I was cut to the heart." Since by that time Josephus had gained the confidence of the Roman general Titus, he says that when "I told him, with tears, what I had seen," Titus allowed him to have them taken down for medical treatment, after which "two died, but one survived." Citing this anecdote, Crossan acknowledges that the gospels' report that an influential member of the Jewish Council retrieved and buried Jesus's body, though extremely unlikely, is not impossible. But since every one of the New Testament gospels includes a version of the same story of Jesus's burial, apparently uncontested, I find no sufficient reason to doubt it. After all, Jesus was no common criminal; his popularity and public reputation are what made him a threat to Roman power. And as we noted, all the gospel accounts agree that, after Jesus was buried, women returned later to find the tomb open, and the body gone. What actually happened in this case *is,* of course, controversial.

Stories swirled around, varied and contesting. Luke stops short of saying that the first person to have "seen the Lord" was a woman, but three other writers acknowledge that they had heard such a story (Matthew 28:9; Mark's second ending, in 16:9; John 20:14–16). Both Matthew and John agree that Mary Magdalene was the first person to have seen Jesus resurrected (Matthew 28:9; John 20:14–18). Luke qualifies such reports, however, saying instead that when the women found Jesus's tomb empty, all they saw were "two men in dazzling clothes," a description suggesting that they were angels (Luke 24:4). As I've discussed in detail elsewhere, resurrection stories bear multiple meanings, even beyond the startling claim that a dead man had come back to life. Among Jesus's followers, anyone claiming to have received such a vision might qualify for special status, as someone especially close to "the Lord," someone whose authority mattered. We've seen that Paul, previously suspected as a hostile outsider, was especially sensitive about his credibility. When others challenge his authority, he stakes his claim on his vision, demanding that his critics answer to him: *"Am I not an apostle? Have I not seen Jesus, our Lord?"* (1 Corinthians 9:1).

Since claiming to have "seen the Lord" could involve jockeying for position among believers, the writers who select whose stories to tell, and decide how to tell them, effectively highlight the importance of those whose stories they include. Recognizing this, several historians suggest that Mark and Luke downgraded early versions in which women said they had "seen the Lord," in order to diminish their standing. For this reason, Luke admits that they may have seen "two men" standing in the tomb, suggesting that they were angels, but not "the Lord" himself (Luke 24:22–24). Mark says that at Jesus's grave they saw only a "young man," often taken to imply that he, too, was an angel (Mark 16:5). Unlike Matthew, John, and Mark's longer ending, Luke never depicts any woman "seeing the Lord" resurrected. He may have known that Jewish law of the time often disallowed court testimony from women, since they were widely assumed to be unreliable witnesses. In later generations, we see rival groups of believers—some championing women's leadership, others ridiculing it—telling competing accounts of Mary Magdalene's claim to have "seen the Lord."

In the Gospel of Mary Magdalene, for example, Mary declares that she has "seen the Lord" in dreams and visions—a claim that Peter and Andrew flatly deny:

> "I do not believe that the Savior said these things, for indeed these teachings are strange ideas" . . . "Did he, then, speak with a woman in private without our knowing about it? Are we to turn around and listen to her? Did he choose her over us?" (Gospel of Mary BG8502 10.2–3)

In the gospel named for her, Mary wins the argument. But after the fourth century, when Catholic and Orthodox leaders took charge of most churches, they relegated her gospel, previously translated into many languages and circulated throughout the Christian world, to bonfires and trash heaps as "heresy."

Since the New Testament writers invariably prioritize men's authority, Luke, as we've noted, reports that after Peter and the others dismiss the women's stories as nonsense, the male disciples are galvanized by what they do treat as important news: "the Lord *has risen, and has appeared to Peter!*" (Luke 24:34). Hearing this, Luke says, the men began talking excitedly about other appearances—to two men on the road, then to the group of disciples gathered at dinner, while hiding in a locked room. Luke ends this story by telling how the risen Jesus leads the male disciples to Bethany and blesses them before being "carried up into heaven" (24:51) as they watch him ascend, astonished.

What, then, do people who say they have "seen the Lord" actually claim to have seen? To paraphrase a question asked of Paul: *With what body does Jesus come?* We noted already that the stories are not consistent. Not surprisingly, commentators like Wright, who insist that Jesus rose *bodily* after his death, his corpse resuscitated and physically raised into heaven, focus on stories of the empty grave. The sixteenth-century German painter Hans von Kulmbach marvelously pictures the scene we just noted (Luke 24:51; Acts 1:9), the disciples staring upward as only Jesus's feet remain in sight while he ascends into the clouds beyond their view.

Interpreters who envision the risen Jesus in more ethereal ways, though, like someone seen in dreams, visions, or hallucinations, more often take their cues from Paul. Noting this, the New Testament scholar C. H. Dodd distinguishes between two different types of resurrection accounts. Some, he notes, are told as "visionary stories," in which someone claims to have "seen the

Lord" without recognizing him at first, either because, like Paul, the recipient had never met him, or else because Jesus appears in a different form. So, for example, John reports that when Mary Magdalene, grieving, went to Jesus's grave, "she turned around and saw Jesus standing there, *but she didn't know that it was Jesus*" (John 20:14). Mistaking him for the gardener, she bursts out, asking where he has moved the body, and pleads with him to bring it back. Among many others who have pictured this scene, the Dutch painter Rembrandt famously painted Jesus wearing a gardener's hat and holding a trowel. Only when Jesus speaks her name—"Mary!"—does she recognize him. As Dodd points out, such "visionary stories" typically end with a sudden and joyous moment of recognition before Jesus disappears. Here, Mary exclaims, "My rabbi!" But before she can embrace him, he warns, "Do not touch me," and vanishes (20:16–17).

Luke includes a similar account, telling of two followers of Jesus who, grieving his death, are walking toward Emmaus. Luke says, "Jesus himself came near and walked with them . . . but their eyes were kept from recognizing him" (Luke 24:13–16), since, as Mark notes, he appeared to them "in another form" (Mark 16:12). While talking with the two men on the road, Luke says, "he interpreted to them the things about himself in all the scriptures" (Luke 24:27). Only later, after they invite him to share dinner, when he "took bread, blessed, and broke it . . . their eyes were opened, and they recognized him" (24:30–31) as the one with whom, not long before, they had shared a Passover meal on the last night of his life. Then, as in John's account, "he vanished from their sight" (24:31).

Dodd contrasts these "visionary" accounts with "bodily appearance" stories, which various people take as proof of Jesus's *physical* resurrection—stories correlated with reports of the empty grave. Although Mark tells no stories like that, every one of the later gospel writers includes at least one. Luke, for example, says that, while the disciples were still in hiding, suddenly "Jesus himself stood among them" (24:36). But instead of greeting him with joy, Luke says, "they were startled and terrified, and thought they were seeing a ghost" (24:37). Then Jesus speaks:

> Why are you frightened, and why do doubts arise in your hearts? Look at my hands and feet—that it is I, myself! Touch me, and see: a ghost does not have flesh and bones, as you see that I have. (Luke 24:38–39)

In this account, unlike the Emmaus story, Luke emphasizes Jesus's *bodily* resurrection. He displays his wounds, inviting his disciples to "touch me and see" that he is, indeed, physically present. Luke goes so far as to say that, since the disciples were still frightened and incredulous, Jesus asks, "Do you have anything here to eat?" When they offer him a piece of broiled fish, Luke says, "he took it and ate it in their presence" (24:41–43). Now they understand: ghosts don't eat!

John, like Luke, also reports both kinds of stories. Immediately after telling the "visionary" story involving Mary Magdalene, John follows with a "bodily appearance" story that echoes the one we just noted in Luke's gospel. Here again, Jesus suddenly appears to disciples gathered in a locked room, openly displaying the wounds on his hands and side. As John tells it, though, his astonished disciples greet him with joy, not fear; and before departing, Jesus breathes on them, infusing them with the power of the Holy Spirit (John 20:19–23).

After telling this story, John makes a special point of adding that the disciple Thomas "was not with them when he came" (20:24). When the others tell him, "We have seen the Lord!" Thomas adamantly refuses to believe them: "Unless I see the mark of the nails in his hands, and put my finger in the mark of the nails, and my hand in his side, *I will not believe*" (20:25). Next, for emphasis, John adds a second episode. The following week, he says, when the disciples gathered, "although the doors were shut," Jesus appears a second time, ordering Thomas to verify the empirical proof that he demands: "*Put your finger here, and see my hands. Reach out your hand, and put it in my side. Do not doubt, but believe!*" (20:27). This scene famously ends as "Doubting Thomas" capitulates, acknowledging the miracle, and Jesus rebukes him, blessing those—John's future readers!—who accept this testimony without physical evidence, "*those who have not seen, and yet believe*" (20:29).

When first recognizing the difference between "visionary" and "bodily appearance" stories, I wondered: Aren't the gospel writers aware of this? Why do they treat both kinds of stories as if they are interchangeable? Don't they notice that the stories they tell are making different claims about how Jesus was "raised"? After puzzling over these questions for some time, I concluded that since Jesus's followers were intensely aware of critics like Celsus, who ridiculed their claims, they chose to collect and include as many resurrection accounts as they could. Regardless of whether the details agree, the cumulative effect of various reports could bolster the conviction that mattered most to them: that *many* people had "seen Jesus" alive, however they reported what happened. The same concern seems to have motivated the anonymous writers who added three additional resurrection accounts to the abrupt end of Mark's gospel—each of these a widely circulated story that Luke and John would tell later in more detail.

As every Christian knows, the evangelists' stories of the empty grave remain, to this day, a primary element in Easter celebrations. And when Luke writes the script for Peter's first public preaching, he makes Jesus's resurrection from the grave the main point— not only a unique event in Israel's history but in the history of the world:

> Fellow Israelites, I say confidently that our ancestor David both died and was buried, and his tomb is with us to this day . . . [But] David spoke of the resurrection of the Messiah, saying, "He was not abandoned to Hades, not did his flesh experience corruption." This Jesus God raised up; of that we are all witnesses! (Acts 2:29–32)

Allison, who focuses his most recent study of resurrection primarily on the "empty tomb" stories, concludes that, although historical evidence cannot tell us what actually happened, "when Jesus' followers learned of his empty grave, faith in his resurrection entered the world."

What happened to Paul, however, shows that a *visionary* experience of "seeing the Lord" also could ignite such faith, quite *apart* from any story of an empty grave. For, as Paul's life demonstrates, his visions served him as incontrovertible proof that Jesus was alive in some inexplicable way, transformed in "a mystery." And when I began to explore the secret texts discovered at Nag Hammadi, I was surprised and intrigued to see that many Christians later called "heretics" consistently follow the path that Paul has set out. The influential poet and teacher Valentinus, for example, widely known as a disciple of Paul, claimed to have received not only Paul's letters but also the "divine wisdom" he taught secretly "to the initiates" (1 Corinthians 2:6–7). And as we'll see, Valentinus's followers, far from focusing on the "empty tomb" stories, conspicuously leave these out, and take up instead a distinctly Pauline trajectory of "visionary" resurrection accounts.

Since Paul's letters, written some twenty to fifty years earlier than Mark, Matthew, Luke, or John, were the first writings to circulate widely among Jesus's followers throughout the Roman world, they became enormously influential. To this day, they constitute over 60 percent of the New Testament writings. But since "the great apostle" often writes in convoluted and polemical language, his letters also ignite intense controversy. From the start of the Christian movement, opposing groups of his admirers argued about what Paul meant to say. Someone even slipped into the New Testament a letter pseudonymously attributed to Peter that admits as much. Its second-century author, one of the first to characterize Paul's letters as "Scriptures," nevertheless acknowledges that, although "our beloved brother Paul wrote to you according to the wisdom given of him, speaking of this as he does in all his letters, *there are some things in them hard to understand, which ignorant and unstable people twist to their own destruction,* as they do the other Scriptures" (2 Peter 3:15–16).

Many people would agree, since Paul's letters have spawned conflicting interpretations of Christianity for two millennia. About a hundred years after Paul's death, for example, a charismatic Christian named Marcion preached that "the great apostle" had jettisoned the Hebrew Bible, urging believers to abandon Israel's limited and angry God, who created a world so deficient that it includes scorpions and mosquitoes. Marcion declared that Paul intended to turn believers to worship instead a higher, previously unknown God of love, whom Jesus revealed for the first time. And, more than fourteen hundred years after Marcion, the Catholic monk Martin Luther (c. 1517) split Western Christian churches apart by criticizing his own church for insisting that believers must do good works, insisting that Paul's primary message is "justification by faith alone."

Perhaps the most explosive of these controversies, though, concerns resurrection—arguments that heated to a fever pitch within decades of Paul's death and remain unresolved among Christians to this day. Noting these controversies, let's begin where "orthodox" Christians often start, with Bishop Irenaeus, self-styled spokesman for "straight-thinking" believers. Confronting an intricate tangle of conflicting claims about Paul, Irenaeus claims the apostle's authority for himself, infuriated that his primary targets, those he calls "the disciples of Valentinus," counter his claims and boast that they themselves have received access to "divine mysteries." Of these, they say, Irenaeus, although a bishop, knows nothing.

When Irenaeus begins to write the magisterial treatise he calls *The Refutation and Destruction of Falsely So-Called Gnosis* (hereafter called by its Latin title, *Adversus Haereses*), he devotes the first four large and unwieldy volumes to what he may regard as their lesser errors. But in the fifth and final volume, Irenaeus takes direct aim at the worst of their offenses: his opponents "deny the salvation of the flesh, and reject its regeneration, saying that it is not capable of incorruptibility" (*Adversus Haereses*, V.2.1). Challenged to refute their interpretation, Irenaeus sets forth his own in detail, echoing the apostle's words throughout:

> Just as a grain of wheat [1 Corinthians 15:37] is sown into the earth . . . so our bodies . . . *buried in the earth, and having decomposed there, shall rise at the appointed time*, since . . . God gives "to this mortal immortality, and to this corruptible incorruption" [15:53] . . . because God's "strength is perfected in weakness." [cf. 2 Corinthians 12:3]

How can bodies of flesh and blood transform into immortal, imperishable bodies capable of rising into heaven, as Irenaeus declares that Jesus's body has risen? To explain this, he offers an early interpretation of the eucharist, intending to show how physical substances transform into nonmaterial ones—a theory that medieval Catholic theologians later would develop into more philosophically based theologies of transubstantiation. Just as

Jesus unites in himself both human flesh and divine spirit, Irenaeus says, so the eucharist, the Christians' sacred meal, unites two realities (Greek: *pragmata*) into one. For when Jesus declares at the last supper that the bread he offers "is my body," and the wine "is my blood," what he means, Irenaeus says, is:

> The bread, when it receives the invocation from God, is no longer ordinary bread, but the Eucharist, consisting of two realities, earthly and heavenly; so also our bodies, when they receive the Eucharist, are no longer corruptible, having the hope of resurrection to eternity. (*Adversus Haereses,* IV.18.5)

Far from taking Jesus's words as metaphor, Irenaeus suggests that this is how the eucharist uniquely works. As I understand him, he says that when we receive the eucharist, ingesting bread and wine that miraculously have *become* Christ's body and blood, "our bodies are nourished" in such a way that they are gradually being transformed into incorruptible and imperishable bodies, incorporated into Christ. Eating these transformed substances throughout our lifetime, then, eventually enables ordinary bodies, even after they have died, to become "capable of receiving the power of God . . . muscles, arteries and veins," heart and lungs, restored, "made perfect in weakness" (2 Corinthians 12:9), so that they may be raised in resurrection. After a long and convoluted exposition, Irenaeus concludes, "Our opinion is in accordance with the Eucharist, and the Eucharist in turn establishes our opinion" (*Adversus Haereses,* IV.18.5). Irenaeus ends his five volumes of polemic pronouncing a solemn curse upon Valentinus's followers, consigning them to Satan, above all for distorting Paul's teaching on resurrection and "refusing to believe in the salvation of their flesh":

> Let those persons who blaspheme the creator ... like Valentinus' followers, and all the falsely so-called gnostics, be recognized as agents of Satan by all who worship God; through them Satan, even now ... speaks against God, who has prepared eternal fire for every kind of apostasy. (Adversus Haereses, V.26.2)

In concluding, he assures believers that "when Christ returns to earth to reign in Jerusalem," he shall raise the decomposed bodies of the righteous dead, perfectly restoring them with their newly equipped imperishable bodies. And when that day comes, he declares, they shall go on living for a thousand years, enjoying the glory of Christ's long-promised reign on earth—a conviction Irenaeus shares with other believers of his time.

Having strongly pressed his case, Irenaeus acknowledges, as if in passing, what his critics raise as their most obvious objection—that passage in 1 Corinthians 15 in which Paul says precisely the opposite:

> Among other [truths] proclaimed by the apostle, there is also this one, "That *flesh and blood cannot inherit the kingdom of God*" [1 Corinthians 15.50]. *This is [the passage] which is adduced by all the heretics in support of their folly,* with an attempt to annoy us, and to point out that the handiwork of God is not saved. (Adversus Haereses, V.9.1)

Did Irenaeus, then, get it wrong? Is Paul saying simply that a physical body shall *become* a resurrection body? Or is he saying something different when he insists, "We shall all be changed" (1 Corinthians 15:51–52)? Is he suggesting that after death a transformation occurs, one that we cannot now understand—a mystery in which our former existence is "swallowed up" into something much greater (15:51–54)?

What Paul means to say in this powerful passage is surely not obvious. But, here again, the Nag Hammadi texts surprised us. For when our research team opened up Codex 1, the first of the collection of thirteen heavy, leather-bound treatises found there in 1945, we found on the first page a "Letter on Resurrection"—the most powerful and direct interpretation of Paul's teaching that I had ever seen. Since all of us were familiar with Irenaeus's polemics, we were amazed—incredulous, at first—to find that every one of the texts bound into Codex 1, together with the "Letter on Resurrection," strongly affirms faith in resurrection. Only after asking many questions, rereading and discussing the sources, did we realize that, although Irenaeus and others accuse Valentinus's followers of "denying resurrection," what they actually do is different. Most often they leave out stories of *bodily* resurrection and the "empty tomb," to follow instead the path that Paul has set out.

Before taking a look at how this "Letter" interprets resurrection, let's consider how Christians were reading it nearly two thousand years ago. As we've noted in our introduction, Codex 1, along with other sacred books, was found hidden in a cave, where monks from a nearby monastery went to meditate and pray. Pachomius, a former soldier turned spiritual mentor, had built this monastery near the town of Nag Hammadi, only two or three years after Roman emperors ended state persecution. Just as Christians were beginning to feel safe to admit their faith in public, Pachomius announced that angels had inspired him to build this monastery as a "new Christian society" on earth—an early outpost of the coming kingdom.

As I envision the scene, one of the monks who had learned to read would carry this big leather volume from the monastery library into the open courtyard where his monastic brothers, having finished a day's work and shared an early supper of vegetables and bread, would gather as the day begins to darken into night, sitting together on the ground for evening devotions. Standing before them, and placing the heavy book on a lectern, the reader would open to the first page and read the "Prayer of the Apostle Paul," echoing the apostle's words as he led the monks in prayer, asking the Lord to attune their ears to what the Spirit was about to teach through these sacred readings:

> My Redeemer . . . I am yours . . . You are my consciousness; bring me forth! You are my treasury; open to me! You fulfill me; take me to you! . . . Give me healing for my body, . . . and redeem my eternal-light soul and my spirit . . . Grant what no angel's eye has seen, and no ruler's ear has heard, and what has not entered into the human heart . . . Amen. In peace: Christ is holy.

Now the celebrant begins the next reading, "The Apocryphon [Secret Revelation] of James," which tells how Jesus, having died more than a year and a half earlier, unexpectedly appears to his brother James and to Peter, in resurrected form. When, startled, they ask, "Have you come back to us?" he urges them instead to "come toward me" by opening their hearts, then sending heart, mind, and spirit upward, so that they may hear the angels singing joyfully in heaven—a possibility that this Secret Revelation offers to the monks listening in the dark.

After this, following a familiar pattern of Christian worship, the celebrant goes on to read "the gospel." But since his listeners are monks devoted to spiritual practice, instead of reading the New Testament gospels used in ordinary church worship, the reader opens the Gospel of Truth, a mystical interpretation of "the gospel" that claims to reveal what the Spirit taught to Paul.

The reader turns next to the "Letter on Resurrection," a spiritual interpretation of Paul. Here an anonymous teacher, a follower of Valentinus, responds to questions raised by a student named Rheginos: "Do we have to believe in resurrection? Is it an essential element of Christian faith, or not?" The teacher replies that, although "many people don't believe it," faith in resurrection *is* essential. "So," he says, "let's talk about it."

Acknowledging that what he has to say is hard to understand, this teacher, like Irenaeus, echoes Paul's words, but interprets them differently. Whereas Irenaeus insists that our present, earthly bodies are essentially the *same* as our future resurrection bodies, Rheginos's teacher notes Paul's focus on *discontinuity*. When Paul speaks of what was "sown" into the ground like seed as perishable—that is, the physical body—and what comes forth from it as imperishable (1 Corinthians 15:42), he is not, Rheginos's teacher explains, speaking of one body in two forms. Rather, he points out, Paul differentiates two distinct kinds: a "physical body . . . made of dust," which perishes, and a "spiritual body," which is imperishable. And just as Paul declares that "death shall be swallowed up in victory," so, Rheginos's teacher declares, "the Savior swallowed up death," destroying its power, so that "we shall all be changed" (15:51):

> He transformed himself into an imperishable being, and opened the way to our immortality . . . We are embraced by him until our setting, that is to say, like our human death. Then we are drawn to heaven by him, like beams of the sun . . . This is the spiritual resurrection, which swallows up what is psychic [*psychikos*] as well as what is fleshly [*sarkikos*].

"What, then, *is* resurrection?" Recalling the gospel story that tells how Peter, James, and John suddenly saw Jesus transfigured before them, speaking with Moses and Elijah, the teacher says:

> Do not think that resurrection is an illusion. It is not an illusion, but the truth! Indeed, it is more accurate to say that the world is an illusion, rather than the resurrection . . . Rather, *resurrection is the revelation of what is actually real; a transformation of things, and a transition into newness.*

Since spiritual awakening is the beginning of resurrection life, even here on earth, this teacher encourages Rheginos to recognize that, although still a beginner in faith, he already has begun a process of transformation. Then the teacher ends with a challenge. Instead of asking more questions, plunge more deeply into spiritual practice: "Why am I ignoring your lack of exercise? Everyone needs to practice!"

What, then, might resurrection mean—miracle, suspension of natural law, radical transformation at death? Among Christians from the first century to the present we find no single consensus, nor should we expect to find one. Yet, while reading this "Letter," I was surprised to find myself much in agreement with it. Although I once unthinkingly accepted the rationalistic assumption that visions of life after death were nothing but projection or delusion, I now question that assumption—but not, as Rheginos's teacher notes, because of any kind of logical argument, or "persuasion."

Instead, those assumptions changed when I myself was shaken by "experiences that I cannot explain"—by experiencing the presence of people who had died. These were not mediated by ordinary vision or hearing but by some other mode of perception, one that I found inexplicable, yet it felt "more real than real," as Rheginos's teacher suggests. Consequently, like countless others who once assumed that death was simply, as Steve Jobs once put it, "lights out," and who later report that unexpected experiences have brought them to envision some kind of afterlife, I now remain open to wonder, and even to hope for some kind of unimaginable transformation. What also seems clear to me is that Paul is not talking about decomposed bodies restored to life and raised into the heavens, as Irenaeus posits. Instead, what Paul calls "mystery" remains just that.

Even rationally inclined historians, though, find one fact on which nearly all agree. The historian Ed Sanders speaks for many when he says, "That Jesus' followers . . . had resurrection experiences is, in my judgement, a fact. What the reality was that gave rise to the experiences I do not know." The movement that began with Jesus faltered after his death; and it wasn't primarily his *teachings* that breathed new life into his followers, infusing them with what many experienced as superhuman power. Instead, as for Paul, it was the conviction that the Jesus who died had been resurrected. Sanders says, "They believed this, they lived it, and they died for it. In the process, they created a movement . . . that in many ways went far beyond Jesus' message." And although Christians' interpretations of resurrection have fluctuated throughout two millennia in far more ways than we could mention here, as Adolf von Harnack writes:

This could not affect the certainty of the conviction that the Lord would raise his people from death. This conviction, whose reverse is the fear of that God who casts [people] into hell, has become the mightiest power through which the Gospel has won [its reception throughout the world].

In other words, the Christian movement became powerful because Christians could claim to offer "eternal life"—not only to an emperor like Augustus, pronounced divine after his death by a vote in the Senate, but potentially to everyone, even to women, slaves, children dying young, former criminals. And whereas

Rome's gods and goddesses appeared in sculpture and poetry looking more like Rome's imperial rulers than anyone else, stories of Jesus, whose followers called him "Son of God," pictured someone humble and ordinary, with whom the vast majority of Rome's inhabitants might identify.

Furthermore, although leaders like Irenaeus worked hard to promote their own views of resurrection, insisting that Christians all over the world must agree with them, their efforts have failed to shut down continuing speculation. To this day, when Roman Catholic, Episcopal, Orthodox, Methodist, and Lutheran Christians "say the creed," they alternate between two well-known versions, most participants noting no difference between them. What's called "the Apostles' Creed," reputed to go back to Jesus's earliest disciples, agrees with Irenaeus and others, professing faith "in the resurrection of the body." But contemporary versions of the Nicene Creed, currently used in churches from England to Ethiopia, Ukraine to Argentina, more often profess faith in "the resurrection of the dead"—an ambiguous phrase that could refer *either* to bodily resurrection, *or* to Paul's view of transformation.

What seems to matter more than either interpretation, however, is the possibility that faith can challenge death's finality, offering hope for new life, not simply in some shadowy version of Hades but in an unimaginably glorious and joyful victory over death, which Paul calls "the last enemy to be destroyed" (1 Corinthians 15:26). Even without understanding what that might mean, I find this, although not easy to believe, to be a hope that many may appreciate.

Whether one embraces the Biblical stories we've been exploring or rejects them, we can understand how they remain vivid and
powerful for many people. Diverse as they are, they follow a common pattern. These stories begin in the world in which we live,
often plagued by disease, war, natural disasters, and overwhelming loss, and then shift, often unexpectedly, into the key of hope.
The poet Dylan Thomas embodies this shift in his powerful poem
"And Death Shall Have No Dominion," having taken his title from
the King James translation of Paul's discussion of resurrection,
"Knowing that Christ, being raised from the dead, dieth no more;
death hath no more dominion over him" (Romans 6:9):

> And death shall have no dominion.
> Dead men naked they shall be one
> With the man in the wind and the west moon;
> When their bones are picked clean and the clean bones
>   gone,
> They shall have stars at elbow and foot;
> Though they go mad they shall be sane,
> Though they sink through the sea they shall rise again;
> Though lovers be lost love shall not;
> And death shall have no dominion.

Such visions, a primary reason for the astonishing success of
this unlikely movement, continue even now to attract new converts, as we shall see in our final chapters.

6

How Did Jesus "Become God"?

Who is Jesus? Is he God? We've seen that only John's gospel, written later than the others, actually envisions Jesus as God in human form. The historian Bart Ehrman, reporting how this exalted view of Jesus became dominant among Jesus's followers, shows that it was increasingly accepted during the third and fourth centuries, and so could be seen as a latecomer's vision. Paul of Tarsus, though, having first encountered Jesus as a brilliant heavenly presence, was already preaching "Jesus Christ, our Lord," as a divine being, effectively "equal to God," only a decade or two after Jesus's death (Philippians 2:6–11). Yet Paul did not imagine that faith in Christ compromised monotheism. Instead, he seems to assume that Jesus Christ, being God's Son, manifests the glory of God himself.

Our uncertainty points to a reality on the ground. Only some twenty years after the crucifixion, when the views of various groups of Jesus's followers were shaped by their different leaders' perspectives, Paul complains that though some say, "I am from

Paul's group," others insist that they are "from Peter's" (1 Corinthians 1:12–13). What did they have in common? And since many writings were circulating among Christian groups—not only what Paul actually wrote but other "letters of Paul" written in Paul's name by his anonymous admirers, along with a profusion of "gospels"—how could such groups reach unanimity?

One of Justin Martyr's students, a second-century Syrian convert named Tatian, decided to make things simpler. Stitching anecdotes and teachings from four or five gospel accounts into a single narrative, he created a unified text that he called the Diatessaron ("Harmony of the Four Gospels"). But this apparently was too much of a patchwork, thus losing literary coherence; few people adopted it.

Next, around ten years later (180 C.E.), Irenaeus, whom we've met as a Syrian missionary to the barbarians in Gaul (present-day France), expressed dismay that one group of believers, predominantly Jewish, focused only on Matthew's gospel, and a growing network of Gentile groups threw out the Hebrew Bible and read only Luke. Even worse, Irenaeus says, disciples of the Egyptian poet and visionary Valentinus primarily read John's gospel—and, he insisted, they misunderstood it.

Irenaeus proposes a different solution to the question of which gospels are Spirit-inspired, and which, he says, "Satan planted to deceive people." He warns that "the gospels of the heretics" are like poison, or shiny pieces of broken glass that only fools would mistake for genuine jewels. But instead of endorsing only one gospel, or trying to combine them into a single text, Irenaeus suggests that each of the four—Mark, Matthew, Luke, and John—

contributes a different element of the truth. So, he explains, whereas Mark presents Jesus as a prophet, Luke pictures him as a compassionate healer and priest. Matthew, he adds, traces Jesus's genealogy back to King David, setting forth his *human* lineage, and only John's gospel reveals Jesus's *divine* genealogy, as Son of God.

Consequently, Irenaeus declares, although John's gospel is the most important, since it pictures Jesus as God incarnate, "orthodox" believers need all four. And since the term "gospel" originally referred to what Jesus *preached,* and not to any written text, Irenaeus champions what he called the "four-formed gospel"— a quartet of texts that *collectively* support the proclamation of that "good news." Thus, Irenaeus gave shape to the collection of gospels we now find in the New Testament.

Living in the shadow of persecution, Irenaeus was especially concerned to consolidate the bonds between a network of Christian groups throughout the world, from Germany to Spain, Gaul, Egypt, and Africa. Already he had seen close friends and fellow believers in the towns of Lyons and Vienne attacked in public riots. Then he heard how they had been arrested and imprisoned in dank cells, to be held until the emperor's birthday, when they would be publicly tortured and killed in the sports arena as crowds of their local townspeople watched, shouted, and jeered. Irenaeus himself narrowly escaped arrest, having departed for Rome after those held in prison pleaded with him to bring a letter to believers in the capital city to tell them of the danger they were facing. While in Rome, Irenaeus reports, he had a horrifying vision of something taking place back in his home city of Antioch: his own beloved mentor, eighty-six-year-old Bishop Polycarp, led into the central sports stadium packed with spectators who were shouting "Kill him!" "Watch him burn!" as he was bound to a funeral pyre, then torched, stabbed, and burned alive.

For nearly three hundred years after Jesus was crucified, his followers lived under threat of persecution. Although arrests, torture, and horrifying executions were sporadic, not systematic, they were always threatening. For then, as now, totalitarian rulers understood that arresting and killing a few key leaders, and randomly targeting a specific group of them, can effectively terrify and silence countless others. In spite of that, though, the numbers of Christians increased: as the African convert Tertullian boasted to a Roman magistrate, "The more you kill us, the more we multiply; the blood of Christians is seed!"

But in 312 C.E., a miracle happened. Constantine, a military leader and the illegitimate son of one of Rome's rulers, sent shockwaves throughout the empire by becoming emperor, after suddenly shifting his allegiance from Rome's gods to Christ, the divine champion, who, he insisted, had helped him kill his chief rival in battle and given him victory. Other victories followed under Christ's banner, confirming Constantine's conviction that worshipping his new divine patron would ensure his hold on the empire, which Roman rulers saw as "the whole world." Soon after that, Constantine and his allies ordered an end to persecution of Christians. During the decades that followed, they did much more: offering restitution for what Christians had suffered, restoring confiscated property, helping rebuild their churches, and appointing believers to favorable positions in government.

As Christian leaders gained legitimacy, they began to structure their groups more formally, adopting the model of a three-tiered hierarchy from the Roman army. Now "overseers" (*episcopoi,* "bishops") wielded authority over "elders" (*presbyteroi,* "priests") and over "servants" (*diakonoi*). And now that Constantine was eager to enlist bishops as his allies in governing the empire, he was frustrated and angry to hear that, even after he had freed Christians from persecution and showered them with favors, some of them refused to agree among themselves on the most basic questions: Is Jesus God? Or is he less than God? If he is divine, in what way?

Hearing of endless wrangling over such questions, Constantine determined to create a unified network of churches throughout the empire. He summoned over three hundred Christian leaders throughout the Eastern empire to a conference at his summer palace in Nicaea, Turkey, and offered them free travel in the imperial system and generous hospitality. When they arrived, he personally stood to welcome them, and ordered them to compose a document specifying what Christians should believe. What a committee of bishops wrote, and more than three hundred finally endorsed, came to be called the Nicene Creed, which has enormously influenced Christian doctrine ever since.

Constantine then ordered his closest ally among them, Bishop Eusebius of Caesarea, "Get me fifty copies of the [Christian] Scriptures," so that he could send a uniform collection to major churches throughout the empire. First, though, Eusebius had to answer the question, "Which ones?" What belonged on such a list? Which writings should he designate as "recognized" books, and which as "disputed"? The questions of what belonged in the creed, and what belonged in the *canon* (literally, "standard list") of Christian Scriptures, ignited intense arguments. Carefully checking which books most regional bishops regarded as holy and read in church during worship, Eusebius began with Irenaeus's list of the "fourfold gospel," Matthew, Mark, Luke, and John, then added Paul's letters, and raised questions about other texts, like the "Letters" attributed to James, John, and Peter. He could not decide about the book of Revelation, which he realized was a wild card—revered and "recognized" by some, "disputed" by others.

From Eusebius's tentative lists, how did certain texts—John's gospel foremost among them—come to be revered as the canon of gospel truth? During the next fifty years, various bishops throughout the empire held their own councils to vote on this question. But since the vast majority of deliberations, arguments, and controversies about which writings to include in the New Testament have left no surviving written record—scholars today can only trace a few highlights of a process that largely remains obscure—the best we can do is to piece together some central moments in that process from sources left by some of the key players. The interested reader can find hundreds of books meant to work through the details of canonization, but here I offer the briefest possible sketch of what happened—or, maybe better, two contrasting sketches, since the establishment of the New Testament canon is by no means a simple story, and far beyond what I can offer here.

When I was a visiting graduate student at Oxford University, I asked my tutor how the canon was formed. Who better to ask than Professor Henry Chadwick, an Anglican priest and dean of Christ Church Cathedral, a scholar famous for the learning that he had set forth in seven volumes in his influential history of the Christian Church? Chadwick referred me to a book in which he wrote that, around 180 C.E., "the canon of the New Testament emerged out of the mist."

What surprised me was hearing Professor Chadwick speak in uncharacteristically poetic language. Was he imagining the New Testament descending from heaven as an epiphany, unaided by human effort, to clear away "the mist" of human uncertainty? I was hoping for a more down-to-earth answer. But at that moment, having just met this lofty, white-haired man who exuded confidence in his own authority, I hesitated to press him. Later, rereading his book *The Church in Ancient Society: From Galilee to Gregory the Great,* I found another traditional answer: "Admission to the canon was inextricably linked with the orthodoxy of the doctrine contained in the text." Here again, he had chosen only passive verbs: no hint of human intervention.

Let's note what Chadwick left out: human agency. His account avoids any suggestion of how the messy process of "canonization" actually happened. Who made the decisions about what to include as "Scriptures" and which writings to discard, censor, and destroy? On what basis were some classified as "orthodox" (literally, "straight-thinking"), and others as "heterodox" ("thinking otherwise")? Who qualified as the guardians of "admission"— or exclusion—whether of texts or, more to the point, of human beings?

Ramsay MacMullen, Professor of Classics at Yale, offers a

startlingly different view of how church leaders constructed what Chadwick calls "orthodoxy of doctrine." What MacMullen shows in his 2006 book, *Voting About God in Early Church Councils,* is that the results of the Nicene Council proved intensely controversial for hundreds of years after it ended. Working through ancient records of church councils convened between 325 and 553 C.E., MacMullen documents the proceedings, as groups of bishops, some of them working farmers, merchants, and teachers, engaged in heated arguments, with antagonists shouting at each other, sometimes breaking into fistfights. Even at the august and formal Council of Nicaea, summoned and attended by Constantine, St. Nicholas (not the one who climbs down chimneys on Christmas Eve, fortunately) became so angry at another bishop that he got up and publicly slapped him in the face.

Emperor Constantine, attending every session, often found himself impatient as bishops argued over Greek philosophic terms to describe Jesus's relationship to God. The following question was one of the sticking points: What does it mean to say that Jesus is "of one essence, or substance" (*homoousios*) with God? And what is the difference between that and saying that Jesus and God are "of similar substance" (*homoiousios*)? After sitting through days that stretched into exhausting hours of debate over issues that Constantine regarded as trivial, when he finally heard what he likely thought was a majority opinion he said, in effect, "Let's go with that." To no one's surprise, nearly all three hundred bishops voted in favor of the proposal that the emperor endorsed. Thus, they effectively adopted Irenaeus's view that Jesus is, indeed, God—a view almost always expressed in copious quotations from the Gospel of John. The one outspoken dissenter, an African priest named Arius, who insisted that all believers— potentially, at least—are sons of God, was abruptly dismissed from the Council, along with a single supporter. After that, the Council voted to consign both dissenters to eternal damnation.

In the process, John's gospel became the lens through which Christians defending the Nicene Creed chose to read all the gospels—a perspective that Catholic Christians, and many Protestants as well, have adopted ever since. Notably, what the bishops endorsed at Nicaea was a framework insisting that only the Catholic ("universal," in Greek) faith offers salvation. From then on, what would become the church of the Holy Roman Empire was invested with what Matthew's gospel says Jesus received after he ascended into heaven: "all power on heaven and on earth"—or, at least, all that the Roman Empire could claim and summon.

Yet, after the Nicene bishops worked to consolidate Christianity into a single universal communion, confirming Irenaeus's statement that "outside of the church there is no salvation," believers in every generation have continued to reflect, reimagine, and reinterpret who Jesus was, and what his message might mean. Those who gathered at Nicaea generally agreed to read in worship the four narrative gospels—Mark, Matthew, Luke, and John—while ignoring the differences among them, which fueled ongoing arguments, many of which continue to this day. Even then, there was no immediate agreement on what belonged in the "canon"—that is, the closed collection of texts that we call the New Testament. That question would remain a source of contention, as noted above, for more than fifty years.

Consequently, what we call "Christianity" today, far from being a single movement, spills out instead into countless streams leading in different directions and denominations, and emphasizing different interpretations. Today more than one-third of the world's population identifies as Christian, making Christianity the largest of all religious traditions. But when we trace how Christianity spread throughout two thousand years, we can see a distinct lack of unanimity, and often conflict, between communities.

The two groups attracting most converts today—on the one hand, Roman Catholic and Orthodox churches and, on the other, Pentecostals—are nearly polar opposites. The former emphasize tradition, the ritual mystery of the sacraments, and hierarchical authority, whether of the Catholic pope or of the patriarchs of Orthodox churches from Greece to Egypt, Ethiopia, and Russia, whereas Pentecostal Christians reject claims to clerical authority, insisting instead that the Holy Spirit directly empowers individual believers and groups.

Even after the sixteenth century, when Martin Luther began "protesting" papal authority, giving rise to "Protestant" Christianity and the Reformation, many groups that were spawned from that movement maintained the Nicene Creed and the sacred meal as the center of worship, while endorsing the authority of "Scripture alone." Especially from the seventeenth century through the nineteenth, other religious reformers, part of the "Radical Reformation," took Christianity in new directions, creating groups as diverse as the Society of Friends (often called Quakers), Unitarians and Universalists, the Church of Latter-day Saints, and Christian Science. And today, many evangelical Christians who reject denominational labels claim to hold to "the fundamentals" of faith, endorsing the literal truth of the Bible.

We cannot possibly trace this process of diversification through two millennia here. But as the topic of our final chapter, I want to explore "who *is* Jesus" today by investigating how he is seen by a range of recently converted believers from different parts of the world, and by artists, writers, and filmmakers among our contemporaries.

7

Who *Is* Jesus—to New Converts, Artists, and Filmmakers Engaging Him Today?

WHAT IS IT about Jesus, and what people say about him, that still engages me and countless others? I began to ask this question after I first encountered evangelical Christianity—an experience intense, powerful, and brief. When that church's outsized claims to offer ultimate truth and salvation suddenly showed an underside I hadn't expected—harsh rejection of anyone not "born again," and a habit of shutting down questions—I had to leave, but could not entirely shake its allure. Having discovered the power of religious experience, I knew that something had happened—something transformative.

Recognizing that Jesus not only *was*, but still *is* a powerful presence in the lives of people today, I wondered: Which Jesus is each one seeing? What, specifically, about him and his message are people today finding most powerful? For, just as his earliest followers were constantly revising their visions of Jesus, those who engage him today continually adapt what they find in tradition. For although many Christians insist that they know—and know better than anyone else—exactly "what Jesus really meant," on the ground, Christianity is still a work in progress.

Who is Jesus today for people who are choosing to convert? What attracts a group, or a person, to Jesus, and to stories about him? Starting with this question, I found answers that take us—literally—all over the map, from Southern California to remote villages in Madagascar, from the Amazonian jungle of Brazil to the crowded streets of Benares, from South Africa to northern Spain. Christianity is still the most populous religious tradition in the world, and it is quickly gaining new members, especially in Asia, Africa, and Latin America; what ignites such enthusiasm?

What I found first was a group close to home. The Stanford anthropologist Tanya Luhrmann began to question some of her relatives who said that they have close personal relationships with Jesus. Seeking to understand how they came to make such claims, she asked, "How does God—or Jesus—become real for people? How are sensible people able to believe in an invisible being who has a demonstrable effect on their lives?"

Luhrmann chose to investigate the Association of Vineyard Churches in Southern California—a new Protestant denomination that, since its founding in 1982, has attracted thousands of new converts, most of whom previously had nothing to do with religious institutions, or else had abandoned them. Rather like my own experience of evangelical Christianity, Vineyard Christians invite people to encounter Jesus as their closest friend. Luhrmann heard that members think of God "as someone who interacts with them like a friend. He speaks to them. He listens to them; He acts when they pray to him . . . because he cares." She set out to understand how they come to think this way.

Recently, when I visited Stanford, she invited me to speak in her seminar, and then arranged a lunch for me to meet with twelve psychiatrists at Stanford Medical Center. Since psychiatrists tend to view the mind as a private sphere, I asked, "When you hear someone describing an interior conversation—or confrontation—with God or with Jesus, do you assume that the person is delusional?" Startled by the question, nearly every one of them paused, nodded, and said, "Yes."

Luhrmann, having written a book about schizophrenia, is aware of such views and raises a similar question in her book about religious practice, *How God Becomes Real.* How do experiences of "talking with God" or with Jesus differ from insanity, in which mentally unbalanced people interact with invisible spirits?

As she describes it, Vineyard members envision Jesus as someone who, having been human himself, has experienced everything that we experience, yet who, also being God, can meet all of our needs. Characterizing this as "a shift in the American imagination of God," she cites a Vineyard member who celebrates this shift, declaring, "Jesus died so that we could rebuke *religion,* and embrace *relationship!*" Rather than simply offering a set of beliefs, Vineyard leaders explain that learning to embrace a relationship with Jesus takes *practice.* They teach beginners a series of steps to enable them to "develop a new [understanding of their] mind[s]"—steps that are the operating principles for members of this group. Luhrmann shows that these practices, like those involved in psychotherapy, are meant to gradually transform our emotional experience. "All of them," she says, "are ways of practicing the experience of feeling loved by God."

Beginners are encouraged to discriminate between their own thoughts and emotions and "God's voice," seen as a deeper, interior presence that requires patience and skill to recognize. The Franciscan monk Richard Rohr describes this skill as "returning to the heart," to find one's deepest center and "to awaken the profoundest depths of our being in the presence of God, the source of our . . . life." To do this, these California evangelicals use intentional practices—such as meditation, prayer, and chanting—that Christian and Buddhist monastics, among others, have honed for over two millennia.

By engaging persistently and intentionally in these practices—that is, interior questioning, talking with God, asking for direction, visualizing Jesus as present and real—a person actually may transform their sense of reality. In the process, Luhrmann says, the presence of God and Jesus often becomes real in the experience of believers, even when doubt recurs. She observes that many Vineyard Christians who persist became capable of maintaining the sense of a personal relationship with God, whom they see as "always there, always listening, always responsive, and always with you."

Luhrmann's research shows that what often impels people to abandon traditional churches ("organized religion"), as I did, is their *passion to find something that resonates experientially as true.* Rather than embracing the empty wind of atheism, many are seeking a sense of meaning, transcendence of self—something that the experientially focused Vineyard offers.

Since the result of such practice effectively "diminishes whatever isolation there is in modern life," she notes that it has enabled many Vineyard members to recover from addiction, abusive relationships, and depression. Above all, she corrects outsiders' assumptions that such converts have simply accepted a set of irrational beliefs. Instead, they have embraced practices that have transformed their perception of themselves and given them the experience of connecting with a divine source.

Concluding her book, Luhrmann speaks from her own experience of exploring such practice: "I do not presume to know ultimate reality . . . through the process of this journey, in my own way, I have come to know God." She writes that, though she doesn't call herself a Christian, her work with the Vineyard has given her an experience of "unconditional love"; although it is hard to understand, "once grasped, it changes whatever else you thought you understood. It changed me."

African Methodist Episcopal Christians of Arkansas also see Jesus as a close friend, but in a radically different situation, with a sharply different tone. Professor James Hal Cone, who founded Black liberation theology, describes how members of his own family's church often picture Jesus as a "man of sorrows . . . and acquainted with grief." Having grown up Black in the small town of Bearden, Arkansas, during the 1950s, Cone reports that when he was a teenager, he was terrified to hear of the lynching of fourteen-year-old Emmett Till. He goes on to tell how, whenever someone in that town was caught and hung on a tree to be lynched, often tortured and burned alive in a bizarrely festival scene, Black Christians would turn to Jesus.

Deprived of any effective path to justice, Cone says, "my people," hearing of such an event, would immediately gather in their local church, grieving, crying, and singing of Jesus—for them, a deeply human yet divinely powerful ally. But instead of envisioning him as the "best friend" with whom they might share coffee, as some Vineyard Christians do, these AME Christians share Jesus's suffering, focusing on his arrest, torture, and unjust death, confident that he would understand the suffering of one of their own, and their own devastating grief.

In such times of crisis, Cone notes, the familiar spiritual song that asks, "Were you there when they crucified my Lord?" bears double meaning: Jesus's crucifixion is superimposed on the persons lynched, many of whom, in their dying moments, have cried out in Jesus's words, *"My God, my God, why have you forsaken me?"* or even *"Father, forgive them . . ."* Members of the congregation hear the pastor passionately preach of how Jesus has shared the worst that they have seen their own people suffer—at least in his first act, in human form. But when God raises him from death, they envision Jesus arising as a triumphant warrior, whose enemies tremble before him. Now the divine Judge and King reigns supreme in heaven: *"Ride on, King Jesus; no man can a-hinder thee!"*

Since acts of violence against Black people still occur, traditionally minded African American Christians continue to draw solace from the deep reservoir of the gospel stories, both in times of rending grief and in times of celebration. As in the Roman

Empire, where many enslaved people and others despised as "the rabble" rejected the traditional Greek and Roman gods to worship instead the humble, suffering Son of God, so, today, marginalized people are often drawn to the crucified Jesus. Then, as now, the passion story lends hope that those who "suffer with him, die with him," and shall be raised with him, earthly suffering ensuring heavenly joy.

These African American rituals follow the earliest form of Christian worship, when Jesus's followers first began to enact his "last supper," gathering for all-night Easter vigils like those sung and danced between Good Friday and Easter morning to the "Round Dance of the Cross." Throughout the following centuries, Christians continued to lament his death and celebrate his resurrection in plainsong chant that they originally developed from synagogue services. Such Holy Week rituals have continued since medieval and Renaissance times, inspiring the choral music of composers from Palestrina and Bach to Mozart and Beethoven, and continuing today in the work of such Christian composers as the Roman Catholic Olivier Messiaen and the Eastern Orthodox Arvo Pärt. Such music, sung in Christian ritual, is a through-line in history, and, like countless others, I've often experienced its power.

Moving now to less familiar regions of the world, let's consider how the Bicolano people, who live in remote villages in the Philippines, meet Jesus. Evangelized by Catholics since the sixteenth century, as the anthropologist Fenella Cannell notes, they focus worship on an image of Jesus they call the Amang Hinulid, or, familiarly, the Ama, whom they, too, often visualize crucified and dying. Like Catholics throughout the world, they revere him, having carved his image from wood in a nearly life-sized reclining statue, painted to look like a mestizo (a mixed-race person)— that is, with pale skin, bony features, and long brown hair, his eyes nearly closed. Beneath the splendid clothes that village women make for him, they see his arms, chest, and legs painted with bloodstains; for he is "Christ taken down from the cross and laid out in death, but not yet buried."

Having created a series of songs in their own language to retell Jesus's passion, these rural Filipino Christians celebrate Holy Week as the primary festival of the year. On Good Friday, after the women bathe the Ama's image, caring for him as for a beloved relative who has died, the men place him in a glass case and carry him from his shrine to the church; crowds follow them, singing and weeping. After keeping vigil all night on Holy Saturday, they carry him back to his shrine as Easter morning dawns.

Noting the focus on Easter ritual, the anthropologist Vicente Rafael suggests that what attracts Bicolanos to Christianity is hope for a glorious afterlife. Unlike traditionally minded Romans, who envisioned that only emperors and heroes would ascend into the heavens after death, Christians democratized heaven. Ever since the apostle Paul first preached, anyone baptized might anticipate being raised to eternal life. That hope has drawn many people to embrace faith in Christ, and still does. The anthropologist Aparecida Vilaça, for example, notes that her adoptive tribal father, Paletó, a leader, holy man, and healer among the indigenous Amazonian Wari, who accepted Christianity as a young man, later decided to "quit God." But when he grew old, realizing that many of his relatives would be in heaven, he "returned to God," hoping "to be resurrected and be near to God."

In the past, many anthropologists dismissed Christianity as if it were nothing but the imperialists' stamp on indigenous traditions, effectively obliterating them. Yet, as Cannell shows, the Bicolano people have chosen to integrate the story of Jesus's passion with ancient Filipino traditions, apparently to make them even more powerful. From ancient times, Bicolano healers sought to counter hostile spirits, sensed as especially dangerous when someone is dying. Now, the afternoon of Good Friday through the night of Holy Saturday, when Jesus dies and descends into the underworld, the healers seek to pacify dangerous spirits with traditional sacrifices and vows of service. Then they banish them by speaking Jesus's name and making the sign of the cross. On Easter morning, when he rises from death, they praise him above all as *Jesus the healer*, who offers healing and health through God's power.

By contrast, converts among the Piro people of the Peruvian Amazon have met Jesus in several other forms. First Catholic missionaries introduced him as the Crucified One and Lord in heaven, who offers eternal life through the sacraments of his church. After some Catholic missionaries were killed by the Piro, others succeeded in baptizing members of the tribe, as did the Adventist missionaries who followed them. But since the 1940s, evangelical Christians from Wycliffe Bible Translators have met with much more success, preaching Jesus as Mark's gospel portrays him—the beloved Son of God who announces "good news for all people": God's kingdom is coming, and soon!

What did this message mean to the Piro people? What it meant to the missionaries was clear: "Bible believing Christians" had founded Wycliffe Bible Translators in 1934 to fulfill what Matthew's gospel describes as Jesus's final command ("Go, and teach all nations, and baptize them . . ." [Matthew 28:19]). But unlike earlier missionaries, whether Catholic or Protestant, members of Wycliffe Bible Translators were the first to learn and speak the Piro language, and to translate the Bible into it, to gain converts for Christ. Seeing these outsiders show respect for their culture as they struggled to learn and speak Piro, many of the local people accepted their invitation.

Within a generation, the Wycliffe group's efforts ignited major change. The Piro credit these new American missionaries with enabling them to "liberate themselves from slavery." Traditionally, their people had lived in the forest, working as debt farmers, virtually enslaved to "white" bosses (primarily those of Spanish and mestizo descent), who despised them as illiterate *"indios,"* effectively less than human. Accepting baptism, though, changed their status; as the anthropologist Peter Gow notes, "Spanish speaking people used the term *cristiano* to mean '*human*,' by contrast with the category '*animal*,' or even '*diablo*,' 'demon.'" Since "the racial hierarchy was mapped onto one of religious faith, white people and mixed blood people were *Christians,* and Indians were *pagans.*" But when members of the Piro people accepted baptism, they began to identify themselves as *cristianos,* that is, as *human,* like "white people."

As the Piro increasingly built homes clustered around the schools, and acquired the powerful skill of literacy in their own indigenous language, as well as Spanish, many celebrated their "new way of thinking and living." Gow suggests that new converts could see Jesus's promise of "*God's kingdom coming*" beginning to take place for real in what they called "*the good world to come.*" In this new world, from around 1950 to 1990, the Piro stopped working for the bosses, and began to live in their own villages, where both children and adults learned to read and write. Beginning in the 1970s, they also developed indigenous networks of commerce and community life that enabled them to negotiate directly with Peruvian government officials, increasing their social and economic power.

No doubt the Piro gained social and financial advantages from conversion, as Gow shows. But, to a remarkable extent, the Piro were also living the "*good news*"—a transformed world that brought them as God's people into their full humanity, and joined them in communion with Christians all over the world.

Even more intriguing to me are reports of how recent converts find Christianity infusing their lives with new meaning. For example, Eva Keller, engaged in fieldwork in two small towns in Madagascar, writes that what attracts converts there is *intellectual excitement*. These new believers, enthusiastic members of Christian Adventist churches, testify that they have met Jesus as *God's Word in human form*—the divine teacher who has opened them to a whole new world.

What surprised me is that the Adventist missionaries there, who accept the literal truth of the Bible, refrain from presenting a single dogmatic perspective. Instead, they encourage new converts to "seek the Scriptures" through intense study, in order to understand its meaning for themselves, questioning what every word and passage might mean. For, although the missionaries present the Bible as an infallible guide to understanding the world's origin, purpose, and destiny, they also explain that its answers are not obvious, and not on the surface. Consequently, as Keller describes it:

> Adventist Bible study is not a matter of the truth being taught by some to others . . . Rather, it is a matter of everyone discovering the truth contained in the Bible for themselves by way of study, reflection, and discussion. The goal . . . is not to establish one correct answer, but rather to open each person's understanding.

Adventists are taught to discard information that directly contradicts the Bible, like the theory of human evolution from apes, but they welcome evidence from their own observation, and from science. Keller notes that new converts eagerly discuss such questions as how different ethnic groups arise, how the solar system has developed, and how the universe is expanding, while choosing to understand these within the context of Biblical views about the beginning and end of time. Since Adventists believe that Satan, active in the world, constantly schemes to hide God's truth, these recent converts also believe that they must carefully discriminate between God's truth and Satan's lies. Among these Madagascar Christians, Keller says, "I found people who, despite their lack of literacy and education, are enthusiastically engaged in study and learning, rather like scientists in search of truth about the world."

Keller's research offers rare insight into the possible effects of missionary work—and into Jesus as *teacher of all wisdom*.

For the Urapmin people of New Guinea, Jesus shines especially as a *teacher of righteousness*. The anthropologist Joel Robbins recognizes that ancient Urapmin traditions have long engaged issues about morality, and that as a result, Urapmin Christians are now "caught between two cultures." Robbins sees many converts seeking to resolve questions of how to live a good life:

> Living with the counterposed paramount values of these two cultures is what troubles them, and makes their experience of cultural change so wrenching, especially since moral transformation is the overriding preoccupation of contemporary Urapmin life.

Beginning around 1950, Urapmin men began to enroll in distant Christian schools, before returning home to teach. These indigenous leaders helped their people integrate into a wider cultural world. But when a charismatic revival broke out in the 1970s, some Christians among them ecstatically announced that the Holy Spirit inspires them directly. From that time, the community no longer needed to depend on the teaching of foreigners. And since then, many others, notably many women, have received the Spirit of Christ, which infuses them with authority to "work the spirit" in states of trance, to receive revelations, and to offer powerful prayers and healing, increasing the respect they have gained within the community.

To the Dalit people of India, long an extremely marginalized group, Jesus comes as a loving and all-powerful friend, much as he had to those who first walked into Christian gatherings in ancient Rome. Like many enslaved early converts, the Dalit traditionally have been shunned by other Indians as "untouchables," literally "outcasts," since they belong to none of the castes that Hindu tradition recognizes as human. The anthropologist Nathaniel Roberts, who lived among them for many years, observed, "All over India, Dalits are stereotyped as lazy, stupid, licentious, dishonest, suitable only for manual labor, unclean, and repulsive." As he traces their history, Roberts notes that twentieth-century Hindu politicians, including Mahatma Gandhi, found it necessary to integrate "untouchables" into the Hindu population only when they were contending with Muslims for a majority. Even more recently, Roberts adds, in order to claim India as a Hindu nation, government leaders finally found it in their interest to include the Dalit people as human, classifying them as Hindu only during the late twentieth century and into the twenty-first.

Not surprisingly, the great majority of Indian Christians are Dalit, attracted to rare groups like Christians who have welcomed them and offered to join them by spiritual power into a worldwide Christian family. Since Matthew's Jesus taught that practicing compassion toward everyone in need is what qualifies a person to enter his heavenly kingdom (Matthew 25:31ff.), the Dalit have embraced his teachings. Within their own communities, in slums throughout India, they traditionally have seen caring for others as a natural impulse, based on the moral responsibility to recognize the common humanity of all. The American writer Isabel Wilkerson, who recently borrowed the term "caste" to characterize the situation of African Americans descended from enslaved people, notes that her people have long shared the same conviction: what it means to be human is to be a person of intrinsic value, regardless of status, ethnicity, or merit.

Like so many others, Dalit Christians find powerful hope in Jesus's suffering. The Christian gospel has challenged them to transform suffering from a passive experience into an active one, to engage it as a meaningful task:

> What slum Christianity [tells] believers [is] that they are not just life's losers, but the "the dear children of God." Slum dwellers' degradation [is] no longer an inexplicable injustice, but a harbinger of their own inevitable triumph, like that of Jesus Christ.

Until that day comes, Dalit converts, like African American Christians, embrace the passion for justice that Israel's prophets proclaim. Although outsiders ridicule them for shouting and "babbling" in church, "speaking in tongues," Roberts notes that many Dalit Christians, previously illiterate, now have bought Bibles, and carefully read every word. Some, like the Madagascar Adventists Keller describes, declare, "Before, we had nothing, we knew nothing . . . Only now we have begun to learn. What is Christ? *Knowledge!*" Here, too, Jesus's message brings inspiration—and education, leading his followers out of servitude and poverty.

Roberts often participated in worship in the slums of India's Anbu Nagar. When he encountered the Bible in that context, he writes, he discovered for the first time "a book that reverberates with the drums of revolutionary justice and the promise of human equality." He reports hearing believers in church shout out verses like these, "as a kind of ecstatic battle cry":

> He who raises the poor and weak from the dust (Ps. 113:7), we praise you! . . . He who rescues the oppressed, and brings down those with haughty glares (Ps. 18:27), we praise you! . . . He who rescues the weak from the hands of the strong (Ps. 35:10), we praise you! . . . He who pursues justice for the poor (Ps. 140:12), we praise you! . . . For these promises, we praise you!

Like many others, the Dalit love the Jesus who promises justice. All of these, of course, are not different "Jesuses." Instead, they are all recognizable refractions from the light of the gospel stories, with overlapping perspectives—"liberationist" Christians countering previous versions that served colonialist agendas.

In our previous chapters, I've been tracing these perspectives using a new approach in religious studies called "reception history," in which we examine how early texts are received and adapted by later writers. We have seen how Mark's earliest written narrative was received and adapted by the writers we call Matthew, Luke, and John. Unlike other scholars in this field, I included several "secret gospels," to show how those who wrote them received what they found in the four narrative gospels and revised them to include new insights. As someone who loves history, I am endlessly intrigued to see how these ancient sources strike new fire.

In this chapter, we have dipped into another new scholarly field, one that, since about 2010, has been called the "anthropology of Christianity." Here I found a way to engage in a different kind of "reception history." Instead of comparing texts and variations, I've been fascinated to see how, in various accounts of new converts, each group seeks to receive and revise "the gospel" for themselves.

But I cannot conclude this exploration of Jesus without mentioning the amazing and marvelous work created by artists, filmmakers, and poets—many of them not converts, and some not even Christian—who draw upon the gospel stories to speak their own truths. What I especially enjoy is that artists are often less concerned to "get Jesus right" than to invite imagination, spiritual insight, sometimes even caricature, and to explore and play with gospel stories, reinventing as they go. Since we cannot begin to review two thousand years of Christian art, let's look briefly at how three twentieth-century painters, working within a few years of one another, chose to picture Jesus.

For the Spanish surrealist painter Salvador Dalí, who was raised Catholic, the crucifixion was an intensely personal story. Born into a Catholic family shortly after the death of his older brother at age two, Dalí was given his brother's name: Salvador ("Savior" in Spanish). Throughout his life, he deeply identified with the Savior for whom both were named, and with his deceased brother: "He was probably the first version of myself, but conceived too much in the absolute." In *Christ of Saint John of the Cross*, painted in 1951, Dalí mingles private family reflections with those of a sixteenth-century Catholic mystic, picturing a perfectly unblemished young Spaniard with light-brown hair, suspended on a cross high above earth, "angelically ascending into heaven," as Dalí imagined his brother, or Christ, may have done. As the psychoanalyst C. G. Jung has noted, many people in Western culture envision Christ as "the symbol of the self," one's spiritual essence.

In contrast to Dalí's identification with Christ, we consider how a Jewish artist powerfully appropriated the image of Jesus's crucifixion, aiming it as a political and moral challenge to Christians. Marc Chagall fled to France as Nazism rose in Germany, after authorities there denounced his painting as "degenerate." From 1938 until the end of the war, Chagall obsessively painted crucifixion scenes—dozens of them—picturing Jesus embodying the entire Jewish people. In his famous *White Crucifixion* of 1938, Jesus's loins are covered with a prayer shawl, a lighted menorah at his feet. Inscribed on the cross above his head is a sign, written in Hebrew, that identifies him as "Jesus of Nazareth, King of the Jews." Above the cross, as if floating in space, are three men and a woman, often interpreted as Abraham, Isaac, Jacob, and Rebekah, one of Israel's matriarchs. Below and behind the crucified Jesus, Chagall pictures European Jewish villages on fire as rabbis carrying Torah scrolls run to protect them, desperate mothers hold their children close, and terrified refugees seek escape.

While reclaiming Jesus's image for his own—and Jesus's—people, Chagall turns it into an indictment *against* Christians, many of whom may have echoed in church Matthew's denunciation of "the whole people" (Gk: *pas ho laos*) of Jews (Matthew 27:25), even shouting it out loud while celebrating Easter.

Chagall's crucifixion paintings deploy bitter irony to show how European people shaped by Christian culture could claim that "the Jews killed Jesus"—while using this counterfactual claim as a pretext for killing Jews.

About thirty years later, the Welsh artist John Petts created another challenging vision of Jesus. Petts designed a stained-glass window for the Sixteenth Street Baptist Church in Birmingham, Alabama, to replace one that was shattered in 1963 by a Ku Klux Klan bomb that killed four young African American girls. Petts replaced the previous image of a "white" Jesus, his face blown out by the bomb, with a Black Jesus, crucified. Below him, he placed a saying of Jesus that here reads not only as a potential blessing but as a warning, alluding to America's history of lynching and echoing the verse from Matthew 25:40: *"Whatever you do to the least of these, you have done to me."* Both Chagall and Petts surely recognized—and intended—that the impact of their work depends on the viewers' awareness of the moral power of Jesus's teaching: that he challenged his followers to abandon hatred.

When filmmakers wade into these deep waters, they, too, can amaze us. In 2006, for example, the filmmaker Mark Dornford-May created a spare, quickly moving drama that masterfully transposed the Jesus story into a contemporary context. Having begun his career in London with the Royal Shakespeare Company, Dornford-May, now a citizen of South Africa, chose to set *Son of Man* in a fictional location called Afrika, Judea, and filmed it near Cape Town.

Son of Man opens as Mark opens his gospel, framing the story with cosmic conflict. The first scene opens onto a desert, where

Jesus, in solitude, ponders his divine mission. Then Satan appears, tempting him to abandon it. Jesus sharply rebukes him, declaring, "This is my world!" Satan, thrown down and rejected but not vanquished, defiantly shouts back, "No, this is *my* world!" Rather than retelling the whole Jesus story, Dornford-May selects a narrative line that enables him to interpret the conflict that nearly tore apart his adopted country, especially during the struggle against apartheid. But, to avoid a simplistic mapping of this conflict onto race, the film engages only black actors, who speak in the South African language Xhosa and in English.

Beginning with brief clips of wartime violence, the film moves to a startling scene of the angel Gabriel's annunciation to Jesus's mother. But instead of the peaceful household setting that Luke pictures, here Mary first appears in a panic, running into a school classroom to escape soldiers on a killing rampage. Only then, after taking a breath of relief, does she suddenly see, to her horror, the corpses of recently slaughtered children stacked around the room. By diving down among them to hide as if dead, she escapes their fate. After the soldiers pass by, Mary, grieving, sees the angel Gabriel, played by a child, announce that she will give birth to the Son of God. Shocked and weeping, she quietly begins to sing the Magnificat as if it were a dirge: "My soul magnifies the Lord . . . for he has seen the lowliness of his servant . . . Henceforth, all nations shall call me blessed."

Soon after this, the mood changes; darkness and light interweave throughout the entire film. As the sun rises, a whole host of child angels joyfully sing of the people united, a theme song for the film, as Gabriel announces "good news of great joy" to boys herding goats in the mountains. Shortly after that, Joseph travels with Mary, now fully pregnant; they arrive in a town and are shown a shed where they can take shelter. The child's birth brings joy to Mary, Joseph, and the goatherds who arrive, offering a goat, and, later, to three kings who arrive on horseback to pay homage to the holy child.

Then, again, violence intervenes. As Matthew's gospel depicts soldiers slaughtering male children, here soldiers tear them from their mothers' arms. Mary, watching from afar with tears running down her cheeks, recognizes that they have come for her child. Next, Jesus appears as an adolescent, preparing for the Xhosa circumcision ceremony, a ritual initiation into manhood, which Dornford-May substitutes for the gospels' baptism scene. When he becomes an adult, the South African Jesus is powerfully aware of his mission: he must fight against Satan. Resolving to do so, he gathers some followers, four of them women, here named with feminine forms of the "twelve disciples'" traditional names, and sets out with his itinerant band.

Now he begins to speak in public, hoping to arouse people in the surrounding villages to defy their country's governing coalition, which consists of ruthless leaders empowered by the world's imperialist regimes. Before starting, Jesus orders his followers to turn over their guns, insisting that their power lies in truth alone: "We cannot kill; we do not need weapons." Now he speaks openly what no one else dares say aloud, about the frequent "disappearances" of those who defy government leaders: "*When you are told that people just disappear, I say you have been lied to!*"

At the same time, he wields divine power, raising a dead man from his coffin and exorcising demons from a possessed girl. Finally, as he is addressing a large crowd, urging them to rise and demand liberty, Judas secretly videotapes his activities, and reports them to the authoritarian rulers, whose leader, "Pilate," spills water on his hands as he tacitly assents to their plot to kill this incendiary preacher: "This has nothing to do with me."

Then, as in the gospels, the story moves quickly toward its inevitable end, as an armed search posse finds Jesus at night. After they seize and torture him to death, the soldiers throw his body into a truck to bury in a remote area—a scene that recalls the death of Steve Biko, a hero of the black South African anti-apartheid movement. Since that inference is unmistakable, how, I wondered, could this film then move toward resurrection? Or would Dornford-May leave that out?

What he did surprised me, and shows how contemporary realities can both resonate with and reshape ancient stories. At the film's conclusion, Jesus's mother, like her son, refuses to capitulate to fear. Instead of allowing him to "disappear," she digs up his body with her bare hands and carries it back to town on her lap, sitting in the back of a truck—a scene that visually echoes Michelangelo's *Pietà*. Next, accompanied by crowds of women, she defies the authorities, raising her son's body to hang on a cross as testimony to the truth of what they had done. Although surrounded by soldiers with raised guns, threatening to shoot, she leads the demonstrators who join her to stand up and defiantly stamp their feet and dance the *toyi-toyi*, as demonstrators did to challenge apartheid, while chanting the Black South African anthem of resistance. Since tyrants rule by instilling terror, the film suggests that people who dare to defy despotic leaders by exposing their lies may finally triumph over evil, and even over death, allowing life to return and flourish.

The film's coda shows Jesus, alive again, running up a hill, followed by a crowd of children dressed as God's angels, as he raises his fist in triumph. And as the credits roll, Dornford-May shows images of a new kind of everyday life in Africa, lived without fear: children in school and others playing games; mothers tending families; young lovers walking, dancing, singing, renewing ordinary life—miraculous resurrection.

Son of Man prominently features women, not only placing them among Jesus's twelve disciples but picturing Jesus's mother, along with her son, as a hero. The 2018 film *Mary Magdalene,* cowritten by Helen Edmundson, goes a step further, focusing on the most intriguing woman in the gospel stories. The New Testament gospels describe her as a woman who followed Jesus from Galilee, and helped support him "out of [her] resources," indicating that she was wealthy. Mark and John both report that she participated in his burial, and was the first to see him resurrected.

Five centuries later, though, Pope Gregory I denigrated Magdalene's image in his Easter sermon of 591 C.E., conflating her with the nameless "sinful woman" who anointed Jesus's feet (Luke 7:36–50). His sermon ignited a false and widespread belief that Mary Magdalene was a prostitute—a rumor that gave painters license to picture her either as seductive and stunningly beautiful, or else as a shamed and ragged penitent. And although Pope Paul VI officially retracted Gregory's denigration of Mary over a thousand years later, in 1969, many Christians still envision her either as seductress and prostitute, as Martin Scorsese does in *The Last Temptation of Christ,* or as a promiscuous "sinful woman," as Dornford-May does in *Son of Man.*

Aware of such stereotypes, the British playwright and film-maker Helen Edmundson challenges them. From the opening scene of a woman diving deep into the sea, her film shifts the focus from Jesus to Mary, portraying her as a woman who refuses to be defined by sexuality or gender. When first seeing the film, I thought, "Her Magdalene acts like a twenty-first-century woman caught in an ancient culture." But since the film invites us to identify with Magdalene, it reminds us that women today still struggle with patriarchal culture, in some parts of the world more than others. Much of the following discussion is owed to Helen Edmundson, who generously agreed to talk with me about how she created her film.

As *Mary Magdalene* shows, acting as an independent person would have been enormously difficult for a rural Jewish woman in first-century Judea. When Magdalene rejects marriage with the older man her family has chosen for her, her father and brother, shocked, then enraged, first accuse her of being demon-possessed, and then nearly drown her while attempting an exorcism. Failing at that, they call in an itinerant healer.

"Your family says you grapple with demons," Jesus of Nazareth says to her. "I wish they were demons," she replies. "What do you fear?" "I fear that I have shamed my family . . . I'm not as I'm supposed to be." "What do you long for?" "I am not sure: to know God." As they talk, he calms her fear, reassuring her, "There are no demons here," and telling her to rest. Simple and clear, such dialogue reveals what the two have in common. He senses, as she does, what it means to feel God's presence; and he, like her, has seemed strange from his youth. His mother later tells Magdalene, "His friends said he had the devil in him," since Jesus, also engaged with the spiritual world, was sometimes seen as deranged, as Mark's gospel shows.

Portraying this similarity between them resonates with me as true. For, whatever else we don't know about Jesus, he was neither conventional nor ordinary, nor were all people drawn to him. As Edmundson pictures the next scene, when Jesus calls fishermen from their nets to follow him, Magdalene defies her family to join them. Her father and brother arrive to seize her and bring her home—just as Mark's gospel describes Jesus's family trying to do to him (Mark 3:20).

As in *Son of Man*, a sense of danger hovers over Jesus. Crosses hung with dead men are seen from a distance; and in a chaotic scene, desperate crowds push and shove to get close to him as he enacts a healing. But Magdalene persists, wading into the river to join the men being baptized. When she arrives to join Jesus's group, Peter scowls, complaining that a woman among them "will divide our community," and warning that "people will judge us," but Judas, younger and more naïve than the others, befriends her.

Sometime later, Mary approaches Jesus when he is alone, telling him what he seems not to realize: "the women were too afraid to be baptized with the men, and they cannot follow you." After that, Edmundson shows Jesus directing his message—the coming Day of the Lord—to a group of women gathered around a well. In Cana, where the gospels set a marriage scene, Edmundson presents a counterpoint: women complaining to Jesus about what marriage often means for them: "We are women; our lives are not our own!" Undeterred, he declares, "Your spirits are your own, as precious as your husbands' . . . You must follow God." Now Mary adopts the role of teacher, baptizing many women and urging them to "awake, for the Day to come!"

When it comes to healings, all three filmmakers recognize that engaging the gospel's power requires openness to miracle. Here, after healing the sick, Jesus raises a dead man, speaking a Hebrew incantation into his ear, then offering a new prayer—the "Lord's Prayer"—for the kingdom's coming, God's will done, "on earth, as in heaven." But what does the kingdom's coming actually mean? Edmundson invites the viewer to experience the disciples' arguments and confusion about when, or how, it might come.

Next she creates an original scene in which Magdalene and Peter are traveling and unexpectedly encounter a cave in which they find people left for dead among many corpses, crying pitiably for water. Although Peter urges her to leave, Mary stops to bring water from a nearby stream to relieve their thirst. Startled, Peter recognizes that Magdalene is acting on Jesus's teaching, which he himself has failed to do.

As Jesus's followers approach the Holy City, Edmundson pictures another chaotic scene, in which none of the disciples knows what might happen next, their hope alternating with terror. As Jesus leads them toward the Jerusalem Temple, Judas, ecstatic, expects that Jesus is about to vanquish all opposition and inaugurate his reign: "It's beginning!" Other disciples share his hope, but with more trepidation, as they struggle to enter Temple court-

yards packed with pilgrims arriving for Passover. When they pass
the stalls of money changers and merchants selling doves, goats,
and lambs for the required sacrifices, Jesus, suddenly frenzied
with the spirit, or with rage, grasps and shakes some pillars, as if to
pull them down. The scene quickly devolves into wild confusion,
as people in the crowd shout, "He's mad!" Then Temple officials
arrive, and armed Roman soldiers advance; Magdalene, terrified,
turns and runs with others into the warren of the Old City's tun-
neled streets, seeking a place to hide.

Later, Judas, shocked and desperate, attacks Jesus for having
failed: "I have seen you heal the sick, raise the dead . . . One word
from you, and the poor, the suffering, the dead, will rise . . . Say
the word, and you will be crowned king!" When Magdalene tries
to quiet him ("Perhaps we have misunderstood"), he turns to
Jesus, pleading, "Tell her she's wrong!" During his final gathering
with his disciples, Magdalene hears Jesus intoning a traditional
Jewish prayer promising that God's "steadfast love is eternal,"
even when what happens is "beyond our understanding."

Edmundson conveys Jesus's torture and crucifixion in extremely
brief and graphic flashes. During the moments that picture him
dying, I silently pleaded with the filmmaker, *Please, no words!*:
pain like that would plunge anyone far beyond the capacity to
speak, much less utter the noble sayings that the gospels insert as
Jesus's last words. To my relief, Edmundson leaves all those words
out, focusing instead on Magdalene's response.

As in a dream sequence, Magdalene dives into the sea, falling
into deep waters. But when dawn returns, she suddenly sees Jesus
as she had during his life, and greets him joyfully. Rejoining the

others, she announces, "As the sun rose, I saw him . . . It wasn't a dream!" When the other disciples scoff at her, saying, "He's gone from us," she insists:

> He's not gone; it's not what we thought . . . *The kingdom is here now . . . It's not something we can see with our eyes; it's within us . . . It grows with us, with every act of love and care* . . . No new world could end oppression, bring justice for the poor. *We have the power to relieve their suffering!*

One of the men turns to respond: "I believe you, Mary . . . It was a sign; he will return. He chose you even before us . . . gave you a special message." But Peter angrily shouts, "Your message is not his . . . You weakened him, Mary; it's your fault that he failed us!" Assuming control of the gathering, Peter scolds and dismisses her: "It's not right that you come to tell us this . . . *Every man in this kingdom has one message.*" Insisting that he alone understands Jesus's message, Peter paraphrases what many Christians today— Catholic, Protestant, Orthodox—agree is the "gospel truth": that "Jesus *had to die,* to save people from sin . . . Now we shall lead them!"

Startled, Mary turns from Peter to plead with the others: "Pray that you see me as I am . . . You are all my brothers, and I love you." But when most turn away, ignoring her, Mary defies them: "I will not stay and be silent: I will be heard!" She rejects Peter's message, and declares again that Jesus's message will come to fruition: "The kingdom is like a seed, and it grows."

In this final scene, as in others, Edmundson takes her cues

not only from the New Testament but also from the Gospel of Thomas and the Gospel of Mary, sources rejected by Roman Catholic authorities and other "orthodox" Christians who insist that Jesus founded "his church" upon Peter ("On this rock I will build my church" [Matthew 16:18]). To this day, virtually all Christian leaders who claim to wield Peter's authority recognize only one interpretation of "the gospel"—*his*, which they make *theirs*. Edmundson also compellingly reimagines the role of women in Christ's legacy. Even though for two thousand years nearly all Christian leaders have succeeded in denying spiritual authority to women, Edmundson champions Mary Magdalene and her understanding of Jesus's message.

Our third film, *The Last Temptation of Christ*, comes from the 1980s. Around that time, when Martin Scorsese was considering making a film about Jesus, he called me to say that he was intrigued by my book *The Gnostic Gospels*, and invited me to talk about it. Knowing his work, I was honored and delighted. Like other artists, he was thinking of a film that would reflect on his own complicated relationship with Christianity. He had long participated in his family's Roman Catholic church in New York's Little Italy, and in the process had met a charismatic and thoughtful priest who encouraged him, at age fifteen, to enter a school that would prepare him for priesthood. Later, he told me, he decided not to proceed: "The movies saved me from the priesthood." But his involvement with rituals and stories of Jesus remains.

At our initial meeting, he spoke of possibly making a film about a Roman senator's son who converts to Christianity, encountering fierce family resistance and facing the danger of joining a persecuted minority. But later, impressed with the clear and vivid storyline in the Greek novelist Nikos Kazantzakis's *Last Temptation of Christ,* he chose to adapt that work. Recently, while reflecting on the Jesus stories for this writing, I was glad to be able to talk with him again, before writing these notes on his film. Like Dornford-May and Edmundson, Scorsese has created one of the most original and powerful adaptations of the gospel stories of our time.

The film opens with text from Kazantzakis's novel, reflecting on his theme:

> The dual substance of Christ—the yearning, so human, so superhuman, of man to attain to God . . . has always been a deep inscrutable mystery to me . . . the incessant, merciless battle between the spirit and the flesh . . . and my soul is the arena where these two armies have clashed and met.

The first scene shows a young man asleep on the ground, thrashing around with disturbing dreams, troubled by visions and voices questioning him, some taunting: "Jesus, who are you?" When Judas pressures him to join other young Jews taking up weapons to fight against Rome, Jesus hears dissonant internal voices saying the opposite: "the Messiah won't come that way"— by war. Terrified that God seems to be demanding something of him, he cries out, "I want Him to stop; I fight Him," but his mother asks, "You are sure it's God? What if it's the devil?"—an ambivalence that weaves through the whole drama.

Next, Jesus ventures into a whorehouse and waits in line for his turn to approach Mary Magdalene, a magnificently sensuous prostitute—not to have sex with her, he insists, but to ask forgiveness for having offended her when they were friends as children. Are his intentions as pure as he claims, or, as she taunts him, is he afraid of being overcome with sexual passion? Nothing is clarified; Kazantzakis's "incessant, merciless battle" continues. Driven into the desert alone, Jesus hears conflicting voices tormenting him: "Who is my God?" "Fear!" "Lucifer is inside me!" Black cobras snake out of his body, softly speaking in Magdalene's voice, then mocking, before Satan appears, first as a serpent, tempting him with love of women and family, and next as a lion, tempting him with power. Finally, in flames of fire, Satan terrifies him by saying what he hardly dares imagine—that he himself is God, "God's only Son."

When he emerges from the desert, Jesus discovers that he has power to heal, to exorcise demons, to stop a mob from killing. He is gentle at first, speaking of love, but then suddenly turns violent, brandishing an ax. Who is this man, torn with inner conflict? Throughout the film, Scorsese creates two compelling visions of Jesus's life—but they are opposites. First he pictures the man who is also God, Jesus Christ, who, after intense struggle, offers his life to atone for human sin. This version of Jesus acts out the ancient view that God requires blood sacrifice, a view that Kazantzakis interprets as spirit battling against flesh—that is, all-powerful divinity pitched against all natural human desire.

The film now reprises the gospel accounts, as Jesus claims his God-given power—even the power to demand that Lazarus return from his grave back to life. When he storms into the Jerusa-

lem Temple, throwing down tables, scattering money, and defying the Temple authorities, he declaims in hyperbolic language
like that found in John's gospel: *"I am the end of the old law—and
when I say 'I,' I say God!"* Here the film suggests that he offends
other Jews by offering access to God to all people: "God belongs
to everyone . . . God is not an Israelite!" At the same time, Jesus
knows that offering such access to God would require a terrible
price: he must die.

Meanwhile, Peter and the others, having arrived in Jerusalem,
anticipate that they are near their goal: to see Jesus triumph over
Rome, and reign as king. But when he enters Jerusalem, hailed
by crowds shouting his praises, Scorsese's scene highlights the
disconnect between their hopes and his secret awareness that
he is approaching his death. Arriving in the Temple courtyard,
Jesus suddenly bursts out again, violently disrupting its order, and
shouting, "God is here!" Suddenly, though, he looks confused,
turning to Judas for help, and barely escapes a second time.

Strikingly, instead of picturing Jesus hunted down to his death,
this film follows the scenario that John's gospel sets out, emphasizing his agency. When his enemies fail to capture him, Jesus
decides to engineer—and choreograph—his own betrayal. In a
powerful and moving scene between the closest of friends, he
entrusts Judas with his "terrible secret," begging him to help make
it happen: "I have to die on the cross . . . We're bringing God and
man together; I am the sacrifice!" After a final supper with his
disciples, when Jesus prays alone at night in Gethsemane, he
is racked with fear and pleads with God to spare him ("I never
asked you to choose me"). But by then it is too late. Arrested,

Jesus stands before a sophisticated, bored, and cynical Pilate, who dismisses him as another half-crazed Jewish nationalist, to be stripped naked, beaten, and mocked, before being forced to carry his own cross to Golgotha.

As Kazantzakis and Scorsese depict it, Jesus is offered the "last temptation" on the cross. An angelic being appears, offering him, as God's will, a reprieve. Suddenly gone from the cross, he is spirited away to a peaceful valley: "Now you can see the world's true beauty. Harmony between the earth and the heart, that is God's world!" Now he sees the young Magdalene approaching him, dressed as a bride, arriving for the marriage he once spurned. After she comforts him, tending his wounds, their mutual joy arouses passion, and she conceives his child. He soon learns, though, that this earthly paradise includes ordinary suffering. When she suddenly dies, he grieves, raging at God, then collapses, devastated, and confesses, "I am ashamed of all the mistakes I've made, the wrong ways I looked for God."

Leading him back to the home of Mary and Martha, his angelic companion encourages him to dispel his grief by starting a new life and a new family. Sometime later, surrounded by the children he has conceived with a new wife, he unexpectedly confronts the apostle Paul, a fanatic preaching about him: "Now I bring the good news to you! . . . His mother was a virgin . . . He suffered for our sins, and three days later he rose again . . . Now the road to God is open to everyone!" Irate, Jesus shouts back: "You're a liar . . . I'm a man like everyone else, the son of Mary and Joseph . . . Don't go around telling lies about me!"

Defying him, Paul attacks: "Do you see these people? They

need the crucified Jesus; I'll tell them what to believe . . . My Jesus is much more important and more powerful than yours!" Repudiating Paul, Jesus turns back to stay with his family. When he is old, his disciples, having heard that he survived and now is dying, appear at the door. "Traitor!" shouts Judas. "Your place was on the cross; you got scared and ran . . . You broke my heart . . . I loved you so much." As Jesus protests ("You don't understand; God sent an angel to save me"), Satan appears in a burst of fire.

Was the angelic vision a diabolical trick? It's far from clear; one can interpret the scene either way. As Scorsese tells it, Jesus suddenly feels that he had been terribly wrong. Taunted by Satan, he cries out to God: "Father, will you listen to me . . . a selfish and unfaithful son? I want to bring salvation . . . pay the price . . . I want to be the Messiah!" Instantly transported back onto the cross, with only seconds having passed, he seems to smile, and speaks the final words that John reports: "*It is accomplished!*" Having triumphed at last, he dies.

The Last Temptation offers, then, two opposing visions of Christian life—one that seeks God by sacrificing "the flesh," the other that embraces the human heart's harmony with nature— each compelling, but pictured as antithetical. And though the final scene suggests that the first wins over the second, it allows the paradox to stand, resonating in the viewer's mind and heart.

Any response to the question of "Who is Jesus today?" that does not mention the countless people who take his teachings and his life as a template for their own would be entirely incomplete. Such people are impossible to enumerate, but we may mention, for example, Jimmy and Rosalynn Carter, who, long after his presidency, were joining crews to hammer nails into new floors for Habitat for Humanity, a Christian service ministry started in 1976 by Millard and Linda Fuller to provide homes for homeless people. We might also look back to Mahatma Gandhi, who, in his correspondence with Leo Tolstoy, agreed that Jesus taught nonviolence, which both strove to practice. After writing his most famous novels, Tolstoy wrote *A Confession,* a short and powerful autobiography recounting his midlife struggle with suicidal depression as he sought to embrace the Russian Orthodox faith, until he found his own spiritual resolution. Later, he wrote several books interpreting Jesus's teachings, including one called *The Kingdom of God Is Within You.*

Martin Luther King Jr., taking cues from both Gandhi and Tolstoy, as well as from his lifelong immersion in the Bible, staked his own life on that principle, and on his faith in Jesus, when preaching his vision of the "beloved community." We might also look to Bishop Desmond Tutu of South Africa, who, in the 1990s, declared that his country would have *No Future Without Forgiveness,* as Jesus taught it, when he initiated the Truth and Reconciliation Commission, and to Pope Francis, who has gone into migrant camps to welcome newly arrived Muslims, and has visited prisoners in jail. He also has offered blessings to those his church previously shunned because of their gender differences.

All of these recognize that Jesus's teaching was radical then, as it is now. I am especially moved by those who recall the themes that Luke says Jesus first preached in Nazareth, quoting words of the prophet Isaiah: "The Spirit of the Lord is upon me, because he has anointed me to bring good news to the poor . . . to proclaim release to the captives, recovery of sight to the blind, to let the oppressed go free, and to proclaim the year of the Lord's favor" (Luke 4:18–19).

Like many others, King often echoed the prophets' demands for justice and mercy: "Let justice roll down like a river, and righteousness as a never-ending stream!" (Amos 5:24). More recently, the Reverend William Barber has taken up King's work, leading the Poor People's Campaign as he advocates for economic justice that would enable marginalized people to thrive.

Such messages often remain relatively undiluted by theological dogma about "the nature of Christ," or "atonement theology." More often than in the past, Christians involved with the gospels today tend to leave aside quarrels about whose church is "right"— as if only one group could encompass the power of the vast collection of traditions, stories, liturgies, prayers, hagiographies that we call "Christianity." For, as the psychologist William James points out, people of different temperaments and cultures incline toward different kinds of religious experience, some resonating with formal "high church" worship, and others with Quaker simplicity, or with Pentecostal openness to inspiration. None of these is prescribed, but none are excluded; and all agree that Christian faith requires practicing justice, mercy, and love.

Conclusion

WHO IS JESUS? And how could his humble life and humiliating death inspire a great religion? Having started with these questions, what have we discovered?

We learned that we cannot consider the gospels as accounts of historical events and that likely none of the gospel writers knew Jesus, despite John's claim that he did. They were followers of Jesus, yes, but in the next generation, or the one after that; and they were writing what they had heard people say, often from memory, along with some of his teachings that others had written down. We have seen, too, that the gospel writers were writing for a purpose—to attract new followers—which shaped what they were likely to say. And they were writing in challenging historical conditions—during wartime, or shortly afterward—when it was dangerous to be known as a follower of Jesus.

Knowing all this, we can speculate that his followers created some of the details of Jesus's life to paper over inconvenient facts: That Jesus wasn't illegitimate; his mother miraculously conceived him through the Holy Spirit. That his body was left on the cross; instead, he rose from the dead, and his followers saw him alive; they ate with him, touched him, and spoke with him for more than a month after he died. That he didn't fail to establish God's kingdom; his kingdom is still to come; he lives in us. These details, some historians say, were the very ones that most electrified their listeners, and helped their numbers grow.

My own experience as a historian has made me cautious. We do not know which episodes were made up, and which might be based on actual or visionary experiences. Furthermore, I have shown that some scenes that sound like invention are written as metaphor.

Besides shaping these stories for their own purposes, we've seen that each of the gospel writers took a different approach. That meant that after Constantine converted to Christianity, church leaders had to launch a huge effort to pull all four gospels together, as if they tell a single story—even if all the wrinkles in that story are not ironed out perfectly flat. That multiplicity lent itself to different interpretations, and may be why, even today, stories of Jesus have vast and varied appeal.

As I reflect on this project, what fascinates me is not only the historical mysteries my book seeks to unravel but the spiritual power that shines through these stories. This passionate, charismatic first-century rabbi interpreted the Genesis creation story that "God created humankind in his image" to mean that every member of the human race has sacred value. Other moral teachers, like Plato, had recommended helping people in need, but only people of one's own status—certainly not indigents, the poor, or people enslaved. And other rabbis of Jesus's time preached, as he did, the Scriptural injunction to "love your neighbor as yourself." But instead of focusing such charity primarily on other Jews in his community, he shocked his listeners by urging them to lend compassion and practical help to anyone who is sick, in prison, or hungry, to a disgraced and ungrateful son, or even to an enemy. Is this what extended his reach so far beyond his own community, and even to ours today? His radical, unprecedented reading of Genesis still resonates through our social and political life as indictment—and inspiration.

We have seen that Jesus is still a powerful presence for people today, including those who infuse the gospel stories with new energy. How does this happen? Exploring the gospels with this question, I've come to see that they follow an intriguing pattern. Starting in a world filled with challenge, oppression, and suffering, their stories shift—often suddenly—into hope.

The episodes Mark tells, for example, begin in a world filled with familiar adversity: someone has a fever, is infected with disease, is paralyzed, is blind, or is deeply distressed. When Jesus's healing power intervenes, the story opens onto miracle: a blind man recovers sight; the ill are healed; even the dead come back to life. When Matthew adds the story of a pregnancy so shocking that even the devout and righteous Joseph nearly breaks his marriage contract, *that* turns out to be a blessing. Finally, every one of these "gospels"—not only those in the New Testament but also the "secret gospels"—ends in the most astonishing reversal of all. After Jesus suffers the worst imaginable fate, betrayed by a trusted friend, abandoned by everyone, falsely accused, tortured, and cruelly executed in public, he is raised to glorious new life, reunited with those who love him, and elevated to receive the highest praise in heaven, to reign over a world renewed in justice and peace.

Hebrew Scriptures set the pattern for such shifts: people enslaved are set free; a shepherd boy named David fells a hostile giant with a slingshot; hungry lions spare Daniel's life; and Jonah emerges alive from the belly of a whale. The point is clear as a lightning flash: "*God can make a way out of no way,*" transforming what we suffer into joy. I love this about the gospel stories. Is that what keeps the stories of Jesus alive amid the twists and turns of history? As I see it, they give us what we often need most: an outburst of hope.

Acknowledgments

As every writer knows, writing is often solitary and far more enjoyable when shared. Recalling that this book culminates decades of research and teaching, I am amazed and grateful that so many colleagues and friends have contributed to the process of completing it.

First, I'm grateful to my students, who never let me forget the questions with which I began and still ask: What makes the New Testament stories of Jesus and those in the secret gospels—all of them short and many of them strange—vividly alive for countless people? How are they so compelling and yet so open-ended that they have invited continual improvisation for more than two thousand years, so that storytellers from Dante and Milton to Dostoyevsky and Borges, as well as filmmakers such as Martin Scorsese and Helen Edmundson, can play them in radically different keys?

Here I can mention only a few of my remarkable teachers, each of whom illuminated those basic sources in a new way: in graduate school, Krister Stendahl, George MacRae, S.J., Arthur McGill, and Gilles Quispel. When I first began teaching at Barnard College, I learned a great deal from Theodore Gaster, the remarkable senior scholar who chaired our department, and from other colleagues and friends then at Barnard: David Sperling, Alan Marilyn Harran, and Joel Brereton.

More recently, since teaching at Princeton University, I am enormously grateful for the collegiality of our department faculty and the members of our working group in *Religions of the Ancient Mediterranean*: John Gager, Martha Himmelfarb, Peter Schaefer, Naphtali Meshel, Moulie Vidas, AnneMarie Luijendijk, Liane Feldman, Yedidah Koren, and Jonathan Henry. Each one has heard or read drafts of this work in progress and offered suggestions that much improved, and often corrected, earlier drafts. Many thanks, too, to Jeff Stout, who, from the day we first met, has always been available to give support and sound advice. I am especially grateful to Jonathan Gold for his willingness to dive into the new humanities course that we invented and created, Jesus and Buddha, and for the adventure of teaching it together! And I've so much enjoyed colleagues in our department, although mentioning only a few: Eric Gregory, Jacqueline Stone, Stephen "Buzzy" Teiser, Michael and Elena Wood, Judith Weisenfeld, Bryan Lowe, Esther "Starry" Shorr, Sandra and George Bermann, Nicole Turner, and Kathryn Crown, and meetings with Seth Perry and Tehseen Thaver as we plotted to induce the administration to allow students to minor in religion. And I am especially grateful to longtime friend Wallace Best, whose steadiness and insight have seen me through challenging moments and whose gift for friendship has given all of us wonderful celebrations!

I've also appreciated the opportunity to work with outstanding students. Besides enjoying the seminars and workshops we've shared, I've learned so much from what each one has discovered, here mentioning only a few: David Frankfurter, Annette Reed, Kirsti Copeland, Lance Jenott, Geoffrey Smith, Philippa Townsend, Eduard Iricinschi, Sarit Kattan, Tony Alimi, Elena Dugan, Ari Lamm, Rebekah Haight, Yitz Landes, and Eliav Grossman.

Scholars at other universities, many of whom are longtime friends and conversation partners, have helped shape the research and writing: Harold Attridge, Bernadette Brooten, Laura Nasrallah, Paula Fredricksen, Jeffrey Kripal, and Elizabeth Clark. Colleagues well known for their contributions to Nag Hammadi scholarship have also become essential collaborators: Karen King, Michael Williams, Louis Painchaud, Einar Thomassen, Antii Marjanen, Ismo Dunderberg, David Brakke, Hugo Lundhaug, Tuomas Rasimus, Ismo Dunderberg, April de Conick, and Nicola Denzey.

Meanwhile, I owe special thanks to two friends and scholars who have seen this work through from start to finish for more than six years. Dale Allison, the Dearborn Professor of New Testament at Princeton Theological Seminary, has generously engaged in many wide-ranging conversations with his characteristic good humor and open-minded approach, neither of which succeeds in hiding how enormously learned he is in his study of the New Testament and its literary and historical contexts. I am also very grateful to Lance Jenott, director of religious studies at Washington University. Even after receiving his PhD from Princeton University with highest honors and achieving international recognition, he has willingly continued to offer indispensable corrections and perspectives on this work and on scholarly articles with which we have collaborated.

Thanks, too, to the members of the Stanford Humanities Center, who invited me to spend a semester there while giving a public lecture on Satan and what I called his "social history"—a topic that surprised us by packing the lecture hall! While there, I learned much from Tanya Luhrmann's anthropological writing, as well as from the issues her research raises. I especially enjoyed the hospitality that she and her husband, Richard Saller, professor of classics, offered during that visit. I am grateful, too, that she also agreed to chair a session of the Cambridge University Seminar, "Science in the Forest, Part IV: Regeneration," in June 2024, in which I presented the fourth chapter of this book for discussion. Now I look forward to comments from other members of that lively and distinguished seminar as we prepare papers from that seminar for publication.

To Deborah Whitehead, chair of the Department of Classics and Religion, and our friend Samuel Boyd, together with their colleagues, who invited me to deliver a lecture at the University of Colorado Boulder during the writing of this book.

To Adele Reinhartz, who invited me to give the McMartin Lecture at the University of Ottawa, when, to my surprise, many hardy faculty and students showed up to hear it, even in a Canadian snowstorm; and for the lovely hospitality we shared with her husband and other colleagues.

Many thanks, too, to the Very Rev. Randolph Hollerith, dean of the Washington National Cathedral, who kindly invited me to speak from the pulpit at the cathedral, even knowing that the result would be a "gnostic sermon" inspired by the Gospel of Truth found at Nag Hammadi; and to Letitia Mills, executive assistant, and Kathy Predergast, director of the Office of the Dean, who kindly arranged that event.

To Sylvia Kaufmann and her remarkable late husband, Richard Kaufmann, who together founded the Interfaith Institute, Grand Rapids, Michigan—who often gather an enthusiastic audience for lectures and dialogue featuring Jewish, Christian, and Muslim speakers—for their kind invitation to speak at the tenth anniversary of the Interfaith Institute in 2024.

To the National Endowment for the Humanities for a grant that allowed for time and research to work on this book. And I am grateful to Judith Weisenfeld, professor and chair of the Department of Religion at Princeton, and Kerry Smith, our department manager, for their help in securing a grant from the university to provide resources to help with final publication details. Mary Kay Bodnar, executive secretary to the department, has managed countless details, resolved dozens of crises, and accomplishes everything she does with great competence and generous good cheer; Florian Fues, who, along with Jeffrey Guest, has rescued me from computer disaster more times than any of us could count; and Michelle Minter, who manages many details of our teaching and arranges festivities for our department.

Acknowledgments

When I first began to think about the topic of this book, discussing it with my agents, John Brockman and Katinka Matson, and their son, Max Brockman, was indispensable as the work began to take shape. Besides the expert advice that they always offer from their outstanding publishing experience, they have seen this book through to its completion, and I am especially grateful for our longtime friendship.

Many thanks to Martin Scorsese for taking the time to meet and talk at length about his film *The Last Temptation of Christ* (1988) and his ongoing interest in the Christian stories. Many thanks, too, to his close collaborator, film editor, and producer Thelma Schoonmaker for her kindness in arranging a screening of his new masterpiece, *Killers of the Flower Moon.* I am very grateful to Helen Edmundson, screenwriter and filmmaker, for graciously agreeing to talk with me about her film *Mary Magdalene* (2018), offering unexpected insights about decisions she made about the script and the characters.

From the time I first met Bill Thomas, publisher and editor in chief of Doubleday, and his close associate Kris Puopolo, vice president and editorial director of nonfiction, to the time of publication, their enthusiasm for the topic of this book has been a great encouragement. From the start, too, Kris, as my editor, has given enormous energy and time to smooth out rough edges, raise questions, while enormously improving the clarity of the writing. Ana Espinoza, assistant editor, has contributed to the work when we were making final decisions on publication details, and Elizabeth Eames expertly sorted out the details for publishing photographic images. Dr. Jolyon Pruszinski, a colleague for many years, has been an essential partner in checking the manuscript and endnotes for accuracy, and collecting the bibliography. Without his expertise and that of the team at Doubleday, the book would not have come together; I send them heartfelt thanks.

In Princeton, the Rev. Paul Jeanes, rector of Trinity Church, has often given the time to talk about issues raised in this book, as well as many others of common concern. And many friends, some of whom are fellow writers, have offered indispensable gifts of friendship and encouragement. Elizabeth Diggs and Emily McCulley, close friends since graduate school, generously read and reread the chapters, raising questions and making suggestions that helped improve them, as have Emily Mann, Gary Mailman, Catherine Mauger, Jane Shapiro, and Eric Motley. I deeply appreciate the members of our New York *sangha,* who have so often shared their wisdom in meetings for meditation: Linda Donn, Barbara Asher, Lisa Schubert, Alexandra Isles, Jeannette Sanger, Flora Biddle, and Noni Pratt.

During summers in Colorado, Timothy Brown was the first who offered to read and comment on earlier drafts of these chapters, noting necessary corrections and suggesting many others to clarify and smooth out academic writing. Many lovely friends have lightened the days with generosity and celebrations of every kind, especially Michael Lipkin, Jody Guralnik, and their wonderful family, Judith Schramm, Richard Carter and Sharon Wells, Daniel and Isa Shaw, John and Janie Bennett, Natasha and Patricia Blanchet, and Timothy and Teresa Brown. Dear friend Barbara Conviser, an artist and photographer, generously offered her time and expertise to take the photograph that appears on this book. And I am very grateful to Diane Morris and Melony Lewis, whose clarity and generosity of spirit have helped so much to think out the issues during our gatherings sparked by questions of what spirituality might mean.

Most personal thanks go to family members for the support and encouragement they often give: to my daughter, Sarah, and her husband, Mark; my son, David; our extended family, Len and Danielle Strickman; my brother, Ralph Hiesey, and his wife, Jane; Alan's daughter, Julia, and her family and son, Orion, and his wife, Ashley.

Deepest gratitude to Alan Trist, my husband and dearest friend. During the writing of this book, he has been my first reader and editor. He has read every page, improving them with notes and corrections, drawing upon a natural reservoir of patience and wit, essential in dealing with frequent computer crises! But as he and our families and friends know well, I am far more grateful for so much else; above all, for the joy he brings to our shared life together.

Notes

ABBREVIATIONS

ANF: *Ante-Nicene Fathers,* texts written before the Council of Nicaea (325 C.E.) by Christian leaders that Catholic Christians revere as "Fathers of the Church"

LCL: *Loeb Classical Library,* series of ancient texts in Greek and Latin with English translations included

NHC: *The Coptic Gnostic Library: A Complete Edition of the Nag Hammadi Codices,* the definitive scholarly edition here published with complete Coptic texts, annotations, and commentary, in five volumes by Brill Press in Leiden, Holland, in 2001

NHL: *The Nag Hammadi Library,* translations of secret gospels and other texts discovered at Nag Hammadi, translated into English and published in one volume in 1977, ed. James M. Robinson

1. THE VIRGIN BIRTH

11 But when I went back: Brown, *The Birth of the Messiah;* Boslooper, *The Virgin Birth;* Schaberg, *The Illegitimacy of Jesus;* Miller, *Born Divine.*

12 The same is true: For discussion that reviews the work of some major interpreters, see Fitzmyer, *The Gospel According to Luke I–IX,* 3–34; Luz, *Matthew 1–7,* 1–131.

12 "virgin birth": For examples of miraculous birth in Greek and Roman sources, see Cartlidge and Dungan, *Documents and Images for the Study of the Gospels,* 133–39; Brown, *Birth of the Messiah,* 564–70; also Miller, *Born Divine.*

15   Roman Catholic scholar: Brown, *Birth of the Messiah,* 169.

15   silver coin honoring Julius Caesar: Ibid., 170.

15   Kepler sighted a conjunction: See Brown's discussion of the star, and other heavenly portents, in ibid., 170–73, 189–90.

16   Matthew assimilated into his narrative: Ibid., 186–87.

16   searched in vain: Ibid., 188–89.

17   he had previously executed: Josephus, *Jewish Antiquities,* 15.7, 16.1.

17   Instead, here again: Brown, *Birth of the Messiah,* 214–19.

17   As for the third event: Ibid., 396.

17   This similarity between their gospels: Ibid., 189–90.

18   He suggests instead that Matthew: Ibid., 111–12.

20   Mark reports that: Emphasis added.

20   As Mark tells it: Emphasis added.

20   "Where did this man": Emphasis added.

21   Hearing the tale: Meier, *A Marginal Jew,* 1.226ff.

21   As he revises Mark's story: Emphasis added.

21   Luke, too: Emphasis added.

21   Finally, John: Emphasis added.

22   "These facts make it probable": Smith, *Jesus the Magician,* 26.

22   "he would have been a ridiculed child": Ibid., 26–27.

22   "There is a psychological": Flusser, *Jesus,* 20.

23   *"Anyone who comes to me"*: Emphasis added.

23   *"Whoever loves father"*: Emphasis added.

23   the distinguished Rabbi Eliezer: Smith, *Jesus the Magician,* 46.

24   Jesus had learned magic: Ibid., 47.

24   "Jesus ben Pantera": Ibid., 48; Schäfer, *Jesus in the Talmud;* also "Jesus' Origin, Birth and Childhood According to the Toledot Yeshu and the Talmud," 139–61. See also Zeichmann, "Jesus 'ben Pantera': An Epigraphic and Military-Historical Note," commenting on a wide rage of views and concluding that this soldier is unlikely to be Jesus's father.

24   *On the True Doctrine:* The Greek title (transcribed as *ho alethes logos)* also could be translated as "On the True Word."

25   "Let us imagine": Celsus, *On the True Doctrine,* trans. Hoffman, 57; excerpt drawn from *Origen: Contra Celsum,* vol. I, pp. 28–32. Emphasis added.

26   Luke, assumed to be: See, for example, Townsend, "Who Were the First Christians?," 212–30.

26   a hostile polemic: Schaberg, *Illegitimacy of Jesus.*

27   Reaction to Boslooper's book: See Fuller, "*The Virgin Birth.* By Thomas Boslooper," 254–55.

27   Furthermore, as many historians: See notes in Brown, *Birth of the Messiah,* 123–24.

27   "Many think that the difference": Ibid., 124; Josephus, *The Jewish War,* 17.11.2; Isaac, citing a third-century ruling of R. Judah Nesi'ah, noting that Jewish women captured by soldiers were assumed to have been raped, *The Limits of Empire,* 86.

29   In the fighting that followed: Josephus, *The Jewish War,* 1.32–2.1.

29   "The whole district": Josephus, *The Jewish War,* 2.5.1 (Thackeray, LCL 203:349).

30   "They make a desert": Tacitus, *Agricola,* 32 (Hutton, LCL 35:81).

30   Roman commanders often chose: Josephus, *The Jewish War,* 2.5.

31   "had often been disorderly": Josephus, *Jewish Antiquities,* 17.10.10 (Marcus, LCL 410:305).

31   "Many young people": Marianne Sawicki, *Crossing Galilee,* 192. See the entire chapter for her full discussion of what this would mean for how Jesus would have been treated by his family and neighbors in Nazareth.

32   Jewish sources that speak of rape: Isaac, *The Limits of Empire,* 85–86.

32   "cohort of archers": Deissmann, *Light from the Ancient East,* 73–74, made this inference, apparently assuming that this cohort was among the auxiliary troops that Varus brought into Judea c. 4 B.C.E., and later transferred to Germany c. 7–9. Zeichmann challenges such assumptions: "Though we cannot say precisely where (cohors I sag) was at the time of Jesus' conception, it largely remained in Germany 9–69 C.E.," "Military Forces in Judea 6–30 C.E.: The *Status Quaestionis* and Relevance for New Testament Studies," 149. See also Zeichmann, "Jesus 'ben Pantera,'" 141–55. On treatment of this tradition in the Talmud, see Schäfer, *Jesus in the Talmud,* 15–24, and Schäfer, "Jesus' Origin, Birth and Childhood According to the Toledot Yeshu and the Talmud," 139–61. Tentea's study of Syrian units among the Roman military agrees with Zeichmann that evidence of the cohort's early movements is lacking, *Ex Oriente ad Danubium,* 59–63.

33   Jesus's biological father: Tabor, *The Jesus Dynasty,* 63–70.

34   only thirteen generations: Brown, *Birth of the Messiah,* 69–70, 74–80.

35   liable to the death penalty: Ibid., 137; Schaberg, *Illegitimacy of Jesus,* 91–101.

37   He even declares: For the full story, see Genesis 38:1–26.

37   And when they realize: Joshua 2–6.

Notes

37   He agrees, legitimizing: Ruth 1–4.

38   Even after that, David: 2 Samuel 11:1–26.

38   Before mentioning: Brown, *Birth of the Messiah,* 71–77; Schaberg, *Illegitimacy of Jesus,* chap. 2.

39   Breaking the conventional pattern: Emphasis added.

40   *"The Lord himself"*: Emphasis added.

40   "he left her unmolested": Diogenes Laertius, *Lives of Eminent Philosophers,* 3 (Hicks, LCL 184:277–79).

40   "dreamed . . . that a thunder-bolt": Plutarch, *Lives,* Alexander, 2.1–3.1 (Perrin, LCL 99:227–29).

41   "a serpent glided up": Suetonius, *Lives of the Caesars,* II.94.4 (Rolfe, LCL 31:287–89).

41   just myths invented: Here paraphrasing Justin, *Apol.* 1.55ff.

41   Most likely, Trypho: Justin, *Dialogue with Trypho,* 67.

42   About ten years after: *Origen: Contra Celsum,* 1.34. For discussion, see Brown, *Birth of the Messiah,* 145–49.

42   Yet many who share: For one, Meier (*A Marginal Jew,* 1.1) states that his "method follows a simple rule: it prescinds from what Christian faith or later Church teaching says about Jesus, without either affirming or denying such claims," and he runs through an impressive list of Catholic theologians who have treated the virgin birth in terms not dictated by Catholic doctrine (222, 244–45 n. 76).

43   "a theological statement": Brown, *Birth of the Messiah,* 529.

45   Then, surprisingly, the Lord: See Stephen J. Patterson's discussions of Jesus pictured as a "hero" in *Beyond the Passion.*

47   "[Mary] had been violated": Schaberg, *Illegitimacy of Jesus,* 95–101.

48   Instead, like Matthew: Emphasis added.

49   "Why were you looking": Emphasis added.

50   "And a voice came": Emphasis added.

51   *"John, John, why"*: Apocryphon [*Secret Revelation*] *of John* II 2,1–14. Emphasis added. *NHL,* 105.

51   "into the Father": *Gospel of Truth* I 24,7–9. *NHL,* 43.

52   he was "born again": Gospel of Philip II 61, 30. So, Philip adds, when you come to be baptized in water and anointed with oil, "do not seek only to become a Christian, but a Christ" (Greek *chrestos,* "anointed one")—that is, not merely *named after* Jesus ("*Christianos*" in Greek) but, like Jesus himself, spiritually reborn.

2. WHO IS JESUS?

53 "This is the good news": Mark 1:1. Emphasis added.

54 This ancient ceremony: See Meier, *A Marginal Jew*, 1.218–19; Fredriksen, *Jesus of Nazareth*, 119–49.

54 Plutarch's biography: Plutarch, *Lives*.

55 African American Christians: Cullen, *The Black Christ and Other Poems*.

56 "what Andrew or Peter": Papias, as preserved in Eusebius, *Ecclesiastical History*, III.39.1 (Lake, LCL 153:293).

56 The writer we call Mark: Allison, *Constructing Jesus*, passim; Koester, *Ancient Christian Gospels*, 220–30.

56 as cognitive psychologists suggest: Dale Allison makes this point in *Constructing Jesus*, 423–24, citing psychiatric studies of bereavement including Gibson, *Order from Chaos*, 63; Littlewood, *Aspects of Grief*, 46; and Rynearson, *Retelling Violent Death*, ix, x, xiv.

58 "turned him into": 1 Samuel 10:6–12.

59 *"What do you have to do"*: Emphasis added.

59 *"What is this?"*: Emphasis added.

60 All the gospel writers agree: On the need for medical help—and the lack of it, for most people in the ancient world—see Smith, *Jesus the Magician*, 8ff.

61 "Whenever the unclean": Emphasis added.

62 *"To you is given"*: Emphasis added.

62 *"Let anyone with ears"*: Emphasis added.

62 "He did not speak": Emphasis added.

63 *"Who then is this"*: Emphasis added.

63 *"Son of the Most High God"*: Emphasis added.

63 "It was thought that demons": Smith, *Jesus the Magician*, 84.

63 *"Send us into the swine"*: Emphasis added.

66 Later in his life: Flavius Philostratus, *The Life of Apollonius of Tyana*.

66 "There was a girl": Ibid., IV.45.1 (Jones, LCL 16:419).

66 Hanina ben Dosa: Vermes, *Jesus the Jew*, 72–76.

66 Even the respected: Tacitus, *Histories*, 4.81.

67 Anyone familiar with magical: See, e.g., Betz, *The Greek Magical Papyri in Translation Including the Demotic Spells*; Meyer et al., eds., *Ancient Christian Magic*; Naveh and Shaked, *Amulets and Magic Bowls*; Naveh and Shaked, *Magic Spells and Formulae*.

Notes

68   "fits the psychological facts": Smith, *Jesus the Magician*, 16.

68   the placebo effect: Davies, *Jesus the Healer*. See also Harrington, *The Placebo Effect*.

69   "I presume that Jesus": Crossan, *Jesus: A Revolutionary Biography*, 82.

70   In 1879, she founded: Eddy, *Science and Health with Key to the Scriptures*, 3.

70   "resulted from the sudden": Smith, *Jesus the Magician*, 10–11.

71   "Whatever else": Allison, *Constructing Jesus*, 92.

73   Jews regarded Fretensis's banner: See Dabrowa, *Legio X Fretensis*; Weksler-Bdolah, "The Camp of the Legion X Fretensis," 19–50; Marcus, *Mark 1–8*, 351–52; Ginzberg, *The Legends of the Jews*, 5.294.

73   Forced to submit: Eusebius, *Chron.* Hadr. XX, cited in Smallwood, *The Jews Under Roman Rule*, 457–58 n. 116.

74   When, to their astonishment: See the discussion by Levenson, *Creation and the Persistence of Evil*.

76   "The vision of Christ": Blake, *The Everlasting Gospel and Other Poems*.

77   *"This is the good news"*: Emphasis added.

77   *"Don't tell anyone!"*: Emphasis added.

77   "The *Son of Man* must": Emphasis added.

77   "a human being": Sanders, *The Historical Figure of Jesus*, 246–48, describes the various meanings that "Son of Man" (Aramaic: *bar-adam*) can have in the literature of this time.

79   *"May no one ever"*: Emphasis added.

80   "curse miracle": Meier, *A Marginal Jew*, 2.876–80.

80   "completely senseless cursing": Quoted in Schweitzer, *The Psychiatric Study of Jesus*, 38.

80   "Everything we know": Quoted in ibid., 40.

80   Noting that John's gospel: Ibid., 42.

80   "religious paranoia": Quoted in ibid.

81   *"I found Israel"*: Emphasis added.

82   *"By what authority"*: Emphasis added.

82   Instead, she suggests: Fredriksen, *Jesus of Nazareth*, 207–13, 225–34.

83   *"Yes, I am"*: Emphasis added.

83   *"the secret of the kingdom"*: Emphasis added.

3. WHAT IS THE "GOOD NEWS"?

86   "asked him privately": Emphasis added.

87   As Mark tells it: Emphasis added.

89   Meanwhile, outsiders: E.g., The *Apocryphon of John*, II 1.5–17.

89   "the future church": He describes the initial appearance of this fundamentally compensatory idea in the early church (Reimarus, *Fragments from Reimarus*, 50–51), which later theologians further embellished.

90   "people would flock": Albert Schweitzer summarizes Reimarus's position here in *The Quest of the Historical Jesus*, 19.

90   "the people in Jerusalem": Reimarus, paraphrased in ibid.

91   *"My God"*: Emphasis added.

91   Two years later: See Leyden, "5 Years After Death, Messiah Question Divides Lubavitchers"; Gonzalez, "Lubavitchers Learn to Sustain Themselves Without the Rebbe"; and the various accounts and explanations of the phenomena included in Allison, *Constructing Jesus*, 57 n. 113.

92   Furthermore, since the movement: Wodziński, *Historical Atlas of Hasidism*, 192–96.

92   by no means the only one: Allison, *Constructing Jesus*, 143–53; Landes, "On Owls, Roosters, and Apocalyptic Time," 49–69. On the death of Charles Russell and the survival of Jehovah's Witnesses, see Penton, *Apocalypse Delayed*. On the reinterpretation of prophecies by his followers after the death of Muhammad Ahmad, see Holt, "Islamic Millenarianism and the Fulfillment of Prophecy," 335–48.

94   "lit a fire": Justin, *Dialogue with Trypho*, 8.1.

94   "bursting with power": Ibid., 8.2.

94   "deny Christ": "Acts of Justin and His Companions," in H. Musurillo, ed., *Acts of the Christian Martyrs*, 42–61.

96   "the most pestilential": His invective (delivered orally at a meeting of the Church Pastoral Aid Society and recorded in his diary of May 12, 1866) was aimed at a different, and somewhat later book, *Ecce Homo*, which sought similarly to examine Jesus's life using critical tools, but his response is indicative of the general tenor of reception of Strauss's critical approach in English church circles of the time.

96   Read this way: The idea as summarized by Howard Clark Kee, *Jesus in History*, 9, quoted in Schweitzer, *The Quest of the Historical Jesus*, 84.

96   What gives ongoing meaning: See, for example, Frank Kermode's incisive analysis of gospel writing in *The Sense of an Ending*.

98   So, he declares: Emphasis added.

98   "You have heard": Emphasis added.

99   Aren't these teachings: Fredriksen, *Jesus of Nazareth,* 110.

99   *"Be perfect"*: Emphasis added.

101   *"What you give"*: Emphasis added.

101   *"and the measure you give"*: Emphasis added.

104   *"Whatever you did"*: Emphasis added.

105   *"Today* this [good news]": Emphasis added.

105   *"for the kingdom of God"*: Emphasis added.

105   Rather than expecting: Borg, *Jesus: Uncovering the Life,* 258.

106   *"today* you shall be with me": Emphasis added.

106   this very ambiguity: Kermode, *The Sense of an Ending,* 162–63.

107   He often seeks: See the classic account of this phenomenon in Leon Festinger et al., *When Prophecy Fails.*

107   Each of these goes beyond: For discussion of the reasons for calling them "dueling gospels," see Pagels, *Beyond Belief,* especially chapter two.

107   "These are the secret sayings": *NHL,* 126.

107   *"the secret of the kingdom"*: Emphasis added.

108   "If those who lead you": Emphasis added. *NHL,* 126.

109   *"If you bring forth"*: Emphasis added. Cf. *NHL,* 134.

109   Having discussed: See Pagels, *The Gnostic Gospels;* Pagels, *Beyond Belief.* See also Quispel, *Het Evangelie van Thomas;* Quispel, *Gnostica, Judaica, Catholica;* Koester, *Ancient Christian Gospels,* 75–172; Gathercole, *The Gospel of Thomas;* Dunderberg, *The Beloved Disciple in Conflict?*

109   So there's still much: See, for example, Gathercole, *The Composition of the Gospel of Thomas;* Marjanen, "Is Thomas a Gnostic Gospel?"; Patterson, *The Gospel of Thomas and Christian Origins.*

110   "It is I who am": *NHL,* 135.

111   *"There is light within"*: *NHL,* 129. Emphasis added.

111   "If they ask": Cf. *NHL,* 132.

111   "the kingdom [of God] is inside": *NHL,* 126.

112   *"will become like me"*: Emphasis added.

112   "Say, then, from the heart": *NHL,* 47.

113   "His disciples said to him": *NHL,* 138.

114   *"see the kingdom of God"*: Emphasis added.

114   He actually has Jesus declare: Emphasis added.

114   *"I AM"*: Emphasis added.

115   *"The Father and I are one"*: Emphasis added.

115   *"only begotten Son"*: Emphasis added.

115   *"God so loved"*: Emphasis added.

115   The line that follows: Emphasis added.

115   *"My kingdom is not"*: Emphasis added.

116   *"God from God"*: Emphasis added.

116   Having struggled to understand: Pagels, *The Johannine Gospel in Gnostic Exegesis;* Pagels, "Exegesis of Genesis 1 in the Gospels of Thomas and John," 477–96; and, in more accessible language, Pagels, *Beyond Belief,* 30–73.

4. THE CRUCIFIXION

119   *"I will not drink wine"*: Emphasis added.

120   *"I shall strike the shepherd"*: Emphasis added.

121   Charged with making threats: Emphasis added.

122   "Ironic though it be": Brandon, *Jesus and the Zealots,* 1. Emphasis added.

122   "despicable death": Tacitus, *Annals,* 15:44; *Hist.,* II, 72.

122   Jewish historian Josephus: Josephus, *Jewish Antiquities,* 18.3.3.

122   "This, they insist": Justin, 1 *Apol.,* 13.

123   "most horrible": Cicero, *In Verrem,* 2.5.166.

123   "a billboard": A "broadcast" of a "zero-tolerance policy," as Fredriksen describes it in *Jesus of Nazareth,* 150.

123   Jesus's followers, shocked: Samuelsson, *Crucifixion in Antiquity;* Chapman, *Ancient Jewish and Christian Perceptions of Crucifixion;* Hengel, *Crucifixion in the Ancient World and the Folly of the Message of the Cross;* Hewitt, "The Use of Nails in the Crucifixion," 29–45; Smith, "An Autopsy of an Autopsy," 3–6, 14–15; Zugibe, "Two Questions About Crucifixion," 34–43.

125   Furthermore, in cases: For discussion, see Paul Winter's classic study, *On the Trial of Jesus.*

125   In an influential article: Millar, "Reflections on the Trials of Jesus," 355–81.

126   Pointing out that the gospel writers: Crossan, *The Historical Jesus,* 367–94.

126   "it makes . . . historical sense": Allison, *Constructing Jesus,* 391.

126   "people in all cultures": Ibid., 423.

126   *"Further, memories"*: Here Allison (ibid., 423) quotes Parkes, *Bereavement,* 40.

See Allison, *Constructing Jesus,* 423–27, for an extensive bibliography on this subject.

126   "eclipses the retelling": Rynearson, *Retelling Violent Death,* ix, x, as quoted in Allison, *Constructing Jesus,* 424.

126   When Mark set out to write: Koester, *Ancient Christian Gospels,* 288–89; Allison, *Constructing Jesus,* 403–5.

127   the troubles in Judea: Fredriksen, *Jesus of Nazareth,* 12–17. See also Koester, *Ancient Christian Gospels,* 288–89; Allison, *Constructing Jesus,* 403–5; Pagels, *The Origin of Satan,* 7–8.

129   "You have been deceived": As reconstructed from portions of Origen's *Contra Celsum,* 2.9–44, by Hoffmann in his translation of Celsus, *On the True Doctrine,* 60–66. Emphasis added. See also discussion by Niehoff, "A Jewish Critique of Christianity from Second-Century Alexandria," 151–75.

130   "Jesus prayed the Psalms": Richard B. Hays, "Christ Prays the Psalms: Paul's Use of an Early Christian Exegetical Convention," in *The Future of Christology,* ed. Abraham J. Malherbe and Wayne A. Meeks (Minneapolis: Fortress Press, 1993), 122–36.

130   "Many devout Jews": Hays, "Christ Prays the Psalms," 108. Emphasis added.

130   Instead, he replaces it: Emphasis added.

131   *"My own familiar friend"*: Emphasis added.

131   "one of the twelve": Emphasis added.

131   John's gospel takes this: Emphasis added.

131   Both Mark and Luke: Emphasis added.

132   One phrase of the original: See Roberts, "A New Root for an Old Crux, Ps. XXII 17c," 247–52; Barré, "The Crux of Psalm 22:17c," 287–306. Christian translators likely assumed *ka'aru* was intended to be *karu,* the perfect tense of *karah,* "to dig," which we assume was understood to being closer to "pierced" than any other likely options. Justin relies on this translation rhetorically in *Dialogue with Trypho,* 32, 97–98, 104.

133   *"Do you not know"*: Emphasis added.

135   *"The whole people"*: Emphasis added.

135   *"handed him over"*: Emphasis added.

136   *"I find no basis"*: Emphasis added.

136   *"I have not found this man guilty"*: Emphasis added.

136   *"no basis for the death sentence"*: Emphasis added.

137   "We, here, are condemned": Emphasis added.

137   *"Certainly this man"*: Emphasis added.

137   Even Josephus: E.g., Josephus, *The Jewish War,* 2.9.2–4.

138   "inflexible, stubborn, and cruel": Philo, *Embassy to Gaius,* 38 (Colson, LCL 379:151–53). Emphasis added.

139   "[For] those who are converted": Tacitus, *Hist.,* 5.5 (Moore, LCL 249:183). See also Tertullian, *Apology,* 10.

139   "regard as profane": Tacitus, *Hist.,* 5.4 (Moore, LCL 249:179).

139   To deflect such danger: Josephus, *Jewish Antiquities,* 18.3.3; Millar, "Reflections on the Trials of Jesus."

140   "The stern Pilate": Winter, *On the Trial of Jesus,* 88.

140   as I've shown elsewhere: Pagels, *Origin of Satan,* 63–111.

140   "sentenced to hell": Saldarini, *Matthew's Christian Jewish Community,* 44–67.

141   *"What shall I say"*: Emphasis added.

142   *"I told you that I am he"*: Emphasis added.

143   *"The one who handed me over"*: Emphasis added.

143   He despises Jesus: Celsus quoted in Chadwick, trans., *Origen: Contra Celsum,* II.15, p. 81.

144   "prophecies could be applied": Celsus quoted in ibid., II.28, p. 91.

144   "does he utter loud laments": Celsus quoted in ibid., II.24, p. 88.

144   "alter the original text": Celsus quoted in ibid., II.27, p. 90.

144   "secret society": Celsus quoted in ibid., VIII.17, 20, pp. 464, 466.

144   "whose members huddle": Celsus, *On the True Doctrine,* Hoffman, trans., 53.

144   "the death penalty that hangs": Celsus quoted in Chadwick, trans., *Origen: Contra Celsum,* I.3, p. 8.

146   "Christian prejudices": Barnes, *Constantine and Eusebius,* 252.

146   "Satan worshippers." For discussion see Livingstone, *Adam's Anestors,* 19.

146   African American Christians actually endorsed: see Johnson, *The Myth of Ham in Nineteenth-Century American Christianity.*

147   This question, so often: Frankl, *Man's Search for Meaning,* 137.

149   *"died for our sins"*: Emphasis added.

149   "On the night": Emphasis added.

149   *"Behold—the Lamb"*: Emphasis added.

151   a mystical song: *Acts of John,* 94–96, in Schaferdiek, trans., *New Testament Apocrypha,* 2.181–84.

154   Although it was startlingly different: See Schaferdiek's introduction to ibid., *II,* 152–212.

154   "the eucharist is Jesus": *NHL,* 148.

154   *"the one who extends himself"*: Emphasis added.

155   "the cup . . . contains": *NHL,* 154.

155   On the contrary: *Ibid.*

155   The Gospel of Truth: See Pagels, "How the Gospel of Truth Depicts Paul's Secret Teaching," 99–112.

155   *"the true gospel"*: Emphasis added. *NHL,* 40.

156   "the hidden mystery": *NHL,* 40.

156   "show . . . [us] a way": *NHL,* 40–41.

156   "into the Father": *NHL,* 43.

157   "since he knows": *NHL,* 41.

5. RESURRECTION

161   "primary puzzle": Allison, *Resurrecting Jesus,* 200.

162   "Orthodox, Roman Catholic": Ibid., 199.

163   Or were some reports: To note only a few of these perspectives: Pannenberg, *Jesus—God and Man;* also his public lecture at Harvard University, 1968; Lüdemann, *The Resurrection of Jesus;* Lüdemann, *What Really Happened to Jesus.* See also the comments by Sanders in *The Historical Figure of Jesus,* chap. 17, "Epilogue: The Resurrection," 276–81.

163   Yet some people say: Wright, *The Resurrection of the Son of God.*

165   *"seen Jesus our Lord"*: Emphasis added.

167   "something deeply mysterious": Segal, *Paul the Convert,* 134, xii.

167   *"anyone in Christ"*: Emphasis added.

167   *"I died . . . so that"*: Emphasis added.

167   "once at a crash": Hopkins, "The Wreck of the Deutschland."

168   *"Do you not know"*: Emphasis added.

168   And when this happens: Paul, Galatians 1:13–14; note the prayer ("Birkhot Hashahar") incumbent on Orthodox Jewish men to this day: "I thank G—d that thou hast not made me a Gentile, a slave, or a woman."

168   "You are all children": Emphasis added.

169   "our preaching is empty": Emphasis added.

170   *"What is sown"*: Emphasis added.

170   *"flesh and blood cannot inherit"*: Emphasis added.

171   *"this perishable body"*: Emphasis added.

171   "I want you to know": Emphasis added.

172   Suspicious or not: See Koester, *Ancient Christian Gospels,* 6–7, 52; Allison, *Resurrecting Jesus,* 233–38.

173   *"I am the least"*: Emphasis added.

173   What Mark *does* include: Allison notes some of the later commentators who have argued that Jesus's disciples stole his body and faked the resurrection, such as Thomas Woolston (c. 1667–1733) and Reimarus (1694–1768) (*Resurrecting Jesus,* 207–8).

174   We noted earlier: See Kermode, *The Sense of an Ending,* passim. Matthew D. C. Larsen, in *Gospels Before the Book,* takes a different view, arguing that some of the earliest readers of Mark's narrative assumed that it was unfinished, and consequently added endings they considered more appropriate.

174   *"with fear and great joy"*: Emphasis added.

174   *"took hold of his feet"*: Emphasis added.

174   Since ghosts often are assumed: Allison, *Resurrecting Jesus,* 278.

175   "Blessed are you": The second blessing of the Amidah as cited in Allison, *The Resurrection of Jesus: Apologetics, Polemics, History,* 26.

175   "The earth shook": Emphasis added. Cf. Zechariah 14:4.

176   "Jesus' body most likely": Spong, *Resurrection: Myth or Reality?,* 225–26.

177   "Roman crucifixion was state terrorism": Crossan, *Jesus: A Revolutionary Biography,* 127.

177   As evidence, Crossan points out: Ibid., 124–27.

177   "many prisoners who had been crucified": Josephus, *The Life, Against Apion,* 75 (Thackeray, LCL 186:155).

178   As I've discussed in detail elsewhere: Pagels, *The Gnostic Gospels,* chap. three, 48–69.

178   *"Am I not an apostle"*: Emphasis added.

178   Recognizing this, several historians: See Allison's demonstration of how the other gospel writers make this inference, *Resurrecting Jesus,* 250–52.

179   Jewish law of the time: For discussion and details, see the excellent book by Kraemer, *Unreliable Witnesses.*

179   "Did he, then, speak": King, trans., *The Gospel of Mary of Magdala,* 17. Cf. King et al., eds., "The Gospel of Mary (BG 8502,1)," in *NHL,* 523–27.

180   "the Lord *has risen*": Emphasis added.

180   "visionary stories": Dodd, "The Appearances of the Risen Christ," 9–35.

181   when Mary Magdalene: Emphasis added.

182   Dodd contrasts these: Dodd, "The Appearances of the Risen Christ."

183   *"I will not believe"*: Emphasis added.

183   *"Put your finger here"*: Emphasis added.

183   *"those who have not seen"*: Emphasis added.

184   "when Jesus' followers learned": Allison, *Resurrection of Jesus: Apologetics, Criticism, History,* 11.

185   "our beloved brother Paul": Emphasis added.

186   "the disciples of Valentinus": Irenaeus, *Adversus Haereses,* I, pref., 2.

187   "deny the salvation": Here citing the *Ante-Nicene Fathers* translation by Roberts and Rambaut.

187   "Just as a grain of wheat": *Adversus Haereses,* V.2.3.

187   To explain this: Ibid., IV.18.5.

189   *"Let those persons who blaspheme"*: Emphasis added.

189   And when that day comes: Justin Martyr expresses a similar hope for Christ's thousand-year reign on earth in *Dialogue with Trypho,* 80.

189   "Among other [truths] proclaimed": Emphasis added.

191   "new Christian society": Rousseau, *Pachomius.*

191   "My Redeemer . . . I am yours": *"Prayer of the Apostle Paul,"* NHC I,1 A.1—B.10 (my own translation).

192   he urges them instead: *The Apocryphon of James,* NHC I,2.

192   the Gospel of Truth: Elaine Pagels, "How the Gospel of Truth Depicts Paul's Secret Teaching," 99–112.

192   "let's talk about it": "The Letter (or Treatise) on Resurrection," NHC I,4 43.25–44.12.

193   "physical body . . . made of dust": Michael D. Coogan, ed., *The New Oxford Annotated Bible: New Revised Standard Version with the Apocrypha,* 3rd ed. (New York: Oxford University Press, 2001). Richard Horsley translates the Greek term *psychikon* as "physical," which is a questionable translation as it literary means "psychic," that is, "soul body."

193   "He transformed himself": Ibid., NHC I,4 45.19–46.2. Emphasis added.

193   "Do not think that": Ibid., NHC I,4 48.10–37. Emphasis added.

194   "Why am I ignoring": Ibid., NHC I,4 49.29–32. Relevant to this teacher's point is what Tanya Luhrmann demonstrates in her most recent book, which shows how spiritual seekers throughout various traditions often emphasize the same point: that attaining spiritual understanding requires engaging in such practices as fasting, meditation, and prayer (*How God Becomes Real,* especially 72ff.).

194 "experiences that I cannot explain": Elaine Pagels, *Why Religion?* (New York: Ecco, 2018), passim.

195 "That Jesus' followers": Sanders, *Historical Figure of Jesus,* 280.

195 "They believed this": Ibid.

195 "This could not affect": Harnack, *History of Dogma,* vol. I, 85.

6. HOW DID JESUS "BECOME GOD"?

198 a latecomer's vision: Ehrman, *How Jesus Became God,* 8, 232–52. See also his many other books, including *The Orthodox Corruption of Scripture.*

199 Stitching anecdotes: On the Diatessaron, see Barker, *Tatian's Diatessaron: Composition, Redaction, Recension, and Reception;* Petersen, *Tatian's Diatessaron: Its Creation, Dissemination, Significance, and History in Scholarship;* Boismard, *Le Diatessaron: De Tatien à Justin;* Lange, *Ephraem der Syrer: Kommentar zum Diatessaron;* Laurentin, *Nouveau Diatessaron: Les Quatre Évangiles en un Seul.*

199 Even worse, Irenaeus says: Irenaeus, *Adversus Haereses,* I, pref., 2.

199 "Satan planted to deceive people": Ibid., pref.

200 whereas Mark presents: Irenaeus, *Adversus Haereses,* III.11.8.

200 Already he had seen: For a vivid account of what happened, see Musurillo, "Letter of the Churches of Lyons and Vienne," 62–85. For historical context, see Frend, *Martyrdom and Persecution in the Early Church.* See also more recent perspectives by Bowersock, *Martyrdom and Rome;* Boyarin, *Dying for God;* Castelli, *Martyrdom and Memory;* Moss, *The Myth of Persecution.*

200 While in Rome: Musurillo, "The Martyrdom of Polycarp," 2–21.

201 "The more you kill us": Tertullian, *Apology,* 50.

201 During the decades: Historical evaluations of Constantine, his motives, actions, and influence, are many and intensely contested. See, for example, Pohlsander, *The Emperor Constantine;* Cameron and Hall, eds., *Eusebius: Life of Constantine;* Cameron, *The Later Roman Empire;* Lenski, ed., *The Cambridge Companion to the Age of Constantine;* Barnes, *Constantine: Dynasty, Religion and Power in the Later Roman Empire.*

202 came to be called the Nicene Creed: See Drake, *Constantine and the Bishops;* Lenski, *Constantine and the Cities;* Barnes, *Constantine and Eusebius.*

203 He could not decide: Eusebius, *Ecclesiastical History,* 7.25.

204 "the canon of the New Testament": Chadwick, *The Church in Ancient Society,* 105.

204 "Admission to the canon": Ibid.

205   Even at the august: At least, according to legend. For discussion of a number of such assaults, see MacMullen, *Voting About God in Early Church Councils.*

206   After that, the Council voted: On the Nicene Council, many studies are available, including by Rowan Williams, former Archbishop of Canterbury, *Tokens of Trust.*

7. WHO *IS* JESUS?

210   "How does God": Luhrmann, *When God Talks Back,* xi.

210   "as someone who interacts": Ibid., xix.

211   "Jesus died so that": Ibid., 76. Emphasis added.

211   "develop a new": Ibid., xxi.

212   "All of them": Ibid., 111.

212   "returning to the heart": Richard Rohr, as quoted in ibid., 164.

212   "always there, always listening": Ibid., 324.

213   "diminishes whatever isolation": Ibid.

213   "I do not presume": Ibid., 325.

213   "once grasped": Ibid., xxiv.

213   He goes on to tell: Cone, *The Cross and the Lynching Tree,* xiv–xv.

214   *"Ride on, King Jesus"*: Cone, *The Spirituals and the Blues.* Emphasis added.

215   "Round Dance of the Cross": *Acts of John,* 94–96.

216   "Christ taken down": Cannell, "The Funeral of the Dead Christ," 165–82. See also her excellent introduction to the volume she has edited, *The Anthropology of Christianity,* 1–50, and her chapter in the same volume, "Reading as Gift and Writing as Theft," 134–62.

216   Noting the focus on Easter: Rafael, *Contracting Colonialism.*

217   "returned to God": Vilaça, *Paletó and Me,* 14. See also her influential monograph about her research in the Amazon, *Praying and Preying.*

217   Yet, as Cannell shows: See Robbins's perceptive analysis and critique of the utilitarian and intellectualist approaches to anthropological research in his influential monograph, *Becoming Sinners,* especially chap. 2, "Christianity and the Colonial Transformation of Regional Relations," 84ff.

217   On Easter morning: Cannell, "Kinship, Reciprocity and Devotions to the Saints," 183–200.

217   But since the 1940s: Gow, "Forgetting Conversion," 211–39. See also his monograph, *An Amazonian Myth and Its History.*

218   "Spanish speaking people": Gow, "Forgetting Conversion," 227.

218   But when members: Ibid., 226.

219   *"God's kingdom coming"*: Ibid., 232. Emphasis added.

219   For example, Eva Keller: Keller, "Scriptural Study as Normal Science," 273–94.

220   "Adventist Bible study": Ibid., 282.

220   "I found people who": Ibid., 292.

221   "caught between two cultures": Robbins, *Becoming Sinners*, 316–17.

221   These indigenous leaders: Ibid., 119.

222   "All over India": Roberts, *To Be Cared For*, 3.

222   Even more recently: Ibid., 124–25.

222   recently borrowed the term "caste": See Wilkerson, *Caste*.

223   "What slum Christianity": Roberts, *To Be Cared For*, 227.

223   "Before, we had nothing": Ibid., 224.

224   "drums of revolutionary justice": Ibid., 221.

225   "He was probably the first": Descharnes and Néret, *Salvador Dalí, 1904–1989*, 166.

226   "the symbol of the self": Jung, *Man and His Symbols*, 231.

227   Chagall's crucifixion: Pagels, *The Origin of Satan*, passim.

228   to avoid a simplistic mapping: See Walsh, Staley, and Reinhartz, eds., *Son of Man*, especially S. D. Giere, " 'This Is My World'!," 23–33; the introduction by the editors; and other fine essays.

238   "The dual substance": Kazantzakis, *The Last Temptation of Christ*, 1.

243   Later, he wrote several: Tolstoy, *The Kingdom of God Is Within You*.

CONCLUSION

246   That his body wasn't left: Crossan, *The Historical Jesus*, 391–91; Crossan, *Who Killed Jesus?*, 202–10.

246   That he didn't fail: Borg, *Jesus: Uncovering the Life*, 186–90, 251–58.

Bibliography

Adams, Edward. *The Stars Will Fall from Heaven: Cosmic Catastrophe in the New Testament and Its World.* London: T&T Clark, 2007.

Alexander, P. S. "Comparing Merkavah Mysticism and Gnosticism: An Essay in Method." *Journal of Jewish Studies* 35 (1984): 1–18.

Allison, Dale C., Jr. *Constructing Jesus: Memory, Imagination, and History.* Grand Rapids, Mich.: Baker Academic, 2013.

———. *The End of the Ages Has Come: An Early Interpretation of the Passion and Resurrection of Jesus.* Eugene, Ore.: Wipf & Stock, 2013.

———. *The Historical Christ and the Theological Jesus.* Grand Rapids, Mich.: Eerdmans, 2009.

———. *Jesus of Nazareth: Millenarian Prophet.* Minneapolis: Fortress, 1998.

———. *Resurrecting Jesus: The Earliest Christian Tradition and Its Interpreters.* London: T&T Clark, 2005.

———. *The Resurrection of Jesus: Apologetics, Polemics, History.* London: Bloomsbury, 2021.

Altmann, Alexander. " 'Homo Imago Dei' in Jewish and Christian Theology." *Journal of Religion* 48, no. 3 (1968): 23–59.

Anderson, Paul N. *The Fourth Gospel and the Quest for Jesus: Modern Foundations Reconsidered.* London: T&T Clark, 2007.

Angus, Larry. *The Forbidden Gospels: New Gospels: Embracing the Spirit of God.* Shelbyville, Ky.: Wasteland Press, 2023.

Bibliography

Armstrong, Karen. *The Spiral Staircase: My Climb Out of Darkness*. New York: Knopf, 2004.

Arnal, William E. "The Rhetoric of Social Construction: Language and Society in the Gospel of Thomas." In *Rhetoric and Reality in Early Christianities*, ed. W. Braun (Waterloo, Ont.: Wilfrid Laurier University Press, 2005), pp. 27–47.

Attridge, Harold W., and George W. MacRae, trans. "The Gospel of Truth (I,3 AND XXII,2)." In *The Nag Hammadi Library in English*, revised edition, ed. James M. Robinson (New York: HarperCollins, 1990), pp. 38–51.

———. "The Gospel of Truth." In *Nag Hammadi Codex I (The Jung Codex): I. Introductions, Texts, Translations, Indices*, ed. Harold Attridge. *Nag Hammadi Studies, The Coptic Gnostic Library* 22 (Leiden: Brill, 1985), pp. 55–122.

———. "The Gospel of Truth." In *Nag Hammadi Codex I (The Jung Codex): II. Notes*, ed. Harold Attridge. *Nag Hammadi Studies, The Coptic Gnostic Library* 23 (Leiden: Brill, 1985), pp. 39–135.

Augustine. *The City of God Against the Pagans: Books XII–XV*, vol. IV. Translated by P. Levine. LCL 414. Cambridge, Mass.: Harvard University Press, 1966.

———. *Confessions, Books 1–8*. Translated by Carolyn J.-B. Hammond. LCL 26. Cambridge, Mass.: Harvard University Press, 2014.

———. *Confessions, Books 9–13*. Translated by Carolyn J.-B. Hammond. LCL 27. Cambridge, Mass.: Harvard University Press, 2016.

Aurelius, Marcus. *Marcus Aurelius*. Translated by C. R. Haines. LCL 58. Cambridge, Mass.: Harvard University Press, 1930.

Bader, Chris. "When Prophecy Passes Unnoticed: New Perspectives on Failed Prophecy." *Journal for the Scientific Study of Religion* 38, no. 1 (1999): 119–31.

Bagnall, Roger S. *Egypt in Late Antiquity*. Princeton: Princeton University Press, 1993.

Balch, David L. *Let Wives Be Submissive: The Domestic Code in I Peter*. Atlanta: Scholars Press, 1981.

Barker, James W. *Tatian's Diatessaron: Composition, Redaction, Recension, and Reception*. Oxford, U.K.: Oxford University Press, 2021.

Barnes, Timothy. *Constantine and Eusebius*. Cambridge, Mass.: Harvard University Press, 1981.

———. *Constantine: Dynasty, Religion and Power in the Later Roman Empire*. Malden, Mass.: Wiley-Blackwell, 2014.

Barnett, P. W. "The Jewish Sign Prophets—A.D. 40–70: Their Intentions and Origin." *New Testament Studies* 27 (1981): 679–97.

Barré, Michael L. "The Crux of Psalm 22:17c: Solved at Long Last?" In *David and Zion*, ed. Bernard F. Batto et al. (Winona Lake, Ind.: Eisenbrauns, 2004), pp. 287–306.

Barton, Carlin A. *The Sorrows of the Ancient Romans: The Gladiator and the Monster.* Princeton: Princeton University Press, 1993.

Bauckham, Richard. *The Climax of Prophecy: Studies on the Book of Revelation.* London: T&T Clark, 1993.

———. *Jesus and the God of Israel.* Grand Rapids, Mich.: Eerdmans, 2009.

Bazzana, Giovanni B. *Having the Spirit of Christ: Spirit Possession and Exorcism.* New Haven: Yale University Press, 2020.

Beal, Timothy. *The Rise and Fall of the Bible: The Unexpected History of an Accidental Book.* New York: Houghton Mifflin Harcourt, 21.

Berger, David. "The Rebbe, the Jews, and the Messiah." *Commentary* 112, no. 2 (2001): 23–30.

Betz, H. D. *The Greek Magical Papyri in Translation, Including the Demotic Spells.* Chicago: University of Chicago Press, 1992.

Bialecki, Jon. *A Diagram for Fire: Miracles and Variation in an American Charismatic Movement.* Oakland: University of California Press, 2017.

Blake, William. *The Everlasting Gospel and Other Poems.* Edited by Sasha Newborn. Yuma, Ariz.: Bandanna Books, 2011.

Boismard, M.-E. *Le Diatessaron: De Tatien à Justin.* Paris: J. Gabalda, 1992.

Borg, Marcus J. *Jesus: Uncovering the Life, Teachings, and Relevance of a Religious Revolutionary.* San Francisco: Harper, 1989.

———. *Meeting Jesus Again for the First Time: The Historical Jesus and the Heart of Contemporary Faith.* New York: HarperCollins, 1994.

Borg, Marcus J., and N. T. Wright. *The Meaning of Jesus: Two Visions.* New York: HarperCollins, 1999.

Boslooper, Thomas. *The Virgin Birth.* Philadelphia: Westminster, 1962.

Bowe, Barbara Ellen. "Dancing into the Divine: The Hymn of the Dance in the Acts of John." *Journal of Early Christian Studies* 7, no. 1 (1999): 83–104.

Bowersock, G. W. *Fiction as History: Nero to Julian.* Berkeley: University of California Press, 1994.

———. *Martyrdom and Rome.* Cambridge, U.K.: Cambridge University Press, 2002.

Bowler, Kate. *Have a Beautiful, Terrible Day! Daily Meditations for the Ups, Downs, and In-Betweens.* New York: Convergent, 2024.

Boyarin, Daniel. *Dying for God: Martyrdom and the Making of Christianity and Judaism.* Stanford: Stanford University Press, 1999.

———. *The Jewish Gospels: The Story of the Jewish Christ.* New York: New Press, 2012.

Boyd, Samuel L. "Judaism, Christianity, and Islam: The Problem of 'Abrahamic Religions' and the Possibilities of Comparison." *Religion Compass* 13, no. 10 (2019): 1–7.

———. *Language Contact, Colonial Administration, and the Construction of Identity in Ancient Israel*. Leiden: Brill, 2021.

Brakke, David. *The Gnostics: Myth, Ritual, and Diversity in Early Christianity*. Cambridge, Mass.: Harvard University Press, 2010.

———. "Scriptural Practices in Early Christianity: Towards a New History of the New Testament Canon." In *Invention, Rewriting, Usurpation: Discursive Fights over Religious Traditions in Antiquity*, ed. J. Ulrich, A.-C. Jacobsen, and D. Brakke (New York: Peter Lang, 2012), pp. 263–80.

———, trans. *Talking Back: A Monastic Handbook for Combating Demons*. Collegeville, Minn.: Liturgical Press, 2009.

Brandon, S. G. F. *Jesus and the Zealots: A Study of the Political Factor in Primitive Christianity*. Manchester, U.K.: Manchester University Press, 1967.

Braude, Ann D. *Radical Spirits: Spiritualism and Women's Rights in Nineteenth-Century America*. Bloomington: Indiana University Press, 2001.

———. *Sisters and Saints: Women and American Religion*. Oxford, U.K.: Oxford University Press, 2007.

Brock, Ann Graham. *Mary Magdalene, the First Apostle: The Struggle for Authority*. Cambridge, Mass.: Harvard University Press, 2003.

Brown, Peter. *The Cult of the Saints: Its Rise and Function in Latin Christianity*. Chicago: University of Chicago Press, 1981.

———. *Society and the Holy in Late Antiquity*. Berkeley: University of California Press, 1982.

———. *Through the Eye of a Needle: Wealth, the Fall of Rome, and the Making of Christianity in the West, 350–550 AD*. Princeton: Princeton University Press, 2012.

Brown, Raymond E. *The Birth of the Messiah: A Commentary on the Infancy Narratives in Matthew and Luke*. Garden City, N.Y.: Doubleday, 1979.

———. *The Death of the Messiah*, vol. 1. New York: Doubleday, 1994.

———. *The Death of the Messiah*, vol. 2. New York: Doubleday, 1994.

Butterworth, G. W., trans. *Origen on First Principles: Being Koetschau's Text of the De Principiis Translated into English, Together with an Introduction and Notes*. Gloucester, Mass.: Peter Smith, 1973.

Butts, Aaron Michael, and Simcha Gross, eds. *Jews and Syriac Christians: Intersections Across the First Millennium*. Tübingen: Mohr Siebeck, 2020.

Cameron, Averil. *The Later Roman Empire: AD 284–430*. Cambridge, Mass.: Harvard University Press, 1993.

Cameron, Averil, and Stuart G. Hall, eds. *Eusebius: Life of Constantine.* Oxford, U.K.: Clarendon Press, 1999.

Campenhausen, Hans von. *Aus der Frühzeit des Christentums.* Tübingen: Mohr Siebeck, 1963.

———. *The Fathers of the Greek Church.* Translated by Stanley Godman. New York: Pantheon, 1959.

Cannell, Fenella. "The Funeral of the 'Dead Christ.'" In Cannell, *Power and Intimacy in the Christian Philippines* (Cambridge, U.K.: Cambridge University Press, 1999), pp. 165–82.

———. "Introduction." In Cannell, *The Anthropology of Christianity* (Durham, N.C.: Duke University Press, 2006), pp. 1–50.

———. "Kinship, Reciprocity and Devotion to the Saints." In Cannell, *Power and Intimacy in the Christian Philippines* (Cambridge, U.K.: Cambridge University Press, 1999), pp. 183–200.

———. "Reading as Gift and Writing as Theft." In Cannell, *The Anthropology of Christianity* (Durham, N.C.: Duke University Press, 2006), pp. 134–62.

———, ed. *The Anthropology of Christianity.* Durham, N.C.: Duke University Press, 2006.

Cartlidge, David, and David Dungan. *Documents and Images for the Study of the Gospels.* Minneapolis: Fortress, 2015.

Castelli, Elizabeth. *Martyrdom and Memory: Early Christian Culture Making.* New York: Columbia University Press, 2004.

Celsus. *On the True Doctrine: A Discourse Against the Christians.* Translated by Joseph Hoffman. Oxford, U.K.: Oxford University Press, 1987.

Chadwick, Henry. *The Church in Ancient Society: From Galilee to Gregory the Great.* Oxford, U.K.: Clarendon, 2001.

———, trans. *Origen: Contra Celsum.* Cambridge, U.K.: Cambridge University Press, 1953.

Chapman, David. *Ancient Jewish and Christian Perceptions of Crucifixion.* Tübingen: Mohr Siebeck, 2008.

Christian, William A., Jr. *Local Religion in Sixteenth-Century Spain.* Princeton: Princeton University Press, 1981.

Clark, Elizabeth A. *Jerome, Chrysostom, and Friends: Essays and Translations.* New York: Edwin Mellen Press, 1979.

Collins, John J. *The Apocalyptic Imagination: An Introduction to Jewish Apocalyptic Literature.* 2nd edition. Grand Rapids, Mich.: Eerdmans, 1998.

———. *Encounters with Biblical Theology.* Minneapolis: Fortress, 2005.

————. "Jesus and the Messiahs of Israel." In *Frühes Christentum*, ed. H. Canick, H. Lichtenberger, and P. Schäfer (Tübingen: Mohr Siebeck, 1996), pp. 287–302.

Cone, James H. *The Cross and the Lynching Tree*. Maryknoll, N.Y.: Orbis, 2011.

————. *God of the Oppressed*. Revised edition. Maryknoll, N.Y.: Orbis, 1997.

————. *My Soul Looks Back*. Maryknoll, N.Y.: Orbis, 1986.

————. *Risks of Faith: The Emergence of a Black Theology of Liberation, 1968–1998*. Boston: Beacon Press, 1999.

————. *Said I Wasn't Gonna Tell Nobody: The Making of a Black Theologian*. Maryknoll, N.Y.: Orbis, 2018.

————. *The Spirituals and the Blues*. Maryknoll, N.Y.: Orbis, 1991.

Coogan, Michael D., ed. *The New Oxford Annotated Bible: New Revised Standard Version with the Apocrypha*. 5th edition. Oxford, U.K.: Oxford University Press, 2018.

Copenhaver, Brian P. *Hermetica: The Greek Corpus Hermeticum and the Latin Asclepius in a New English Translation, with Notes and Introduction*. Cambridge, U.K.: Cambridge University Press, 1992.

Crossan, Jon Dominic. *The Birth of Christianity: Discovering What Happened in the Years Immediately After the Execution of Jesus*. New York: HarperCollins, 1998.

————. *The Historical Jesus: The Life of a Mediterranean Jewish Peasant*. New York: HarperCollins, 1991.

————. *Jesus: A Revolutionary Biography*. New York: HarperCollins, 1994.

————. *Who Killed Jesus? Exposing the Roots of Anti-Semitism in the Gospel Story of the Death of Jesus*. New York: HarperCollins, 1996.

Cullen, Countee. *The Black Christ and Other Poems*. New York: Harper & Brothers, 1929.

Dabrowa, Edward. *Legio X Fretensis: A Prosopological Study of Its Officers (I–III c. A.D.)*. Stuttgart: Franz Steiner Verlag, 1993.

Daly, Robert J., ed. *Apocalyptic Thought in Early Christianity*. Grand Rapids, Mich.: Baker Academic, 2009.

Davies, Stevan L., trans. *The Gospel of Thomas: Annotated and Explained*. Woodstock, Vt.: Skylight Paths Publishing, 2002.

————. *Jesus the Healer: Possession, Trance, and the Origin of Christianity*. New York: Continuum, 1995.

DeConick, April D., ed. *The Code Judas Papers: Proceedings of the International Congress on the Tchacos Codex Held at Rice University, Houston, Texas, March 13–16, 2008*. Leiden: Brill, 2009.

———. *Comparing Christianities: An Introduction to Early Christianity.* Hoboken, N.J.: Wiley–Blackwell, 2023.

———. *The Original Gospel of Thomas in Translation.* London: T&T Clark, 2006.

Dein, Simon. "Lubavitch: A Contemporary Messianic Movement." *Journal of Contemporary Religion* 12, no. 2 (1997): 191–204.

———. "Mosiach Is Here Now: Just Open Your Eyes and You Can See Him." *Anthropology and Medicine* 9, no. 1 (2002): 25–36.

———. "When Prophecy Fails: Messianism Amongst Lubavitcher Hasids." In *The Coming Deliverer: Millennial Themes in World Religions,* ed. Fiona Bowie and Christopher Deacy (Cardiff: University of Wales Press, 1997), pp. 238–60.

Deissmann, Adolf. *Light from the Ancient East: The New Testament Illustrated by Recently Discovered Texts of the Graeco Roman World.* 4th (German) edition. Translated by L. R. M. Strachan. Grand Rapids, Mich.: Baker Book House, 1978 (reprint).

———. "Der Name Panthera." In *Orientalische Studien T. Nöldeke gewidmet,* ed. Carl Bezold (Giessen, Germany: Alfred Töpelmann, 1906), pp. 871–75.

Deng, Francis Mading. *Dinka Folktales: African Stories from the Sudan.* New York: Holmes & Meier, 1974.

Descharnes, Robert, and Gilles Néret. *Salvador Dalí, 1904–1989.* London: Taschen Verlag, 1989.

Desjardins, Michael. "Where Was the Gospel of Thomas Written?" *Toronto Journal of Theology* 8, no. 1 (1992): 121–33.

Dirkse, Peter A., et al. "The Discourse on the Eighth and Ninth (NHC VI,6)." In *Nag Hammadi Codices V, 2–5 and VI with Papyrus Berolinensis 8502, 1 and 4,* ed. Douglas M. Parrott. *Nag Hammadi Studies, The Coptic Gnostic Library* 11 (Leiden: Brill, 1979), pp. 341–73.

Dodd, C. H. "The Appearances of the Risen Christ: An Essay in Form-Criticism of the Gospels." In *Studies in the Gospels,* ed. D. E. Nineham (Oxford, U.K.: Blackwell, 1955), pp. 9–35.

Dohrmann, Natalie B., and Annette Yoshiko Reed, eds. *Jews, Christians, and the Roman Empire: The Poetics of Power in Late Antiquity.* Philadelphia: University of Pennsylvania Press, 2013.

Drake, H. A. *Constantine and the Bishops: The Politics of Intolerance.* Baltimore: Johns Hopkins University Press, 2000.

———. "The Elephant in the Room: Constantine at the Council." In *The Cambridge Companion to the Council of Nicaea,* ed. Y. R. Kim (Cambridge, U.K.: Cambridge University Press, 2021), pp. 111–32.

Dubois, Jean-Daniel. "Le 'Nom Insigne' d'Après Marc le Mage." In *Noms Barbares I:*

Formes et Contextes d'une Pratique Magique, ed. Michel Tardieu, Anna Van den Kerchove, and Michela Zago (Turnhout, Belgium: Brepols, 2013), pp. 253–64.

Duff, Paul B. *Who Rides the Beast? Prophetic Rivalry and the Rhetoric of Crisis in the Churches of the Apocalypse.* Oxford, U.K.: Oxford University Press, 2001.

Dunderberg, Ismo. *The Beloved Disciple in Conflict? Revisiting the Gospels of John and Thomas.* Oxford, U.K.: Oxford University Press, 2006.

———. *Beyond Gnosticism: Myth, Lifestyle, and Society in the School of Valentinus.* New York: Columbia University Press, 2008.

Dunn, Geoffrey D. "Catholic Reception of the Council of Nicaea." In *The Cambridge Companion to the Council of Nicaea,* ed. Y. R. Kim (Cambridge, U.K.: Cambridge University Press, 2021), pp. 347–67.

Dunning, Benjamin H. *Specters of Paul: Sexual Difference in Early Christian Thought.* Philadelphia: University of Pennsylvania Press, 2011.

Eddy, Mary Baker. *Science and Health with Key to the Scriptures.* Boston: Joseph Armstrong, 1900.

Edwards, Mark J. "The Creed." In *The Cambridge Companion to the Council of Nicaea,* ed. Y. R. Kim (Cambridge, U.K.: Cambridge University Press, 2021), pp. 135–57.

———. "Pseudo-Priscillian and the Gospel of Truth." *Vigiliae Christianae* 70 (2016): 355–72.

Ehrman, Bart D. *How Jesus Became God: The Exaltation of a Jewish Preacher from Galilee.* New York: HarperOne, 2014.

———. *The Orthodox Corruption of Scripture.* Oxford, U.K.: Oxford University Press, 2011.

———, trans. *The Apostolic Fathers II.* LCL 25. Cambridge, Mass.: Harvard University Press, 2003.

Elior, Rachel. "Mysticism, Magic, and Angelology: The Perception of Angels in Hekhalot Literature." *Jewish Studies Quarterly* 1, no. 1 (1993): 3–53.

Emmel, Stephen, et al. "The Dialogue of the Savior." In *Nag Hammadi Codex III, 5,* ed. Stephen Emmel. *Nag Hammadi Studies, The Coptic Gnostic Library* 26 (Leiden: Brill, 1984), pp. 1–127.

Eusebius. *Ecclesiastical History,* vol. I, bk. 1–5. Translated by K. Lake. LCL 153. Cambridge, Mass.: Harvard University Press, 1926.

———. *Ecclesiastical History,* vol. II, bk. 6–10. Translated by J. E. L. Oulton. LCL 265. Cambridge, Mass.: Harvard University Press, 1932.

Evans, Craig A. "Prophet, Sage, Healer, Messiah, and Martyr: Types and Identities of Jesus." In *Handbook for the Study of the Historical Jesus,* 4 vols., ed. T. Holmén and S. E. Porter (Leiden: Brill, 2011), pp. 1217–43.

Eyl, Jennifer. *Signs, Wonders, and Gifts: Divination in the Letters of Paul.* Oxford, U.K.: Oxford University Press, 2019.

Festinger, Leon, et al. *When Prophecy Fails: A Social and Psychological Study of a Modern Group That Predicted the Destruction of the World.* New York: Harper & Row, 1964.

Fitzmyer, Joseph. *The Gospel According to Luke I–IX.* Garden City, N.Y.: Doubleday, 1981.

Flusser, David. *Jesus.* New York: Herder and Herder, 1969.

Frankfurter, David. *Elijah in Upper Egypt: The Apocalypse of Elijah and Early Egyptian Christianity.* Minneapolis: Fortress, 1993.

Frankl, Viktor E. *Man's Search for Meaning.* Boston: Beacon Press, 2006.

Fredriksen, Paula. *From Jesus to Christ: The Origins of the New Testament Images of Jesus.* New Haven, Conn.: Yale University Press, 1988.

———. *Jesus of Nazareth: King of the Jews.* New York: Knopf, 1999.

———. "What You See Is What You Get: Context and Content in Current Research on the Historical Jesus." *Theology Today* 52, no. 1 (1995): 75–97.

———. *When Christians Were Jews: The First Generation.* New Haven, Conn.: Yale University Press, 2018.

Frend, W. H. C. *Martyrdom and Persecution in the Early Church: A Study of a Conflict from the Maccabees to Donatus.* Garden City, N.Y.: Anchor Books, 1967.

Friesen, Steven J. *Imperial Cults and the Apocalypse of John: Reading Revelation in the Ruins.* Oxford, U.K.: Oxford University Press, 2001.

———. "Revelation, Realia, and Religion: Archaeology in the Interpretation of the Apocalypse." *Harvard Theological Review* 88, no. 3 (1995): 291–314.

———. "Satan's Throne, Imperial Cults and the Social Settings of Revelation." *Journal for the Study of the New Testament* 27, no. 3 (2005): 351–73.

Fuller, Reginald. "*The Virgin Birth.* By Thomas Boslooper." *Journal of Religion* 43, no. 3 (1963): 254–55.

Gager, John G. *Kingdom and Community: The Social World of Early Christianity.* Englewood Cliffs, N.J.: Prentice-Hall, 1975.

———. *Reinventing Paul.* Oxford, U.K.: Oxford University Press, 2000.

Gamble, Harry Y. *Books and Readers in the Early Church: A History of Early Christian Texts.* New Haven, Conn.: Yale University Press, 1995.

Garnsey, Peter, and Caroline Humfress. *The Evolution of the Late Antique World.* Cambridge, U.K.: Orchard Academic, 2001.

Garnsey, Peter, et al. *The Roman Empire: Economy, Society and Culture.* 2nd edition. Oakland: University of California Press, 2015.

Gathercole, Simon. *The Composition of the Gospel of Thomas: Original Language and Influences*. Cambridge, U.K.: Cambridge University Press, 2012.

———. *The Gospel of Thomas: Introduction and Commentary*. Leiden: Brill, 2014.

Gibson, Marion. *Order from Chaos: Responding to Traumatic Events*. Birmingham, U.K.: Venture, 1998.

Giere, S. D. " 'This Is My World'! Son of Man (Jezile) and Cross-Cultural Convergences of Bible and World." In *Son of Man: An African Jesus Film,* ed. Richard Walsh, Jeffrey Staley, and Adele Reinhartz (Sheffield, U.K.: Sheffield Phoenix Press, 2013), pp. 23–33.

Ginzberg, Louis. *The Legends of the Jews*. Philadelphia: Jewish Publication Society, 1925.

Goehring, James E. *Ascetics, Society, and the Desert: Studies in Early Egyptian Monasticism*. Harrisburg, Pa.: Trinity Press, 1999.

Goehring, James E., and Janet A. Timbie, eds. *The World of Early Egyptian Christianity: Language, Literature, and Social Context: Essays in Honor of David W. Johnson*. Washington, D.C.: Catholic University of America Press, 2007.

Gonzalez, David. "Lubavitchers Learn to Sustain Themselves Without the Rebbe." *New York Times,* November 8, 1994.

Gow, Peter. *An Amazonian Myth and Its History*. Oxford, U.K.: Oxford University Press, 2001.

———. "Forgetting Conversion: The Summer Institute of Linguistics Mission in the Piro Lived World." In *The Anthropology of Christianity,* ed. Fenella Cannell (Durham, N.C.: Duke University Press, 2006), pp. 211–39.

Gregg, Robert C., and Dennis E. Groh. *Early Arianism—A View of Salvation*. London: SCM Press, 1981.

Gregory, Eric. *Politics and the Order of Love: An Augustinian Ethic of Democratic Citizenship*. Chicago: University of Chicago Press, 2008.

Gribetz, Sarit Kattan. *Time and Difference in Rabbinic Judaism*. Princeton: Princeton University Press, 2020.

Grull, Tibor. "The Fearful Battle Between Good and Evil." Review of M. Goodman, *Rome and Jerusalem: The Clash of Ancient Civilizations* (New York: Knopf, 2007), https://www.academia.edu/26970421/The_Fearful_Battle_between_Good_and_Evil.

Halpern, Daniel, ed. *Holy Fire: Nine Visionary Poets and the Quest for Enlightenment*. New York: Harper Perennial, 1994.

Hanks, William F. *Converting Words: Maya in the Age of the Cross*. Berkeley: University of California Press, 2010.

Harnack, Adolph von. *History of Dogma,* vol. I. 3rd (German) edition. Translated by Neil Buchanan. London: Williams & Norgate, 1894.

Harrington, Ann. *The Placebo Effect: An Interdisciplinary Exploration.* Cambridge, Mass.: Harvard University Press, 1999.

Harvey, W. Wigan, ed. *Saint Irenaeus, Bishop of Lyons' Five Books Against Heresies,* vol. I. Rochester, N.Y.: St. Irenaeus Press, 2013.

———, ed. *Saint Irenaeus, Bishop of Lyons' Five Books Against Heresies,* vol. II. Rochester, N.Y.: St. Irenaeus Press, 2013.

Haupt, Peter, and Sabine Hornung. "Ein Mitglied der Heiligen Familie? Zur Rezeption eines römischen Soldatengrabsteines aus Bingerbrück, Kr. Mainz-Bingen." *Archäologische Informationen* 27, no. 1 (2004): 133–40.

Hays, Richard B. "Christ Prays the Psalms: Israel's Psalter as Matrix of Early Christology." In Hays, *The Conversion of the Imagination: Paul as Interpreter of Israel's Scripture* (Grand Rapids, Mich.: Eerdmans, 2005), pp. 101–38.

Hengel, Martin. *Crucifixion in the Ancient World and the Folly of the Message of the Cross.* Philadelphia: Fortress, 1977.

Herrin, Judith. *The Formation of Christendom.* Princeton: Princeton University Press, 1987.

Hewitt, Joseph. "The Use of Nails in the Crucifixion." *Harvard Theological Review* 25 (1932): 29–45.

Himmelfarb, Martha. *The Apocalypse: A Brief History.* Malden, Mass.: Wiley-Blackwell, 2010.

———. *Ascent to Heaven in Jewish and Christian Apocalypses.* Oxford, U.K.: Oxford University Press, 1993.

———. "Heavenly Ascent and the Relationship of the Apocalypses and the 'Hekhalot' Literature." *Hebrew Union College Annual* 59 (1988): 73–100.

Hock, Ronald F., and Edward N. O'Neal. *The Chreia in Ancient Rhetoric.* Vol. 1, *The Progymnasmata.* Atlanta: Scholars Press, 1986.

———. *The Chreia in Ancient Rhetoric.* Vol. 2, *Classroom Exercises.* Atlanta: Scholars Press, 2002.

Holt, P. M. "Islamic Millenarianism and the Fulfillment of Prophecy: A Case Study." In *Prophecy and Millenarianism: Essays in Honor of Marjorie Reeves,* ed. Ann Williams (Essex: Longman, 1980), pp. 335–48.

Hopkins, Gerald Manley. *The Wreck of the Deutschland.* Bristol, U.K.: Shearsman Books, 2017.

Horsley, Richard A. *Jesus and the Spiral of Violence: Popular Jewish Resistance in Roman Palestine.* San Francisco: Harper & Row, 1987.

Bibliography

Idel, Moshe. *Kabbalah: New Perspectives*. New Haven, Conn.: Yale University Press, 1988.

Irenaeus. *Against Heresies*. Translated by A. Roberts and W. Rambaut. *Ante-Nicene Fathers,* 1. Edited by A. Roberts, J. Donaldson, and A. C. Coxe. Buffalo, N.Y.: Christian Literature Publishing, 1885.

Iricinschi, Eduard, and Holger M. Zellentin, eds. *Heresy and Identity in Late Antiquity*. Tübingen: Mohr Siebeck, 2008.

Isaac, B. *The Limits of Empire: The Roman Army in the East*. Oxford, U.K.: Clarendon, 1992.

Isenberg, Wesley W., trans. "The Gospel of Philip (II,3)." In *The Nag Hammadi Library in English,* revised edition, ed. James M. Robinson (New York: HarperCollins, 1990), pp. 139–60.

James, William. *The Varieties of Religious Experience: A Study in Human Nature*. New York: Macmillan, 1961.

Jenott, Lance. "Clergy, Clairvoyance, and Conflict: The Synod of Latopolis and the Problem with Pachomius' Visions." In *Beyond the Gnostic Gospels: Studies Building on the Work of Elaine Pagels*, ed. E. Iricinschi et al. Tübingen: Mohr Siebeck, 2013.

Jenott, Lance, and Sarit Kattan Gribetz, eds. *Jewish and Christian Cosmogony in Late Antiquity*. Tübingen: Mohr Siebeck, 2013.

Jenott, Lance, and Hugo Lundhaug. *The Monastic Origins of the Nag Hammadi Codices*. Tübingen: Mohr Siebeck, 2015.

Jenott, Lance, and Elaine Pagels. "Antony's Letters and Nag Hammadi Codex I: Sources of Religious Conflict in Fourth-Century Egypt." *Journal of Early Christian Studies* 18, no. 4 (2010): 557–89.

Johnson, Luke Timothy. *The Real Jesus: The Misguided Quest for the Historical Jesus and the Truth of the Traditional Gospels*. New York: HarperCollins, 1996.

Johnson, Sylvester A. *The Myth of Ham in Nineteenth-Century American Christianity: Race, Heathens, and the People of God*. New York: Palgrave Macmillan, 2004.

Josephus. *Jewish Antiquities, Books XII–XIII*, vol. IX. Translated by Ralph Marcus. LCL 365. Cambridge, Mass.: Harvard University Press, 1998.

———. *The Jewish War, Books I–II*, vol. II. Translated by H. St. J. Thackeray. LCL 203. Cambridge, Mass.: Harvard University Press, 1927.

———. *The Life, Against Apion*, vol. I. Translated by H. St. J. Thackeray. LCL 186. London: Heinemann, 1926.

Jung, Carl G. *Man and His Symbols*. New York: Bantam, 2023.

Kaag, John. *Hiking with Nietzsche: On Becoming Who You Are*. New York: Farrar, Strauss and Giroux, 2018.

———. *Sick Souls, Healthy Minds: How William James Can Save Your LIfe.* Princeton: Princeton University Press, 2020.

Kaag, John, and Jonathan van Belle. *Henry at Work: Thoreau on Making a Living.* Princeton: Princeton University Press, 2023.

Kazantzakis, Nikos. *The Last Temptation of Christ.* New York: Simon & Schuster, 1998.

Kee, Howard Clark. *Jesus in History: An Approach to the Study of the Gospels.* New York: Harcourt, Brace & World, 1970.

Keith, Chris. "Memory and Authenticity: Jesus Tradition and What Really Happened." *Zeitschrift für die neutestamentliche Wissenschaft* 102 (2011): 155–77.

Keller, Eva. "Scriptural Study as Normal Science: Seventh Day Adventist Practice on the East Coast of Madagascar." In *The Anthropology of Christianity,* ed. Fenella Cannell (Durham, N.C.: Duke University Press, 2006), pp. 273–94.

Kennedy, George A. *The Art of Rhetoric in the Roman World: 300 BC–AD 300.* Princeton: Princeton University Press, 1972.

Kermode, Frank. *The Sense of an Ending: Studies in the Theory of Fiction.* Oxford, U.K.: Oxford University Press, 2000.

Kim, David. "A Korean Reader's Insight on Thomas and Its Oral Tradition Origin." In *Global Korea, Old and New: Proceedings of the Sixth Biennial KSAA International Conference, New South Wales, Australia, July 2009,* ed. Duk-Soo Park (Sydney: Korean Studies Association of Australasia, 2010), pp. 499–510.

Kim, Young Richard, ed. *The Cambridge Companion to the Council of Nicaea.* Cambridge, U.K.: Cambridge University Press, 2021.

King, Karen L. *The Gospel of Mary of Magdala: Jesus and the First Woman Apostle.* Santa Rosa, Calif.: Polebridge, 2003.

———. *The Secret Revelation of John.* Cambridge, Mass.: Harvard University Press, 2006.

———. "Which Early Christianity?" In *The Oxford Handbook of Early Christian Studies,* ed. S. A. Harvey and D. G. Hunter (Oxford, U.K.: Oxford University Press, 2008), pp. 66–86.

King, Karen L., et al., eds. "The Gospel of Mary (BG 8502,l)." In *The Nag Hammadi Library in English,* revised edition, ed. James M. Robinson (New York: HarperCollins, 1990), pp. 523–27.

Kloppenborg, John S., Marvin W. Meyer, Stephen J. Patterson, and Michael G. Steinhauser, eds. *Q-Thomas Reader.* Sonoma, Calif.: Polebridge, 1990.

Koester, Helmut. *Ancient Christian Gospels: Their History and Development.* London: SCM Press, 1990.

Bibliography

Kraemer, Ross S. *Maenads, Martyrs, Matrons, Monastics: A Sourcebook on Women's Religions in the Greco-Roman World.* Philadelphia: Fortress, 1988.

———. *Unreliable Witnesses: Religion, Gender, and History in the Greco-Roman Mediterranean.* Oxford, U.K.: Oxford University Press, 2011.

Kreps, Anne. "The Passion of the Book: The *Gospel of Truth* as Valentinian Scriptural Practice." *Journal of Early Christian Studies* 24, no. 3 (2016): 311–35.

Kripal, Jeffrey J. *Authors of the Impossible.* Chicago: University of Chicago Press, 2011.

———. *Roads of Excess, Palaces of Wisdom: Eroticism and Reflexivity in the Study of Mysticism.* Chicago: University of Chicago Press, 2001.

———. *The Superhumanities.* Chicago: University of Chicago Press, 2022.

Kugel, James L. *The Great Shift: Encountering God in Biblical Times.* Boston: Houghton Mifflin Harcourt, 2017.

Laertius, Diogenes. *Lives of Eminent Philosophers,* vol. I. Translated by R. D. Hicks. LCL 184. Cambridge, Mass.: Harvard University Press, 1972.

Lambdin, Thomas, trans. "The Gospel of Thomas (II,2)." In *The Nag Hammadi Library in English,* revised edition, ed. James M. Robinson (New York: HarperCollins, 1990), pp. 124–38.

Lampe, Peter. *From Paul to Valentinus: Christians at Rome in the First Two Centuries.* Translated by M. Steinhauser. Minneapolis: Fortress, 2003.

Landes, Richard. "On Owls, Roosters, and Apocalyptic Time: A Historical Method for Reading a Refractory Documentation." *Union Seminary Quarterly Review* 49 (1995): 49–69.

Lange, Christian. *Ephraem der Syrer: Kommentar zum Diatessaron.* Turnhout, Belgium: Brepols, 2008.

Larsen, Matthew D. C. *Gospels Before the Book.* Oxford, U.K.: Oxford University Press, 2015.

Laurentin, René. *Nouveau Diatessaron: Les Quatre Évangiles en un Seul.* Paris: Fayard, 2002.

Layton, Bentley, ed. *The Rediscovery of Gnosticism: Proceedings of the International Conference on Gnosticism at Yale, New Haven, Connecticut, March 28–31, 1978.* Vol. 1, *The School of Valentinus.* Leiden: Brill, 1980.

Layton, Bentley, et al. "Tractate 2: The Gospel According to Thomas." In *Nag Hammadi Codex II, 2–7, Together with XIII, 2* Brit. Lib. Or. 4926(1) and P. Oxy. 1, 654, 655,* ed. Bentley Layton. *Nag Hammadi Studies, The Coptic Gnostic Library* 20 (Leiden: Brill, 1989), pp. 37–128, 264–89.

Layton, Bentley, et al. "Tractate 3: Gospel According to Philip." In *Nag Hammadi Codex II, 2–7, Together with XIII, 2* Brit. Lib. Or. 4926(1) and P. Oxy. 1, 654, 655,* ed. Bentley Layton. *Nag Hammadi Studies, The Coptic Gnostic Library* 20 (Leiden: Brill, 1989), pp. 129–217, 290–320.

Leloup, Jean-Yves. *The Gospel of Mary Magdalene.* Translated by Joseph Rowe. Rochester, Vt.: Inner Traditions, 2002.

Lenski, Noel. *Constantine and the Cities: Imperial Authority and Civic Politics (Empire and After).* Philadelphia: University of Pennsylvania Press, 2016.

———, ed. *The Cambridge Companion to the Age of Constantine.* Cambridge, U.K.: Cambridge University Press, 2005.

Letteney, Mark. *The Christianization of Knowledge in Late Antiquity: Intellectual and Material Transformations.* Cambridge, U.K.: Cambridge University Press, 2023.

Levenson, Jon D. *Creation and the Persistence of Evil: The Jewish Drama of Divine Omnipotence.* Princeton: Princeton University Press, 1994.

Levine, Amy-Jill. *The Misunderstood Jew: The Church and the Scandal of the Jewish Jesus.* New York: HarperCollins, 2006.

———. *Short Stories by Jesus: The Enigmatic Parables of a Controversial Rabbi.* New York: HarperCollins, 2014.

Levine, Amy-Jill, Dale C. Allison Jr., and John Dominic Crossan, eds. *The Historical Jesus in Context.* Princeton: Princeton University Press, 2006.

Leyden, Liz. "5 Years After Death, Messiah Question Divides Lubavitchers." *Washington Post,* June 20, 1999.

Lied, Liv Ingeborg, and Hugo Lundhaug, eds. *Snapshots of Evolving Traditions: Jewish and Christian Manuscript Culture, Textual Fluidity, and New Philology.* Berlin: De Gruyter, 2017.

Lieu, Judith M. "Accusations of Jewish Persecution in Early Christian Sources, with Particular Reference to Justin Martyr and the Martyrdom of Polycarp." In *Tolerance and Intolerance in Early Judaism and Christianity,* ed. G. N. Stanton and G. G. Stroumsa (Cambridge, U.K.: Cambridge University Press, 1998), pp. 279–95.

———. *Neither Jew Nor Greek: Constructing Early Christianity.* London: T & T Clark, 2002.

Lincoln, Bruce. *Discourse and the Construction of Society: Comparative Studies of Myth, Ritual, and Classification.* Oxford, U.K.: Oxford University Press, 1989.

Littlewood, Jane. *Aspects of Grief: Bereavement in Adult Life.* London: Tavistock/Routledge, 1992.

Livingston, David L. *Adam's Ancestors: Race, Religion, and the Politics of Human Origins.* Baltimore: Johns Hopkins University Press, 2008.

Lüdemann, Gerd. *The Resurrection of Jesus: History, Experience, Theology.* Minneapolis: Fortress, 1994.

———. *Untersuchungen zur simonianischen Gnosis.* Göttingen: Vandenhoeck & Ruprecht, 1975.

———. *What Really Happened to Jesus: A Historical Approach to the Resurrection.* Translated by John Bowden. Louisville: John Knox Westminster, 1995.

Luhrmann, Tanya. *How God Becomes Real: Kindling the Presence of Invisible Others.* Princeton: Princeton University Press, 2020.

———. *When God Talks Back: Understanding the American Evangelical Relationship with God.* New York: Vintage, 2012.

Luhrmann, T. M., and Jocelyn Marrow, eds. *Our Most Troubling Madness: Case Studies in Schizophrenia Across Cultures.* Oakland: University of California Press, 2016.

Luijendijk, AnneMarie. "The Gospel of Mary at Oxyrhynchus (P. Oxy. L 3525 and P. Ryl. III 463): Rethinking the History of Early Christianity Through Literary Papyri from Oxyrhynchus." In *Re-Making the World: Christianity and Categories,* ed. T. G. Petry et al. (Tübingen: Mohr Siebeck, 2019), pp. 391–421.

———. *Greetings in the Lord: Early Christians and the Oxyrhynchus Papyri.* Cambridge, Mass.: Harvard University Press, 2008.

———. "Reading the *Gospel of Thomas* in the Third Century: Three Oxyrhynchus Papyri and Origen's *Homilies*." In *Reading New Testament Papyri in Context,* ed. C. Clivaz and J. Zumstein (Leuven: Peeters, 2011), pp. 241–68.

Lundhaug, Hugo. *Images of Rebirth: Cognitive Poetics and Transformational Soteriology in the* Gospel of Philip *and the* Exegesis on the Soul. Leiden: Brill, 2010.

Luther, Martin. *Three Treatises.* Philadelphia: Muhlenberg Press, 1960.

Luz, Ulrich. *Matthew 1–7.* Minneapolis: Fortress, 2007.

Lyman, Rebecca. "Arius and Arianism: The Origins of the Alexandrian Controversy." In *The Cambridge Companion to the Council of Nicaea,* ed. Y. R. Kim (Cambridge, U.K.: Cambridge University Press, 2021), pp. 42–62.

Maccoby, Hyam. *Revolution in Judaea: Jesus and the Jewish Resistance.* New York: Taplinger Publishing, 1980.

Mack, Burton L. "Elaboration of the Chreia in the Hellenistic School." In Burton L. Mack and Vernon K. Robbins, *Patterns of Persuasion in the Gospels* (Sonoma, Calif.: Polebridge, 1989), pp. 31–67.

MacMullen, Ramsay. *Christianizing the Roman Empire (A.D. 100–400).* New Haven, Conn.: Yale University Press, 1984.

———. *Voting About God in Early Church Councils.* New Haven, Conn.: Yale University Press, 2006.

Magid, Shaul, ed. *The Bible, the Talmud, and the New Testament: Elijah Zvi Soloveitchik's*

Commentary to the Gospels. Translated by J. G. Levy. Philadelphia: University of Pennsylvania Press, 2019.

Marcus, Joel. "The Jewish War and the Sitz im Leben of Mark." *Journal of Biblical Literature* 111, no. 3 (1992): 441-62.

———. *Mark 1–8.* New York: Doubleday, 1999.

———. "The Once and Future Messiah in Early Christianity and Chabad." *New Testament Studies* 46, no. 3 (2001): 381–401.

Marjanen, Antti. "Is Thomas a Gnostic Gospel?" In *Thomas at the Crossroads,* ed. Risto Uro et al. (Edinburgh: T&T Clark, 1998), pp. 107–39.

———. *Was There a Gnostic Religion?* Göttingen: Vandenhoeck & Ruprecht, 2005.

Markschies, Christoph. *Christian Theology and Its Institutions in the Early Roman Empire: Prolegomena to a History of Early Christian Theology.* Translated by Wayne Coppins. Waco, Tex.: Baylor University Press, 2015.

Martin, Clancy. *How Not to Kill Yourself: A Portrait of the Suicidal Mind.* New York: Pantheon, 2023.

McGowan, Andrew B., and Kent Harold Richards. *Method and Meaning: Essays on New Testament Interpretation in Honor of Harold W. Attridge.* Atlanta: Society of Biblical Literature, 2011.

Meeks, Wayne A. *The First Urban Christians: The Social World of the Apostle Paul.* New Haven, Conn.: Yale University Press, 1983.

———. *The Origins of Christian Morality: The First Two Centuries.* New Haven, Conn.: Yale University Press, 1993.

Meier, John P. *A Marginal Jew: Rethinking the Historical Jesus.* Vol. 1, *The Roots of the Problem and the Person.* New York: Doubleday, 1991.

———. *A Marginal Jew: Rethinking the Historical Jesus.* Vol. 2, *Mentor, Message, and Miracles.* New Haven, Conn.: Yale University Press, 1994.

Ménard, Jacques E. "La Structure et la Langue Originale de L'Évangile de Vérité." *Revue des Sciences Religieuses* 44 (1970): 128–37.

Mermelstein, Ari. *Creation, Covenant, and the Beginnings of Judaism: Reconceiving Historical Time in the Second Temple Period.* Leiden: Brill, 2014.

Meyer, Marvin, ed. *The Nag Hammadi Scriptures: The International Edition.* New York: HarperCollins, 2007.

Meyer, Marvin, et al., eds. *Ancient Christian Magic: Coptic Texts of Ritual Power.* Princeton: Princeton University Press, 1994.

Miles, Jack. *God: A Biography.* New York: Vintage, 1996.

Millar, Fergus. "Reflections on the Trials of Jesus." In *A Tribute to Geza Vermes: Essays on Jewish and Christian Literature and History,* ed. P. R. Davies and R. T. White (Sheffield, U.K.: Sheffield Academic, 1990), pp. 355–81.

Miller, Robert J. *Born Divine: The Births of Jesus and Other Sons of God.* Santa Rosa, Calif.: Polebridge, 2003.

Moessner, David P., ed. *Jesus and the Heritage of Israel: Luke's Narrative Claim upon Israel's Legacy.* Harrisburg, Pa.: Trinity Press, 1999.

Moss, Candida. *Divine Bodies: Resurrecting Perfection in the New Testament and Early Christianity.* New Haven: Yale University Press, 2019.

———. *The Myth of Persecution: How Early Christians Invented a Story of Martyrdom.* New York: HarperCollins, 2013.

———. *The Other Christs: Imitating Jesus in Ancient Christian Ideologies of Martyrdom.* Oxford, U.K.: Oxford University Press, 2012.

Motley, Eric L. *Madison Park: A Place of Hope.* Grand Rapids, Mich.: Zondervan, 2017.

Mroczek, Eva. *The Literary Imagination in Jewish Antiquity.* Oxford, U.K.: Oxford University Press, 2016.

Murcia, Thierry. "Yeshua ben Panthera: L'Origine du Nom, Status Quaestionis et Nouvelles Investigations." *Ancient Judaism* 2 (2014): 157–207.

Mueller, Dieter. "The Prayer of the Apostle Paul." In *Nag Hammadi Codex I (The Jung Codex): I. Introductions, Texts, Translations, Indices,* ed. Harold Attridge. *Nag Hammadi Studies, The Coptic Gnostic Library* 22 (Leiden: Brill, 1985), pp. 5–11.

———. "The Prayer of the Apostle Paul." In *Nag Hammadi Codex I (The Jung Codex): II. Notes,* ed. Harold Attridge. *Nag Hammadi Studies, The Coptic Gnostic Library* 23 (Leiden: Brill, 1985), pp. 1–5.

Musurillo, Herbert. "Acts of Justin and His Companions." In Musurillo, ed., *The Acts of the Christian Martyrs* (Oxford, U.K.: Clarendon Press, 1972), pp. 42–61.

———, ed. *The Acts of the Christian Martyrs: Introduction, Texts, and Translations.* Oxford, U.K.: Clarendon Press, 1972.

———. "Letter of the Churches of Lyons and Vienne." In Musurillo, ed., *The Acts of the Christian Martyrs: Introduction, Texts, and Translations* (Oxford, U.K.: Clarendon Press, 1972), pp. 62–85.

———. "The Martyrdom of Polycarp." In Musurillo, ed., *The Acts of the Christian Martyrs: Introduction, Texts, and Translations* (Oxford, U.K.: Clarendon Press, 1972), pp. 2–21.

Najman, Hindy. *Losing the Temple and Recovering the Future: An Analysis of 4 Ezra.* Cambridge, U.K.: Cambridge University Press, 2014.

Najman, Hindy, Jean-Sébastien Rey, and Eibert J. C. Tigchelaar, eds. *Tracing Sapiential Traditions in Ancient Judaism*. Leiden: Brill, 2016.

Nasrallah, Laura Salah. *Archaeology and the Letters of Paul*. Oxford, U.K.: Oxford University Press, 2019.

———. *An Ecstasy of Folly: Prophecy and Authority in Early Christianity*. Cambridge, Mass.: Harvard University Press, 2003.

Nasrallah, Laura, and Elisabeth Schüssler Fiorenza. *Prejudice and Christian Beginnings: Investigating Race, Gender, and Ethnicity in Early Christian Studies*. Minneapolis: Fortress, 2009.

Naveh, J., and S. Shaked. *Amulets and Magic Bowls: Aramaic Incantations of Late Antiquity*. Leiden: Brill, 1985.

———. *Magic Spells and Formulae: Aramaic Incantations of Late Antiquity*. Jerusalem: Magnes, 1993.

Newsom, Carol. *Songs of the Sabbath Sacrifice: A Critical Edition*. Atlanta: Scholars Press, 1985.

Niehoff, Maren R. "A Jewish Critique of Christianity from Second-Century Alexandria: Revisiting the Jew Mentioned in *Contra Celsum*." *Journal of Ethnic and Cultural Studies* 21, no. 2 (2013): 151–75.

Novogratz, Jacqueline. *Manifesto for a Moral Revolution: Practices to Build a Better World*. New York: Henry Holt, 2020.

Oates, Joyce Carol. *The Accursed*. New York: HarperCollins, 2013.

Ophir, Adi, and Ishay Rosen-Zvi. *Goy: Israel's Multiple Others and the Birth of the Gentile*. Oxford, U.K.: Oxford University Press, 2018.

Padilla Peralta, Dan-El. *Divine Institutions: Religions and Community in the Middle Roman Republic*. Princeton: Princeton University Press, 2020.

Pagels, Elaine. "Adam and Eve, Christ and the Church: A Survey of Second Century Controversies Concerning Marriage." In *The New Testament and Gnosis*, ed. Alastair Logan and Alexander J. M. Wedderburn (Edinburgh: T&T Clark, 1983), pp. 146–75.

———. *Adam, Eve, and the Serpent*. London: Penguin, 1988.

———. *Beyond Belief: The Secret Gospel of Thomas*. New York: Random House, 2003.

———. "Exegesis of Genesis 1 in the Gospels of Thomas and John." *Journal of Biblical Literature* 118, no. 3 (1999): 477–96.

———. *The Gnostic Gospels*. New York: Random House, 1979.

———. *The Gnostic Paul: Gnostic Exegesis of the Pauline Letters*. Philadelphia: Fortress, 1975.

———. "How Athanasius, Subject to Christian Emperors, Read John's Apocalypse into His Canon." In *Envisioning Judaism: Studies in Honor of Peter Schäfer on the Occasion of His Seventieth Birthday,* vol. 2, ed. Ra'anan Boustan et al. (Tübingen: Mohr Siebeck, 2013), pp. 799–808.

———. "How the Gospel of Truth Depicts Paul's Secret Teaching: A Study in Second-Century Reception History." *Harvard Theological Review* 117, no. 1 (2023): 99–112.

———. "Irenaeus, the 'Canon of Truth,' and the Gospel of John: 'Making a Difference' Through Hermeneutics and Ritual." *Vigiliae Christianae* 56 (2002): 339–71.

———. *The Johannine Gospel in Gnostic Exegesis: Heracleon's Commentary on John.* Nashville: Abingdon, 1973.

———. *The Origin of Satan.* New York: Vintage, 1995.

———. "The Shape-Shifting Bride: Reflecting on Race and Ethnicity in Origen's Exegesis of the Song of Songs." In *A Most Reliable Witness: Essays in Honor of Ross Shepard Kraemer,* ed. Susan Ashbrook et al. (Providence, R.I.: Brown University Press, 2015), pp. 233–42.

———. "The Social History of Satan, Part Three: John of Patmos and Ignatius of Antioch: Contrasting Visions of 'God's People.'" *Harvard Theological Review* 99, no. 4 (2006): 487–505.

Pagels, Elaine, and Karen L. King. *Reading Judas: The Gospel of Judas and the Shaping of Christianity.* New York: Viking, 2007.

Pagels, Elaine H., and John D. Turne. "NHC XI,3: Allogenes, 45,1–69,20." In *Nag Hammadi Codices XI, XII, XIII,* ed. Charles W. Hendrick. *Nag Hammadi Studies, The Coptic Gnostic Library* 28 (Leiden: Brill, 1990), pp. 173–285.

Pannenberg, Wolfhart. *Jesus—God and Man.* Translated by L. L. Wilkins and D. A. Priebe. Philadelphia: Westminster, 1968.

Parkes, Murray. *Bereavement: Studies of Grief in Adult Life.* New York: International University Press, 1972.

Parvis, Sara. "The Reception of Nicaea and Homoousios to 360." In *The Cambridge Companion to the Council of Nicaea,* ed. Y. R. Kim (Cambridge, U.K.: Cambridge University Press, 2021), pp. 225–55.

Patterson, Stephen J. "Apocalypticism or Prophecy and the Problem of Polyvalence: Lessons from the Gospel of Thomas." *Journal of Biblical Literature* 130 (2012): 795–817.

———. *Beyond the Passion: Rethinking the Death and Life of Jesus.* Minneapolis: Fortress, 2004.

———. *The Gospel of Thomas and Christian Origins: Essays on the Fifth Gospel.* Leiden: Brill, 2013.

———. *The Gospel of Thomas and Jesus.* Sonoma, Calif.: Polebridge, 1993.

———. *The Lost Way: How Two Forgotten Gospels Are Rewriting the Story of Christian Origins.* New York: HarperCollins, 2014.

———. "Twice More—*Thomas* and the Synoptics: A Reply to Simon Gathercole, *The Composition of the Gospel of Thomas,* and Mark Goodacre, *Thomas and the Gospels.*" *Journal for the Study of the New Testament* 36 (2014): 251–61.

Pearson, Birger A., and James E. Goehring, eds. *The Roots of Egyptian Christianity.* Philadelphia: Fortress, 1986.

Peel, Malcolm L. "The Treatise on the Resurrection." In *Nag Hammadi Codex I (The Jung Codex): I. Introductions, Texts, Translations, Indices,* ed. Harold Attridge. *Nag Hammadi Studies, The Coptic Gnostic Library* 22 (Leiden: Brill, 1985), pp. 123–57.

———. "The Treatise on the Resurrection." In *Nag Hammadi Codex I (The Jung Codex): II. Notes,* ed. Harold Attridge. *Nag Hammadi Studies, The Coptic Gnostic Library* 23 (Leiden: Brill, 1985), pp. 137–215.

Penton, M. James. *Apocalypse Delayed: The Story of Jehovah's Witnesses.* Toronto: University of Toronto Press, 2015.

Perkins, Pheme. *The Gnostic Dialogue: The Early Church and the Crisis of Gnosticism.* New York: Paulist Press, 1980.

Petersen, William L. *Tatian's Diatessaron: Its Creation, Dissemination, Significance, and History in Scholarship.* Leiden: Brill, 1994.

Petrey, Taylor G., et al., eds. *Re-Making the World: Christianity and Categories: Essays in Honor of Karen L. King.* Tübingen: Mohr Siebeck, 2019.

Philo. *The Embassy to Gaius,* vol. 10. Translated by F. H. Colson. LCL 379. Cambridge, Mass.: Harvard University Press, 1962.

Philostratus, Flavius. *The Life of Apollonius of Tyana, Books I–IV,* vol. I. Translated by C. P. Jones. LCL 16. Cambridge, Mass.: Harvard University Press, 2012.

Pliny. *Letters, Books I–VII; Panegyricus,* vol. I. Translated by B. Radice. LCL 55. Cambridge, Mass.: Harvard University Press, 1969.

———. *Letters, Books VIII–X; Panegyricus,* vol. II. Translated by B. Radice. LCL 59. Cambridge, Mass.: Harvard University Press, 1969.

Plotinus. *Ennead III,* vol. III. Translated by A. H. Armstrong. LCL 442. Cambridge, Mass.: Harvard University Press, 1993.

———. *Porphyry on Plotinus; Ennead I,* vol. I. Translated by A. H. Armstrong. LCL 440. Cambridge, Mass.: Harvard University Press, 1966.

Plutarch. *Lives: Demosthenes and Cicero, Alexander and Caesar,* vol VII. Translated by B. Perrin. LCL 99. Cambridge, Mass.: Harvard University Press, 1919.

Pohlsander, Hans. *The Emperor Constantine.* 2nd edition. London: Routledge, 2004.

Pokorný, Petr. "Words of Jesus in Paul: On the Theology and Praxis of the Jesus Tradition." In *Handbook for the Study of the Historical Jesus,* 4 vols., ed. T. Holmén and S. E. Porter (Leiden: Brill, 2011), pp. 3437–67.

Quispel, Gilles. *Gnostica, Judaica, Catholica: Collected Essays of Gilles Quispel.* Edited by Johannes Van Oort. Leiden: Brill, 2008.

———. *Het Evangelie van Thomas: Uit het Koptisch vertaald en toegelicht.* Amsterdam: In de Pelikaan, 2005.

Rafael, Vicente. *Contracting Colonialism: Translation and Christian Conversion in Tagalog Society Under Early Spanish Rule.* Manila: Ateneo de Manila University Press, 1988.

Reed, Annette Yoshiko. *Demons, Angels, and Writing in Ancient Judaism.* Cambridge, U.K.: Cambridge University Press, 2020.

———. "ΕΥΑΓΓΕΛΙΟΝ: Orality, Textuality, and the Christian Truth in Irenaeus' *Adversus Haereses*." *Vigiliae Christianae* 56 (2002): 11–46.

———. *Jewish-Christianity and the History of Judaism: Collected Essays.* Tübingen: Mohr Siebeck, 2018.

Reeves, John C., and Annette Yoshiko Reed. *Enoch from Antiquity to the Middle Ages.* Oxford, U.K.: Oxford University Press, 2018.

Reimarus, Hermann Samuel. *Fragments from Reimarus.* Translated by G. E. Lessing. Edited by Charles Voysey. London: Williams and Norgate, 1879.

Riley, Gregory J. *One Jesus, Many Christs: How Jesus Inspired Not One True Christianity, but Many.* New York: HarperCollins, 1997.

———. *The River of God: A New History of Christian Origins.* New York: Harper-Collins, 2001.

Robbins, Joel. *Becoming Sinners: Christianity and Moral Torment in a Papua New Guinea Society.* Berkeley: University of California Press, 2004.

Roberts, J. J. M. "A New Root for an Old Crux, Ps. XXII 17c." *Vetus Testamentum* 23.2 (1973): 247–52.

Roberts, Nathaniel. *To Be Cared For: The Power of Conversion and Foreignness of Belonging in an Indian Slum.* Berkeley: University of California Press, 2016.

Robinson, James M., ed. *The Coptic Gnostic Library: A Complete Edition of the Nag Hammadi Codices,* vol. I. Leiden: Brill, 2000.

———, ed. *The Coptic Gnostic Library: A Complete Edition of the Nag Hammadi Codices,* vol. II. Leiden: Brill, 2000.

———, ed. *The Coptic Gnostic Library: A Complete Edition of the Nag Hammadi Codices,* vol. III. Leiden: Brill, 2000.

———, ed. *The Coptic Gnostic Library: A Complete Edition of the Nag Hammadi Codices,* vol. IV. Leiden: Brill, 2000.

———, ed. *The Coptic Gnostic Library: A Complete Edition of the Nag Hammadi Codices,* vol. V. Leiden: Brill, 2000.

———, ed. *The Nag Hammadi Library in English,* revised edition. New York: Harper Collins, 1990.

Rousseau, Philip. *Ascetics, Authority, and the Church in the Age of Jerome and Cassian.* Oxford, U.K.: Oxford University Press, 1978.

———. *Pachomius: The Making of a Community in Fourth-Century Egypt.* Berkeley: University of California Press, 1999.

Royalty, Robert M., Jr. *The Streets of Heaven: The Ideology of Wealth in the Apocalypse of John.* Macon, Ga.: Mercer University Press, 1998.

Rubenson, Samuel. *The Letters of St. Antony: Monasticism and the Making of a Saint.* Minneapolis: Fortress, 1995.

Rynearson, Edward K. *Retelling Violent Death.* Philadelphia: Brunner-Routledge, 2001.

Saldarini, Anthony J. *Matthew's Christian-Jewish Community.* Chicago: University of Chicago Press, 1994.

———. *Pharisees, Scribes and Sadducees in Palestinian Society: A Sociological Approach.* Grand Rapids, Mich.: Eerdmans, 2001.

Samuelsson, Gunnar. *Crucifixion in Antiquity: An Inquiry into the Background and Significance of the New Testament Terminology of Crucifixion.* Tübingen: Mohr Siebeck, 2013.

Sanders, E. P. *The Historical Figure of Jesus.* London: Penguin Books, 1993.

———. *Paul and Palestinian Judaism: A Comparison of Patterns of Religion.* Philadelphia: Fortress, 1977.

Sanders, Jack T. *The Jews in Luke-Acts.* Philadelphia: Fortress, 1987.

Sawicki, Marianne. *Crossing Galilee: Architectures of Contact in the Occupied Land of Jesus.* Harrisburg, Pa.: Trinity Press, 2000.

Schaberg, Jane. *The Illegitimacy of Jesus: A Feminist Interpretation of the Infancy Narratives.* San Francisco: Harper & Row, 1987.

Schäfer, Peter. *Jesus in the Talmud.* Princeton: Princeton University Press, 2009.

———. "Jesus' Origin, Birth and Childhood According to the Toledot Yeshu and the Talmud." In *Judaea-Palaestina, Babylon and Rome: Jews in Antiquity,* ed. Benjamin Isaac and Yuval Shahar (Tübingen: Mohr Siebeck, 2012), pp. 139–61.

———. *Kurze Geschichte des Antisemitismus.* Munich: Piper, 2022.

Bibliography

———. "New Testament and Hekhalot Literature: The Journey into Heaven in Paul and in Merkavah Mysticism." *Journal of Jewish Studies* 35 (1984): 19–35.

———. *The Origins of Jewish Mysticism.* Tübingen: Mohr Siebeck, 2009.

Schaferdiek, Knut, trans. "The Acts of John." In *The New Testament Apocrypha II: Writings Related to the Apostles; Apocalypses and Related Subjects,* ed. W. Schneemelcher, trans. R. Wilson (Louisville: Westminster John Knox, 2003), pp. 152–212.

Schoedel, William R. "NHC V,3: The (First) Apocalypse of James." In *Nag Hammadi Codices V, 2–5 and VI with Papyrus Berolinensis 8502, 1 and 4,* ed. Douglas M. Parrott. *Nag Hammadi Studies, The Coptic Gnostic Library* 11 (Leiden: Brill, 1979), pp. 65–103.

Scholem, Gershom. *Kabbalah.* New York: Meridian, 1978.

———. *Sabbatai Ṣevi: The Mystical Messiah, 1626–1676.* Princeton: Princeton University Press, 1973.

Schüssler Fiorenza, Elisabeth. *The Book of Revelation: Justice and Judgment.* Philadelphia: Fortress, 1985.

Schweitzer, Albert. *The Psychiatric Study of Jesus: Exposition and Criticism.* Translated by Charles R. Joy. Boston: Beacon Press, 1948.

———. *The Quest of the Historical Jesus.* Translated by W. Montgomery. London: Adam and Charles Black, 1911.

Segal, Alan F. *Paul the Convert: The Apostolate and Apostasy of Saul the Pharisee.* New Haven, Conn.: Yale University Press, 1990.

———. *Two Powers in Heaven: Early Rabbinic Reports About Christianity and Gnosticism.* Leiden: Brill, 1977.

Sellew, Melissa Harl. "Reading Jesus in the Desert: The *Gospel of Thomas* Meets the *Apophthegmata Patrum.*" In *The Nag Hammadi Codices and Late Antique Egypt,* ed. Hugo Lundhaug and Lance Jennot (Tübingen: Mohr Siebeck, 2018), pp. 81–106.

Smallwood, E. Mary. *The Jews Under Roman Rule, from Pompey to Diocletian: A Study in Political Relations.* Leiden: Brill, 2001.

Smith, D. E. "An Autopsy of an Autopsy: Biblical Illiteracy Among Medical Doctors." *Westar* 1, no. 2 (1987): 3–6, 14–15.

Smith, Geoffrey S. "Anti-Origenist Redaction in the Fragments of the Gospel of Truth (NHC XII,2): Theological Controversy and the Transmission of Early Christian Literature." *Harvard Theological Review* 110 (2016): 46–74.

———. "Constructing a Christian Universe: Mythological Exegesis of Ben Sira 24 and John's Prologue in the *Gospel of Truth.*" In *Jewish and Christian Cosmogony in Late Antiquity,* ed. L. Jenott and S. K. Gribetz (Tübingen: Mohr Siebeck, 2013), pp. 64–81.

————. *Guilt by Association: Heresy Catalogues in Early Christianity.* Oxford, U.K.: Oxford University Press, 2014.

————. *Valentinian Christianity: Texts and Translations.* Oakland: University of California Press, 2020.

Smith, Geoffrey S., and Brent C. Landau. *The Secret Gospel of Mark: A Controversial Scholar, a Scandalous Gospel of Jesus, and the Fierce Debate over Its Authenticity.* New Haven, Conn.: Yale University Press, 2023.

Smith, Jonathan Z. *Drudgery Divine: On the Comparison of Early Christianities and the Religions of Late Antiquity.* Chicago: University of Chicago Press, 1990.

Smith, Morton. *Jesus the Magician.* New York: Harper & Row, 1978.

Spong, John Shelby. *Resurrection: Myth or Reality? A Bishop's Search for the Origins of Christianity.* San Francisco: Harper, 1994.

Stark, Rodney. *The Rise of Christianity: How the Obscure, Marginal Jesus Movement Became the Dominant Religious Force in the Western World in a Few Centuries.* Princeton: Princeton University Press, 1996.

Stauffer, Ethelbert. "Jeschu ben Mirjam: Kontroversgeschichtliche Anmerkungen zu Mk 6:3." In *Neotestamentica et Semitica: Studies in Honour of Matthew Black,* ed. E. E. Ellis and M. Wolcox (Edinburgh: T&T Clark, 1969), pp. 119–28.

Stroumsa, Gedaliahu A. G. *Another Seed: Studies in Gnostic Mythology.* Leiden: Brill, 1984.

————. "Gnosis and Judaism in Nineteenth Century Christian Thought." *Journal of Jewish Thought and Philosophy* 2 (1992): 45–62.

Suetonius. *Lives of the Caesars,* vol. I. Translated by J. C. Rolfe. LCL 31. Cambridge, Mass.: Harvard University Press, 1998.

————. *Lives of the Caesars,* vol. II. Translated by J. C. Rolfe. LCL 38. Cambridge, Mass.: Harvard University Press, 1997.

Tabor, James. *The Jesus Dynasty.* New York: Simon & Schuster, 2007.

Tacitus. *Agricola, Germania, Dialogus,* vol. I. Translated by M. Hutton (*Agricola, Germania*) and W. Peterson (*Dialogus*). LCL 35. Cambridge, Mass.: Harvard University Press, 1970.

————. *The Annals & The Histories.* Edited by Moses Hadas. New York: Modern Library, 2003.

————. *The Histories, Books IV–V; The Annals, Books I–III,* vol. III. Translated by C. H. Moore (*The Histories*) and J. Jackson (*The Annals*). LCL 249. Cambridge, Mass.: Harvard University Press, 1931.

Tentea, O. *Ex Oriente ad Danubium: The Syrian Units on the Danube Frontier of the Roman Empire.* Cluj-Napoca, Romania: MEGA Publishing House, 2012.

Tertullian. *Adversus Marcionem, Books 4 and 5*. Translated by Ernest Evans. Oxford, U.K.: Clarendon Press, 1972.

Thomassen, Einar. *The Spiritual Seed: The Church of the "Valentinians."* Leiden: Brill, 2008.

———, ed. *Canon and Canonicity: The Formation and Use of Scripture*. Copenhagen: Museum Tusculanum Press, 2010.

Tiede, David Lenz. *The Charismatic Figure as Miracle Worker*. Missoula, Mont.: Society of Biblical Literature, 1973.

Tolstoy, Leo. *A Confession*. New York: W. W. Norton, 1983.

———. *The Kingdom of God Is Within You: Christianity Not as a Mystic Religion but as a New Theory of Life*. Translated by Constance Garnett. Lincoln: University of Nebraska Press, 1984.

Townsend, Philippa. "Who Were the First Christians? Jews, Gentiles and the *Christianoi*." In *Heresy and Identity in Late Antiquity*, ed. E. Iricinischi and H. M. Zellentin (Tübingen: Mohr Siebeck, 2008), pp. 212–30.

Trigg, Joseph Wilson. *Origen: The Bible and Philosophy in the Third-Century Church*. Atlanta: John Knox Press, 1983.

Trocmé, Étienne. *The Childhood of Christianity*. Translated by John Bowden. London: SCM Press, 1997.

Uro, Risto. *Thomas at the Crossroads: Essays on the Gospel of Thomas*. Edinburgh: T&T Clark, 1998.

Valantasis, Richard. *The Gospel of Thomas*. London: Routledge, 1997.

Van Dam, Raymond. "Imperial Fathers and Their Sons: Licinius, Constantine, and the Council of Nicaea." In *The Cambridge Companion to the Council of Nicaea*, ed. Y. R. Kim (Cambridge, U.K.: Cambridge University Press, 2021), pp. 19–42.

Vermes, Geza. *Jesus the Jew: A Historian's Reading of the Gospels*. London: William Collins Sons, 1973.

Vidas, Moulie. *Tradition and the Formation of the Talmud*. Princeton: Princeton University Press, 2014.

Vilaça, Aparecida. *Paletó and Me: Memories of My Indigenous Father*. Translated by David Rodgers. Stanford: Stanford University Press, 2021.

———. *Praying and Preying: Christianity in Indigenous Amazonia*. Berkeley: University of California Press, 2016.

Visotzky, Burton L. *Aphrodite and the Rabbis: How the Jews Adapted Roman Culture to Create Judaism As We Know It*. New York: St. Martin's Press, 2016.

Völker, Walther. *Quellen zur Geschichte der christlichen Gnosis.* Tübingen: Mohr Siebeck, 1932.

Waldstein, Michael, and Frederik Wisse, eds. *The Apocryphon of John: Synopsis of Nag Hammadi Codices II,1; III,1; and IV,1 with BG 8502,2.* Nag Hammadi and Manichaean Studies 33 (Leiden: Brill, 1995).

Wallis, Jim. *Christ in Crisis? Reclaiming Jesus in a Time of Fear, Hate, and Violence.* New York: HarperCollins, 2019.

Walsh, Richard, Jeffrey Staley, and Adele Reinhartz, eds. *Son of Man: An African Jesus Film.* Sheffield, U.K.: Sheffield Phoenix Press, 2013.

Weiss-Rosmarin, Trude, ed. *Jewish Expressions on Jesus: An Anthology.* New York: Ktav Publishing, 1976.

Weksler-Bdolah, Shlomit. "The Camp of the Legion X Fretensis." In Weksler-Bdolah, *Aelia Capitolina—Jerusalem in the Roman Period: In Light of Archaeological Research* (Leiden: Brill, 2020), pp. 19–50.

Wilken, Robert Louis. *The Christians as the Romans Saw Them.* 2nd edition. New Haven, Conn.: Yale University Press, 2003.

Wilkerson, Isabel. *Caste: The Origins of Our Discontents.* New York: Random House, 2020.

Williams, Francis E. "The Apocryphon of James." In *Nag Hammadi Codex I (The Jung Codex): I. Introductions, Texts, Translations, Indices,* ed. Harold Attridge. *Nag Hammadi Studies, The Coptic Gnostic Library* 22 (Leiden: Brill, 1985), pp. 13–53.

———. "The Apocryphon of James." In *Nag Hammadi Codex I (The Jung Codex): II. Notes,* ed. Harold Attridge. *Nag Hammadi Studies, The Coptic Gnostic Library* 23 (Leiden: Brill, 1985), pp. 7–37.

Williams, Michael Allen. *Rethinking "Gnosticism": An Argument for Dismantling a Dubious Category.* Princeton: Princeton University Press, 1996.

Williams, Rowan. *Tokens of Trust: An Introduction to Christian Belief.* Norwich, U.K.: Canterbury Press, 2007.

Wilson, R. McL., and George W. MacRae. "BG,1: The Gospel of Mary." In *Nag Hammadi Codices V, 2–5 and VI with Papyrus Berolinensis 8502, 1 and 4,* ed. Douglas M. Parrott. *Nag Hammadi Studies, The Coptic Gnostic Library* 11 (Leiden: Brill, 1979), pp. 453–71.

Winter, Paul. *On the Trial of Jesus.* Berlin: De Gruyter, 1974.

Wisse, Frederik. "The Apocryphon of John (II,1 III,1 IV,1, and BG 8502,2)." In *The Nag Hammadi Library in English,* revised edition, ed. James M. Robinson (New York: HarperCollins, 1990), pp. 104–23.

Bibliography

Wodziński, Marcin. *Historical Atlas of Hasidism*. Princeton: Princeton University Press, 2018.

Wolfson, Elliot R. "Inscribed in the Book of the Living: *Gospel of Truth* and Jewish Christology." *Journal for the Study of Judaism* 38 (2007): 234–71.

Wright, Tom. *The Resurrection of the Son of God*. Minneapolis: Fortress, 2003.

Yoder, John H. *The Politics of Jesus: Vicit Agnus Noster*. Grand Rapids, Mich.: Eerdmans, 1972.

Zeichmann, Christopher B. "Jesus 'ben Pantera': An Epigraphic and Military-Historical Note." *Journal for the Study of the Historical Jesus* 18 (2020): 141–55.

———. "Military Forces in Judaea 6–30 C.E.: The *Status Quaestionis* and Relevance for New Testament Studies." *Currents in Biblical Research,* 17 (2018): 86–120.

Zerubavel, Eviatar. *Time Maps: Collective Memory and the Social Shape of the Past*. Chicago: University of Chicago Press, 2003.

Zugibe, F. T. "Two Questions About Crucifixion: Does the Victim Die of Asphyxiation? Would Nails in the Hands Hold the Weight of the Body?" *Bible Review* 5 (1989): 34–43.

Index

Index

Illustration Credits

Illustration Credits

Page 9: Marc Chagall, *The Crucified,* 1944. Gouache on paper, 62.5 x 47.5 cm. © Israel Museum, Jerusalem / Loan by the Victoria Babinto America-Israel Foundation / Bridgeman Images, © 2024 Artists Rights Society (ARS), New York/ADAGP, Paris.

Page 10 (*top*): All Rights Reserved

Page 10 (*bottom left*): Alpha Stock / Alamy Stock Photo

Page 10 (*bottom right*): Birmingham, Alabama, Public Library Archives

Page 11: Alpha Stock / Alamy Stock Photo

Page 12: Art Gallery and Museum, Kelvingrove, Glasgow, Scotland. Photograph © CSG CIC Glasgow Museums Collection/Bridgeman Images.

Page 13: © Titus Kaphar, courtesy of the artist and Gagosian

Page 14: © Kino Lorber / courtesy of Everett Collection

Page 15: Photograph Jonathan Olley / © IFC Films / courtesy of Everett Collection

Page 16: © Universal / courtesy of Everett Collection

ABOUT THE AUTHOR

ELAINE PAGELS is the Harrington Spear Paine Foundation Professor of Religion at Princeton University. In 2015 she received the National Humanities Medal from President Barack Obama, and earlier in her career was awarded the Rockefeller, Guggenheim, and MacArthur Fellowships in consecutive years. As a young researcher at Barnard College, she changed the historical landscape of the Christian religion by exploding the myth of the early church as a unified movement. Her findings were published in the bestselling book *The Gnostic Gospels* (Random House, 1979), which won both the National Book Critics Circle Award and the National Book Award. Her subsequent books include *Why Religion?*, *Revelations*, *Reading Judas*, *Beyond Belief*, *The Origin of Satan*, and *Adam, Eve, and the Serpent*. She has been profiled in *Time*, *The Atlantic Monthly*, *Vogue*, *The New Yorker*, and *Newsweek*'s issue on "Women and Power."